W9-AYT-938

Literary Landscapes

Conceived and produced by Elwin Street Productions Limited
14 Clerkenwell Green
London, EC1R ODP
www.elwinstreet.com

First published in North America, October 2018 by
Black Dog & Leventhal Publishers

Black Dog & Leventhal Publishers
Hachette Book Group
1290 Avenue of the Americas
New York, NY 10104
www.hachettebookgroup.com
www.blackdogandleventhal.com

Cover illustration and design by Jim Tierney

Print book interior design by Peter Ross / Counterpunch Inc.

LCCN: 2018950576
ISBNs: 978-0-316-56182-2 (hardcover), 978-0-316-56181-5 (ebook)

Printed in China

10 9 8 7 6 5 4 3 2 1

LITERARY LANDSCAPES

Charting the Worlds of
Classic Literature

General Editor John Sutherland

BLACK DOG
& LEVENTHAL
PUBLISHERS
NEW YORK

CONTENTS

Mapping Modernism 62

Postwar Panoramas 124

Contemporary Geographies 184

Introduction

By John Sutherland

"There is no there there," Gertrude Stein, now by choice a Parisian, once wrote, haughtily, of her home city Oakland. These are words that could not be said of any of the books examined and described in this volume. Indicating that Californian city's historical emptiness, positing the location as, disappointingly, a kind of anywhere, with no features to mark it out as either memorable or categorically distinct, Stein gives us a scornful shorthand for defining the elusive "sense of place": an essential "thereness" or "isness," without which a city's edges fall apart.

Immediately one's mind starts questioning the idea, subverting it. Was Oakland, when Stein was brought up there (where her childhood was, as Philip Larkin said of his hometown, "unspent") the same as where the hippy revolution of the 1960s found its home? Did the Beatniks give Oakland a "there" which wasn't there, and couldn't be foreseen, in Stein's childhood? Is "Cannery Row" still what the name describes as when fish are canned elsewhere and the place lives mainly as a shrine to lovers of John Steinbeck's fiction? This, and many other questions on literary topography, are pondered, illuminatingly and informatively, in the essays that follow.

As a collection of the world's most memorable fictionalized geographies, *Literary Landscapes* can be summed up as an investigation into Stein's "thereness"—the enduring fixity of place ("There'll always be an England") and the fluidities and meltingness that places are subject to. They melt and reform themselves, over social time, historical time, and geological time. Describing literary place, in the dimensions of time and space, requires a fine critical touch—which, one can confidently assert, is displayed in the pages that follow.

All the works described in this volume capture, are even built upon, a sense of their authors having been to, seen, experienced, and been able to relate all the qualities of a place that, in combination, lodge that locale in cultural and geographical specificity. From Hardy's Wessex to Mishima's Japan, from Bulgakov's Moscow to Proulx's Newfoundland, the literary landscapes collected here are singular in their sights, sounds, associations, and representations; they could not be mistaken for anywhere else.

The idea of "literary landscape" was, originally, founded on a paradox. Entering the English language as a loan word by way of the Dutch *landschap* in the early seventeenth century, a "landscape" initially denoted a purely visual representation. The natural world had begun to emerge from its position as an undervalued backdrop, becoming a major artistic genre from Claude Lorrain and Nicolas Poussin onward, but its depiction was a pictorial skill.

By contrast, "literary landscape," the subject of this richly detailed and illustrated volume, cannot, like fine art, be experienced as representation by the eye alone. Literary landscape is composed of words which must be recomposed in a frame of imagination. "The inward eye," British "Lakeland" poet William Wordsworth called it, drawing a distinction between perception and imagination. Just as the painter can choose his balance of verisimilitude—striving for eye-witnessed accuracy—and creative depiction, so the writer must decide how much of an influence his "inward eye" will have on the scene depicted. What one might call "creative bias" comes into it—subjective coloration. And sometimes moral judgement: when Bunyan called London "Vanity Fair" ("a place of ostentation or empty, idle amusement and frivolity") he meant something quite different, morally, from what London-loving William Makepeace Thackeray presents in his novel *Vanity Fair*. Thackeray rather liked amusement and frivolity.

Some writers open up more than others to the demands of imagination combining studious historical research with the literary artist's creative licence—Chinua Achebe's chronicle of pre-colonial life in Nigeria, for instance (1958, page 161), or Eleanor Catton's recreation of Victorian Hokitika on an epic scale (2013, page 238). Interweaving his knowledge of folklore with authentic details of life in postwar Tokyo, Natsuhiko Kyōgoku's portrait of the city (1994, page 218) hovers between fact and fiction—creating a landscape at once familiar and foreign, populated by phantoms.

For others, a more photographically exact portrayal of place yields a greater reward. Often these writers draw upon a personal topography, recreating the intimate corners of their own uniquely felt experience. From August Strindberg, whose Hemsö was recognized as a lightly veiled version of Kymmendö where he had spent his childhood summers (1887, page 49), to Armistead Maupin, who invests his richly vibrant chronicle of San Francisco with his own experiences of the city (1978, page 186), personal biography informs and colors these characterizations of place and renders them all the more fascinating because of that.

Sometimes authors choose to work on a large canvas landscape, powerful and dramatic, dwarfing humanity; others work on a smaller scale. Jane Austen, whose novel *Persuasion* (1817, page 17) begins the collection, could be described as a miniaturist. From Hampshire to Somerset, her novels stay within a narrow range; she herself was a writer "who only England knew." She had sailor brothers who had seen the world, but not Jane, who never left England's shores (except, perhaps, for the adjoining Isle of Wight). Yet her novels display, as Sir Walter Scott wrote of *Emma*, "the art of copying from nature as she really exists in the common walks of life, and presenting to the reader, instead of the splendid scenes from an imaginary world, a correct and striking representation of that which is daily taking place around him." Yet, even the "little bit (two inches wide) of ivory," as she called it, on which she wrote can give us an occasional large canvas landscape. One such is in the Donwell Abbey Picnic scene in *Emma*. The picnickers have nothing much to say to one another, and Emma looks down from the hill on which she is standing:

> half a mile, at the ruined Abbey and the Abbey Mill farm. It was a sweet view—sweet to the eye and mind. English verdure, English culture, English comfort, seen under a bright sun, without being oppressive.

What is Austen saying here in her encomium of the "Englishness" of the "sweet" landscape? Emma Woodhouse has this serene confidence that her country's countryside was the best anywhere in the world: the dates tell us that these were ominous years for Anglo-French relations, with Waterloo, Napoleon's exile, victory, then peace and the inauguration of the "British Century." Not even a parson's daughter in rural Hampshire could be unaware that society was changing. In short, this is an exquisitely described landscape—worthy of the miniature ivory artist—with a heavy historical subtext to it. Though rooted in her own observation, the novel becomes a commentary on a world beyond personal experience, as a vehicle for affirming "Englishness."

Austen acknowledges in her writing that any conception of "landscape" is inextricably bound up with human presence and human purpose and human idiosyncrasy. Throughout this volume runs the presiding conviction that any landscape will be a synthesis of place and people: from Alessandro Manzoni's *The Betrothed* (1817, page 18) to James Joyce's *Ulysses* (1922, page 74), Gerard Reve's *The Evenings* (1947, page 126) to Elena Ferrante's *My Brilliant Friend* (2012, page 132), across this international canvas the creation of place relies not just on physical details of geography, but on shared habits, customs, and values: a constellation of social actions which, in turn, contour the original concrete reality. Louise Erdrich's *Tracks* (1988, page 208), Kate Grenville's *The Secret River* (2005, page 230) and Peter Schneider's *The Wall Jumper* (1982, page 196) make the point particularly plain: land is instrumental in creating a shared sense of identity, whether national, regional, or tribal.

No collection such as this can hope to be wholly comprehensive, although it can aspire to as wide a coverage as possible. This volume's discriminating selection was driven by three criteria: firstly, each book must conjure a land that exists, or has existed. These are "literary" landscapes, but their bounds extend beyond the textual, insofar as they relate to tangible, visually "real" locations, in the specifics of their characterisation if not explicitly by name. Second, as the difference between the Paris of Balzac (1835, page 21) and the Paris of Modiano (1997, page 222) makes clear, these are books which are rooted in historical time as well as locale: "thereness" depends on history as much as on geography. As much as this collection might serve as a travel companion to the different corners of the globe, it is also a time machine, creating different visions of the same city. No one could confuse Edith Wharton's New York (1920, page 70) with Jay McInerney's (1984, page 200). One of the fascinating questions raised by this volume is whether there is, so to speak, a "New Yorkness."

Finally, within the global reach of this literary selection, place is always more than mere "setting." Where that descriptor implies "atmosphere" or "background," landscape becomes a subject in its own right across the books in this collection, to the extent that some of these imaginings of place have, miraculously, even worked their own impact on the environments they describe. Ocean View Avenue was renamed "Cannery Row" in 1958 to commemorate John Steinbeck's novel of the same name (1945, page 120). In Hongoeka Bay, developers gave up their harassment of the local Māori community in the aftermath of the publication of *Potiki* by Patricia Grace (1986, page 203), which allowed the community to build their own ancestral home. Offering commentary, criticism, eulogy, these writers define the countries and communities they describe.

This is a book to read, relish, and learn from. Its intention is to share with the reader insights which have enriched the contributors' pleasures in, and reward from, great literature; specifically the places in which great literature founds itself. No one reading this sumptuous book will be tempted to think of literary landscape as mere "background."

The reader of today has advantages denied, in most cases, their predecessors. I (now aged 80) was seventeen years old before I ever left British shores. My grandparents never left them. My son (born in 1974) had traveled the four corners of the planet before he was seventeen years old. Born in London he lives in Los Angeles and prefers to holiday in South America. He is not atypical of his multi-placed generation.

We are, as never before, a travelling, "sight-seeing," "place-knowing" race of humans. It is a privilege. The contention of this book (grandiose, it may sound, but genuine) is that we should cultivate our historically unique sense of place and use the resource of great literature (more available to us, like travel, than our ancestors) to do so.

Enjoy.

UP TO 1914

1 Romantic Prospects

From vistas of sublime rugged countryside to the grime of moody city streets, the novels of the nineteenth century began the intense engagement with natural surroundings, rooting psychology in setting. In these dramas of sociability, place figures not just as mere backdrop, but a defined character in the cast of interactions.

BATH, ENGLAND

JANE AUSTEN
PERSUASION (1817)

With the end of the Napoleonic Wars in 1815, 26-year-old Anne Elliot renews her acquaintance with Frederick Wentworth, a captain in the Royal Navy. Both remaining single, Anne and the captain navigate a new engagement, setting a happier course for a second chance at marriage.

Draw a line on an English map from the coastal resort of Lyme Regis, located at the western edge of Dorset, to the city of Bath in Somerset, a distance of 60 miles, and this essentially is the world of Jane Austen's final completed novel, *Persuasion*. The three key settings along this line—traditional country, fashionable resort, modern city—each mark not only a change in geography, but also the heroine's growing independence and maturity.

At the beginning of *Persuasion* Anne Elliot's activities are bound by the society of the landed gentry. She is living with her family at Kellynch Hall, which may well have been based on the Tudor manor Barrington Court in Somerset. It is seven years since Anne, under pressure from her family, ended her engagement to the young naval officer Frederick Wentworth, who lacked both the wealth and connections considered socially necessary.

Anne's life changes during a visit to Lyme Regis, 15 miles to the south. By the start of the nineteenth century Lyme Regis had become a popular leisure destination for the upper and newly emergent middle-classes, and Austen is known to have visited Lyme Regis at least twice, in 1803 and 1804. It is here, by the sea, that Anne renews her relationship with her with her former fiancé.

As when Austen visited Lyme, today its most notable feature remains the imposing curved harbor wall, the Cobb. Austen brings a realistic eye to her portrait of Lyme: "...the principal street almost hurrying into the water, the walk to the Cobb, skirting round the pleasant little bay, which, in the season, is animated with bathing machines and company; the Cobb itself, its old wonders and new improvements...."

When the Elliot family suffer reduced financial circumstances, Kellynch Hall is rented and the family relocates to Bath, where Austen herself had lived for the first decade of the nineteenth century. Bath was then one of England's largest towns with a population of around 60,000. Famed for its Roman Baths, the city was undergoing a cultural renaissance, with new Assembly Rooms offering a hub to fashionable society amid distinctive architecture of golden-colored Bath Stone.

Jane Austen (1775–1817) lived with her family in Bath, one of the key locations of *Persuasion*, from late 1800 to mid-1809. She spent the entirety of her life in Hampshire in the south of England.

Austen wrote seven novels in total. *Sense and Sensibility* (1811), *Pride and Prejudice* (1813), *Mansfield Park* (1814), and *Emma* (1815) were published during her lifetime. Following her death, her brother Henry arranged joint publication of *Persuasion* and *Northanger Abbey* in 1818. Her early short novel *Lady Susan*, written in 1794, was not published until 1871.

"A General View of Bath," from *Bath Illustrated by a Series of Views*, 1805. An engraving by John Hill from the same time as the novel was set.

As Austen satirically illustrates, Bath was class-bound and smitten with hollow gossip and social rivalry, despite its elegance. Yet even in the rain Bath could be invigorating:

> ...entering Bath on a wet afternoon, and driving through the long course of streets from the Old Bridge to Camden Place, amidst the dash of other carriages, the heavy rumble of carts and drays, the bawling of newspapermen, muffin-men and milkmen, and the ceaseless clink of pattens, she made no complaint. No, these were noises which belonged to the winter pleasures; her spirits rose under their influence.

Bath was, symbolically, the ideal place for Anne to break away from past values and set her future with Captain Wentworth, Austen's prototype of a new type of "self-made" gentleman, whose wealth and outlook stemmed from personal endeavor rather than inheritance.

In *Persuasion* Jane Austen maps out a vision of an England in the midst of social and economic renewal, from ancestral estates that had barely changed in centuries to a resurgent Bath, a city that was once part of the Roman Empire, now an icon of a rising British Empire. Austen shows this transformation through the psychological development of her heroine, Anne Elliot, whose liberating romantic journey was one her creator was herself never able to make.

LOMBARDY, ITALY

ALESSANDRO MANZONI

THE BETROTHED
(I PROMESSI SPOSI)(1827)

Manzoni's classic Bildungsroman is an enduring love story, set in the turbulent period of seventeenth-century Italy, in which the peasant protagonist grows into adulthood through the experience of the city of Milan.

Alessandro Manzoni (1785–1873) numbers among Italy's most famous writers. He was the son of a rich country nobleman, and his grandfather was a world famous intellectual of the Enlightenment. While *The Betrothed* is his masterpiece, he also wrote two important verse plays.

The Betrothed was first published in three volumes in 1827. A revised edition of the novel in one volume was published in 1842, which reflected more closely Manzoni's preference for the Florence dialect.

The novel is one of the most widely read novels in the Italian language.

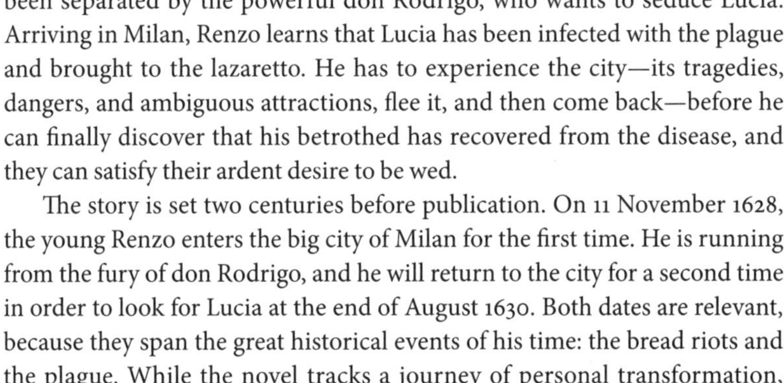

The hero of Alessandro Manzoni's historical novel *The Betrothed* is a young peasant, Renzo, who has never left his native mountain village. Yet the search for his dearly beloved fiancée, Lucia, drives him to the big city. The pair have been separated by the powerful don Rodrigo, who wants to seduce Lucia. Arriving in Milan, Renzo learns that Lucia has been infected with the plague and brought to the lazaretto. He has to experience the city—its tragedies, dangers, and ambiguous attractions, flee it, and then come back—before he can finally discover that his betrothed has recovered from the disease, and they can satisfy their ardent desire to be wed.

The story is set two centuries before publication. On 11 November 1628, the young Renzo enters the big city of Milan for the first time. He is running from the fury of don Rodrigo, and he will return to the city for a second time in order to look for Lucia at the end of August 1630. Both dates are relevant, because they span the great historical events of his time: the bread riots and the plague. While the novel tracks a journey of personal transformation, showing how the hero confronts this new geography and its troubled history, it thus also stamps a new vision of Milan on the atlas of literary imagination, presenting a city that has burgeoned since that incarnation enshrined in Italian literature since the Middle Ages. Renzo's first glimpse of the city registers its otherworldly proportions:

> As Renzo climbed up one of those paths to a higher level, he caught sight of the vast mass of the cathedral standing up alone out of the plain, as if it had been built not in a city but in the middle of a desert.

For Manzoni, one of Italy's preeminent writers in the nineteenth century, Milan is not only the setting for *The Betrothed*, whose map covers the wider Lombardy area, it is also the familiar city where he spent most of his life. He was born there, and his beautifully decorated terracotta townhouse (a stone's throw from the Duomo) still stands in the city today, now a library and a museum. All his works, including *The Betrothed*, were published in

Seventeenth-century Lombardy from the second edition of *The Betrothed*, c. 1840, illustrated by Francesco Gonin. Manzoni lived in Lombardy throughout his lifetime, and his former home in Milan is now a museum.

this city where his life and career were so deeply rooted. The importance of Milan to the book and its story is stated by its subtitle, sadly ignored by most translations: *Storia milanese del secolo XVII secolo* ("A Milanese History of the Seventeenth Century").

In the novel, after Renzo's first sighting of the Cathedral from afar, he journeys further toward the city; towers, roofs, and houses soon begin to sprout before his eyes. He passes a long, low building, the hospital called lazzaretto, and enters Milan from the East Gate, which is now Porta Venezia, and makes his way along the street that is today called Corso Venezia, heading to the Duomo itself.

Before he has an opportunity to continue further, however, he is forced to flee: implicated in the riots, he is pursued from the city by the police. After various adventures, during which time he also catches the plague, he finally hears news of Lucia again. Learning that she is in Milan, he once more makes his way to the city, to be belatedly reunited with her. On this second visit, the hero follows a significantly different path to the town, approaching Milan from the north and finding the city center via "the canal called the Naviglio." Every detail is authentic, carefully chosen by the author from seventeenth-century sources.

But he could discover nothing either way but two reaches of a winding road, and before him a part of the wall: in no quarter was there a symptom of a human being, except than in one spot, on the platform, might be seen a dense column of black and murky smoke, which expanded itself as it mounted, and curled into ample circles, and afterwards dispersed itself through the gray and motionless atmosphere.

Since then, the city's map has not changed, but the urban setting has. When Renzo first visits Milan, his walk is like a time machine: through his eyes, readers see small dusty roads that will in time become alleys and kitchen gardens; washerwomen's little houses are described that are soon to disappear; there is a small square with elm trees that had already been replaced by Manzoni's time by a grand palace. In this way, this fictional Milan is for modern readers the object of an ongoing act of imagination, where three levels of realism entwine: the seventeenth-century city of the characters, the nineteenth-century city of the writer, and the city that will be experienced by future readers.

This movable background is also an agitated, disordered one, because Renzo happens to be in Milan first in the middle of a popular revolt and then during one of the great tragedies of modern European history, the plague of 1630. Because of these extraordinary events, the city becomes the animated setting for apocalyptic visions: a fluctuating world whose strongest symbolic image is maybe that of a cart laden with plague-dead bodies "piled up and interwoven together"—a sort of hyperbole of the grotesque that attracted the praise of Edgar Allan Poe, who mentioned this very passage as an example of the strength of Manzoni's prose.

When Renzo finally finds a recovered Lucia, no longer a victim of the plague, the circle is closed: experiencing the city—its tragedies, dangers, and ambiguous attactions—has made an adult of the novel's young and humble hero, and he is ready for his new life.

PARIS, FRANCE

HONORÉ DE BALZAC

La Comédie humaine (1829–48)

La Comédie humaine *consists of 94 novels and short stories, most of which depict French society in Paris during the post-Revolutionary period.*

Honoré de Balzac was born in Tours, in the heart of the Loire Valley, in 1799. However, it is as a Parisian novelist that he is most often remembered. Balzac first arrived in the capital in 1813, when he began attending classes at the prestigious Lycée Charlemagne in the Marais. After completing his education in 1819, he promptly turned his back on the legal career that his family had planned for him, and instead took up residence in a garret in the Rue Lesdiguières, where he wrote his first play, *Cromwell.* Over the next 30 years, Balzac lived at 18 different addresses in the city. Following his disastrous attempt at establishing a printing business in the 1820s, a venture which saddled him with crushing debts, he led an itinerant life in the capital, moving from one location to the next in an attempt to evade his creditors.

La Comédie humaine was written between 1829 and 1848, but only acquired its definitive title in 1842.

Publication continued after Balzac's death, until 1856, with some works finished by his former secretary Charles Rabou.

Balzac has often been regarded as one of the great social historians of the nineteenth century. German philosopher Friedrich Engels proclaimed in 1888 that he had "learned more [from Balzac] than from all the professed historians, economists, and statisticians of the period together."

Balzac was fascinated by Paris, and viewed its urban landscape as a constant source of artistic inspiration. He described the capital as "the city of a hundred thousand novels," where behind every door was a story waiting to be told. One of his favorite pastimes was to stroll through the Paris streets eavesdropping on conversations in the hope of discovering ideas and plotlines for his work. Shop signs also provided him with inspiration for the names of some of his fictional characters.

La Comédie humaine stands as a towering monument to Balzac's lifelong connection with Paris. Written between 1829 and 1848, the collection comprises 94 novels and shorter fictions, and forms a vast panorama in which Balzac hoped to document every aspect of nineteenth-century French society. Paris occupies a central place in this ultimately unfinished realist enterprise. For Balzac, the capital appears as a place of infinite diversity, and he revels in transporting his readers through its various districts, from the muddy backstreets of the Latin Quarter to the aristocratic salons of the Faubourg Saint-Germain. Balzac was also sensitive to the way in which the city was changing. It was not until the 1870s that the urbanization program of Baron Haussmann swept away much of the medieval city and gave Paris its wide, open boulevards. During his own lifetime, however, Balzac sensed that the old city was already starting to disappear under the dual pressures of

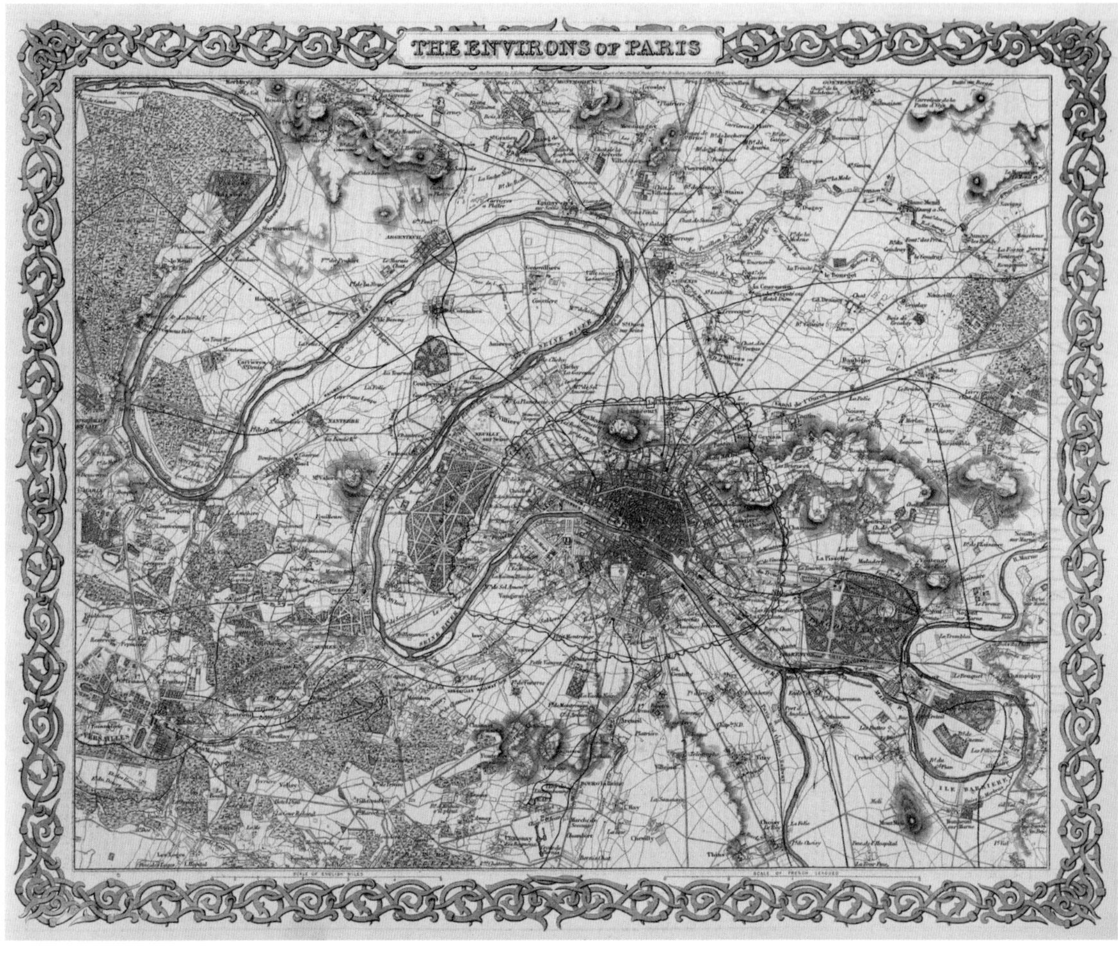

The Seine Valley, with Paris at the center, included in *The Environs of Paris* by J. H. Colton, 1855.

industrialization and new building works. As the novelist warned in his 1845 essay "Ce qui disparaît de Paris" ("What is disappearing from Paris"), "the Paris of yesterday will exist only in the works of those novelists who have the will to depict faithfully the last vestiges of the architecture of our forefathers, since the serious-minded historian cares little for such things."

Balzac's enthusiasm for exploring Paris and Parisian life in his fiction is reflected vividly in *Le Père Goriot* (*Old Goriot*), the 1835 novel that marked the full blossoming of the author's literary talents. Weaving together the stories of Goriot, a retired cereal merchant, and Rastignac, a young law student eager to make his career in the capital, the plot begins in a boarding house in the Latin Quarter (the building that is thought to have inspired Balzac still exists today, at 24 Rue Tournefort). At the outset, the narrative foregrounds the squalor of this corner of the city, where men and women were packed into boarding houses due to a chronic shortage of accommodation, and raw sewage still flowed down the middle of the cobbled streets. This is the Paris that Balzac

mud, a vale of sorrows which are real and joys too often hollow." Casting himself in the role of guide to this urban labyrinth, Balzac wonders aloud whether a story so fundamentally Parisian will even be understood by those unfamiliar with the city.

In its often grim depiction of the capital, *Le Père Goriot* reinvigorates the established literary theme of Paris as a modern hell. Parisians, Balzac had claimed in his 1834 novel *The Girl with the Golden Eyes* [*La Fille aux yeux d'or*], are obsessed with the pursuit of gold and pleasure, and will go to reprehensible lengths in order to satisfy their appetite for them. As the master-criminal Vautrin explains to Rastignac in *Le Père Goriot,* Parisians are prepared "to devour one another like spiders in a pot," and the individual who wants to succeed must fight mercilessly in order to advance his ambitions. Although Balzac did not invent this notion of Paris as a brutal, corrupt city, his view of the capital was colored by his belief that the Revolution had eroded the values of religion and family, and encouraged rampant greed and individualism.

As *Le Père Goriot* also testifies, Balzac presents Paris as a battlefield with its own rules and codes of social engagement. The young southerner Rastignac undergoes a painful learning experience in the capital that identifies this work as one of the defining novels of education of the nineteenth century. His early forays into Parisian life are characterized by a series of blunders, but under the guidance of both Vautrin and his cousin Madame de Beauséant, Rastignac comes to understand how to manipulate the city—and in particular its women—to his best advantage. The final episode in the novel confirms Rastignac's new-found mastery of Paris as he looks down from the hilltop cemetery at Père Lachaise in one of the most memorable and powerful descriptions of the city in French literature: "His eyes turned almost eagerly to the space between the column of the Place Vendôme and the cupola of the Invalides; there lay the shining world that he had wished to reach. He glanced over that humming hive, seeming to draw a foretaste of its honey, and said magniloquently: 'Henceforth there is war between us.'"

Paris has been called a hell. Take the phrase for truth. There all is smoke and fire, everything gleams, crackles, flames, evaporates, dies out, then lights up again, with shooting sparks, and is consumed. In no other country has life ever been more ardent or acute.
[from *La Fille aux yeux d'or*]

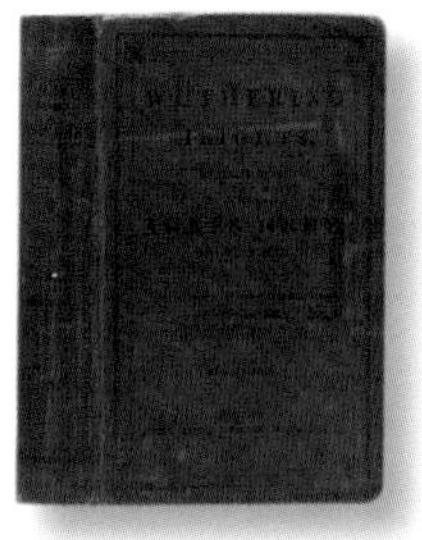

YORKSHIRE MOORS, ENGLAND

EMILY BRONTË

WUTHERING HEIGHTS (1847)

Steeped in the gloomy, gothic mystery of the Yorkshire moors, Brontë's tempestuous romance is a novel of intensities, centering on a love triangle between Catherine Earnshaw, the wealthy Edgar Linton, and the enigmatic Heathcliff.

Wuthering Heights was published in 1847 under the pseudonym "Ellis Bell," and appeared as the first two volumes in a three-volume format along with Anne Brontë's *Agnes Grey*.

A second edition of the novel was published in 1850, edited by Charlotte Brontë who corrected her sister's spelling and punctuation, and altered the servant character Joseph's Yorkshire dialect to make it more understandable.

Mulitple buildings may have inspired Wuthering Heights, one of which is Top Withens, a farmhouse located near Haworth Parsonage, the former Brontë family home now maintained as a museum to the sisters.

Wuthering Heights is a novel with a weather warning in its title. "Heights" is clear enough: many houses carry that epithet. What, though, is "wuthering"? Look it up and you'll be informed that it is "Yorkshire Dialect: the sound strong wind makes as it passes over roofs. Rare."

Wuthering Heights is a novel focused on landscape. But Emily Brontë realized that place and weather are inseparable. No novel comes to mind as conscious of season as *Wuthering Heights*. There are, word search reveals, 25 mentions of "spring," 23 of "winter," and 22 of "summer"—with richly detailed accompanying descriptions. Some things remain the same whatever the weather—the heath (moorland) and the cliff (Penistone Crags) primarily. The novel's antihero, Heathcliff, seems never to have been born of woman, but to have been generated by the landscape in its cruellest moments.

The opening of the novel is given in the form of a journal by the dandiacal gentleman, Lockwood, who has taken up leased residence at Thrushcross Grange. 'This is certainly a beautiful country!" he ejaculates. He will soon change his mind.

He resolves to pay his respects to his landlord, Mr. Heathcliff, four miles off at Wuthering Heights, on foot. It is not, he discovers, a prepossessing habitation. Thrushcross Grange is, as the name implies, a cultivated estate. Wuthering Heights is, by comparison, wilderness. All it has by way of natural scenery is "a few stunted firs [and] a range of gaunt thorns all stretching their limbs one way, as if craving alms of the sun."

Lockwood finds himself snowbound at the Heights and is forced to accept a bed there for the night. His rest is nightmare ridden and the novel's backstory emerges—through a broken window pane, shuddering cold, and a ghostly cut wrist thrusting bloodily through the jagged glass. Consciousness reveals it is no wrist (or was it?) but a branch of a gaunt fir tree rattling against the window in the wuthering wind.

Outside, the next morning, Lockwood finds the landscape a featureless snowy desert. The hill-back on whose top the house rests is "one billowy, white ocean." And a death trap. Winter is a killing place in this region. The heroine, Catherine, whom the antihero Heathcliff loves but his rival Edgar Linton marries, gasping in her sickness for clean air from the moors, throws open the window of her sick-room. The "cold blast" hastens her death. She dies fantasizing of summer, in the spring flowers by her bed. 'These are the earliest flowers at the [Wuthering] Heights," she exclaims. "They remind me of soft thaw winds, and warm sunshine, and nearly melted snow."

The chill Lockwood takes on his first visit to Wuthering Heights plunges him into a similar health crisis. While he convalesces, the Grange housekeeper, Nelly Dean, tells him the epic history of the two houses.

But deathly winter does not prevail: compare the wintry landscape of the opening with the serene, almost Keatsian, final scene, half a year later. It is late summer. Heathcliff is dead, tormented into self-destruction by the ghost of Catherine outside his window. Lockwood cannot forget the story Mrs. Dean has told him of Heathcliff's long, and eventually foiled, campaign to possess the two houses and Cathy. He makes an expedition to look at the churchyard graves of Cathy, her lover and her husband:

> I lingered round them, under that benign sky: watched the moths fluttering among the heath and harebells, listened to the soft wind breathing through the grass, and wondered how any one could ever imagine unquiet slumbers for the sleepers in that quiet earth.

Could landscape—the landscape that killed Cathy—be gentler?

There is a passage in the novel that captures the inseparable connection between weather and landscape. Cathy, as she dies, bears a daughter, Catherine, by the civilized owner of Thrushcross Grange, Edgar Linton. Heathcliff has a son by Linton's sister, Linton Heathcliff. Heathcliff abducts both children, intending they shall marry and cement his ownership of the two great houses. As Catherine recounts to Nelly:

> One time [Linton and I] were near quarrelling. He said the pleasantest manner of spending a hot July day was lying from morning till evening on a bank of heath in the middle of the moors [...] and the blue sky and bright sun shining steadily and cloudlessly. That was his most perfect idea of heaven's happiness: mine was rocking in a rustling green tree, with a west wind blowing, and bright white clouds flitting rapidly above [...] I said his heaven would be only half alive; and he said mine would be drunk [...] At last, we agreed to try both, as soon as the right weather came; and then we kissed each other and were friends.

Capturing the rich landscape of *Wuthering Heights* in its possible tenderness as well as its violent excess, this paragraph presents a rare moment of compromise for Brontë's novel, which is otherwise fraught with contrast and bewilderment, rippling with the windy tumult of the Yorkshire moors.

“This is certainly a beautiful country! In all England, I do not believe that I could have fixed on a situation so completely removed from the stir of society.” *Wuthering Heights (The Witherns, near Haworth)*, 1942. Painting by L. S. Lowry.

LONDON, ENGLAND

CHARLES DICKENS

BLEAK HOUSE (1852–53)

A passionate romance and murder mystery, but like all of Dickens's work it is above all a critical social comment on the failings of Victorian Britain. A long-running legal trial becomes the basis for a satirical damnation of the British judiciary.

Charles Dickens (1812-1870) was born in Portsmouth, moving to London in 1822. A literary celebrity in his own lifetime, he remains one of England's most loved writers, and published 15 novels, five novellas, and numerous short stories.

Bleak House was Dickens's ninth novel, and was published as a serial of nineteen instalments between March 1852 and September 1853.

Bleak House was a great popular success with the reading public from its first appearance, with sales averaging 34,000 per month for each installment.

It's one of the most famous opening scenes in all English fiction; perhaps even the most famous:

> Implacable November weather. As much mud in the streets as if the waters had but newly retired from the face of the earth, and it would not be wonderful to meet a Megalosaurus, forty feet long or so, waddling like an elephantine lizard up Holborn Hill. Smoke lowering down from chimney-pots, making a soft black drizzle, with flakes of soot in it as big as full-grown snowflakes—gone into mourning, one might imagine, for the death of the sun. Dogs, undistinguishable in mire. Horses, scarcely better; splashed to their very blinkers. Foot passengers, jostling one another's umbrellas in a general infection of ill temper, and losing their foot-hold at street-corners, where tens of thousands of other foot passengers have been slipping and sliding since the day broke (if this day ever broke), adding new deposits to the crust upon crust of mud, sticking at those points tenaciously to the pavement, and accumulating at compound interest.

It's the Megalosaurus waddling up Holborn Hill that strikes the fancy most—and Dickens was ahead of the curve here, for the fossils discovered in the eighteenth century had only been classified two decades before he wrote *Bleak House*; and so dinosaurs at the time contained the two extremely distinct characteristics of being both extremely old and extremely new.

And this, in a way, is what he thought about London, and how to portray it: as a place of timeless vice, and also as thoroughly modern. In the census of 1851, just before he started writing *Bleak House*, it was revealed that the British population in cities had overtaken that of the rural population; and an up-to-date novelist would have to realize that tipping point would never be reversed. (Dickens was more modern, and more of an iconoclast than people might nowadays think. In his library. was a book called *The Wisdom of Our Ancestors*; if a guest happened to open it, they'd find the pages entirely blank.)

"A Court for King Cholera," 1852 illustration from *Punch* magazine, published in the same year as *Bleak House* and depicting similar scenes of overcrowding and dirt in Victorian London.

But the point that is often missed is the mud. It's not mud, or not all mud. We are talking about the excrement of thousands of horses and many hundreds of thousands of people, all crammed together in an unimaginably densely populated area. The "general infection of ill temper" is itself a prelude to the general infection of illness such conditions would accelerate. There had been many cholera outbreaks in London before he wrote the novel; the most famous one, the Soho outbreak of 1854, took place in the year after its completion; it was only then that a link was discovered between feces-contaminated drinking water and the disease, by the physician John Snow. Had he read *Bleak House*? It's not exactly a long shot.

Dickens did not predict the outbreak, but it would hardly have been an act of great clairvoyance if he had. Likewise, the mixture of "mud" and fog creates, in his readers' minds, the idea of a kind of miasma, which would take real form in the Great Stink of 1858, during which Parliament was suspended, the foul smell of untreated sewage in the Thames becoming unignorable during that year's hot summer. (It was thanks to this that Bazalgette built the sewage system that still, despite great strains on it, stops London from becoming an olfactorily unlivable city.) Again, Dickens didn't predict this; but anyone living in London knew it was bound to happen sooner or later. (Foreign visitors were always perplexed at how much the city stank, and how the residents could stand it. It wasn't just excreta: it was the disjecta of countless businesses, homes, chimneys, and factories with only an eighteenth-, or in some parts seventeenth-, century infrastructure to cope with them.)

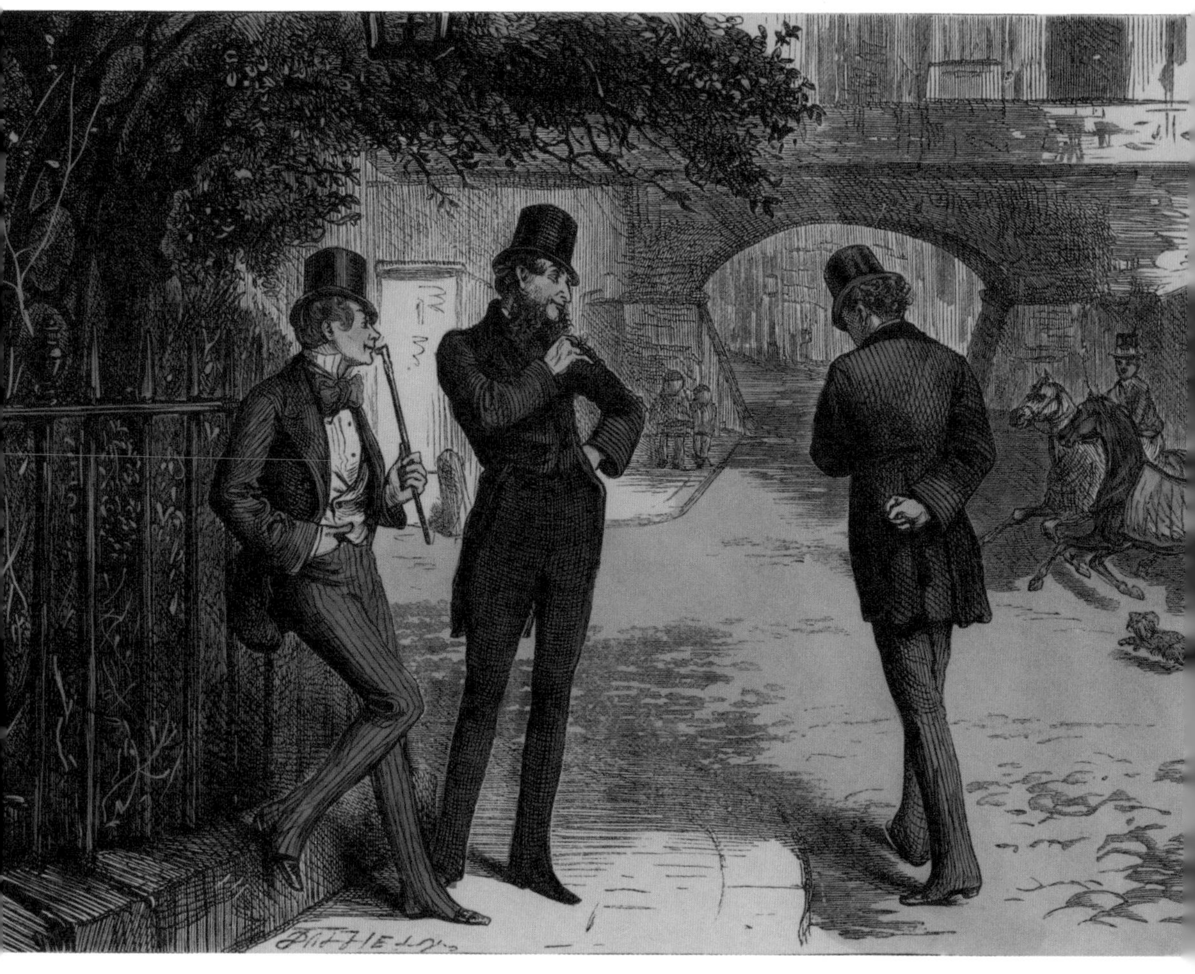

Under the Lincoln's Inn Trees, illustration by Frederik L. Bernard for the *Household Edition of the Works of Charles Dickens*, c.1890.

And there are the mud and fog: or Mudfog—Dickens's name for either the town of Chatham, where he was born, or the workhouse where Oliver Twist spent too much of his childhood (in the serialized version of the book, not the final published volume, that is). You could not call "mud" exactly what Dickens meant by it in a serial publication, and not in a book unless you wanted to scandalize; but contemporary readers knew what he meant.

The point is that he makes the connection between this filth and the corruption of law and establishment. *Bleak House*'s importance resides in the way it links both the highest—Lord and Lady Deadlock—and the lowest—Jo the crossing sweeper. When we first meet the Deadlocks, their estate in Lincolnshire is flooded: in this case, nature's own drainage system has failed to work. And here is where Jo lives:

> Jo lives—that is to say, Jo has not yet died—in a ruinous place known to the like of him by the name of Tom-all-Alone's. It is a black, dilapidated

> street, avoided by all decent people, where the crazy houses were seized upon, when their decay was far advanced, by some bold vagrants who after establishing their own possession took to letting them out in lodgings. Now, these tumbling tenements contain, by night, a swarm of misery. As on the ruined human wretch vermin parasites appear, so these ruined shelters have bred a crowd of foul existence that crawls in and out of gaps in walls and boards; and coils itself to sleep, in maggot numbers, where the rain drips in; and comes and goes, fetching and carrying fever and sowing more evil in its every footprint than Lord Coodle, and Sir Thomas Doodle, and the Duke of Foodle, and all the fine gentlemen in office, down to Zoodle, shall set right in five hundred years—though born expressly to do it.

More disease, described so we hardly know whether it is of the body or the soul; and it is only within walking distance of Chancery Lane ("Dilating and dilating since the sun went down last night, it has gradually swelled until it fills every void in the place;" Tom-all-Alone's gets bigger as it gets darker; that is, ignorance breeds in conditions of darkness, of fog and mud; when, in summer, the weather is drier, Chancery's offices are filled with dust instead).

There are other London locations in *Bleak House*, and indeed you can look up countless books and articles which can tell you how to walk from one to the other. I know of one student whose dissertation's footnotes consisted of nothing but instructions on how to find them. But Dickens was not interested in writing a literary tourist's guide. He was using the city as a metaphor for how the human condition could, unattended, go wrong. Take the Polygon, in Somers Town; in *Pickwick Papers*, this is a pleasant enough place; it had, after all, been designed as a kind of show home, or apartment block. By the time it appears in *Bleak House* (Mr. Slingsby lives there, in genteel poverty) it is beginning to fall apart. (It was demolished in 1894.) That was Dickens's crusade when he wrote about London, seeing it clear and square and for what it was: a crusade against negligence.

Fog everywhere. Fog up the river where it flows among green airs and meadows; fog down the river, where it rolls defiled among the tiers of shipping, and the waterside pollutions of a great (and dirty) city.

PARIS, FRANCE

VICTOR HUGO
LES MISÉRABLES (1862)

Epic in proportion and ambition, Hugo's classic captures an entire Parisian underworld, in all its violence, drama, and poverty. Convict Jean Valjean's changing fortunes provide the backbone to a sensational narrative that teems with characters and heaves with the sprawl of the city.

Victor Hugo was a man of many talents; not only a poet, artist, and novelist, he was also a politician and used his status to campaign for human rights.

Les Misérables has been transformed into one of the world's most successful musicals, with a score by Alain Boublil and Claude-Michel Schönberg. It is the second-longest-running musical in the world.

Despite popular misconceptions, *Les Misérables* is not set during the French Revolution. Rather, the bulk of it is set in 1832: during a failed attempt to overthrow the restored monarchy of Louis Philippe I, several decades after the 1789 revolution.

Victor Hugo's *Les Misérables* takes us through two decades in the long and turbulent lifestory of the good ex-convict Jean Valjean. This central character's escape from the law and his quest for redemption run through the book, but dozens of other strands are also woven through it, as we're introduced to characters like the unfortunate Fantine and her daughter Cosette (whom Valjean eventually comes to adopt), the urchin Gavroche, and the wealthy student Marius Pontmercy, who becomes involved in the Paris Uprising of 1832 (only to have his life saved by Valjean, too). But this is an enormous, wildly digressive novel, about countless other things and other people, and one of those other countless things, looming large over the whole book, is the city of Paris: its roads, its houses, its street children, its tempestuous events, its filth and class and cruel injustices.

Paris is not merely a backdrop for Victor Hugo, it's one of his subjects, and his passions. And that's not only because, in practical terms, steering each of his characters together into this one great, dense city, and recreating it in such rich and unsentimental detail, allows him to paint a complex picture of society, poverty, law, religion, money, and change all on a single (huge) canvas; but also, perhaps, because his own feelings about the city—*his* city—must have been heightened by the fact that the book was substantially created from outside, from elsewhere, from exile.

Much of the Paris that dominates *Les Misérables* is still recognizable today, of course. Most of the streets names mentioned in the book are still on today's maps, and it's possible to trace the characters' movements accordingly. The book's central character rents a big house and garden on the quiet Rue Plumet in the 15th arrondissement (he and Cosette see a chain-gang nearby), and later he lives at the Boulevard de l'Hôpital: both are places a twenty-first-century literary pilgrim might easily find. You could take a stroll, too, in the Jardin de Luxembourg, which is where Cosette is walking when Marius notices her and falls in love.

Not all of this fictional Paris is true to reality, however. Often Victor Hugo begins with an accurate version, only to then distort it to suit his

CONFIER
C'est quelquefois livrer

requirements—yes, Jean Valjean may live on such-and-such real street, but the author has invented a nonexistent house number for him. And much imagination must have gone into one of the book's most memorable Parisian scenes, which takes place not on the city's famous streets but beneath them, when Jean Valjean carries an unconscious Marius (dramatically, if somewhat implausibly) through the Paris sewers. Victor Hugo had done his research and read about the sewers, but he had not visited them himself—though nowadays the city does boast a brilliantly unlikely "Sewer Museum," to entertain some of the novel's more devoted fans.

A garden to walk in and immensity to dream in—what more could he ask? A few flowers at his feet and above him the stars.

Some of the city has changed in the intervening centuries, of course. And indeed, in many ways *Les Misérables* isn't quite about the Paris at the time of its writing, but about a city Victor Hugo already knew to be lost, which had evolved between the years of the book's events and its publication. In the novel, for example, the student barricades are erected on the old Rue de la Chanvrerie, which had already disappeared by the time of its writing. Victor Hugo even acknowledges these transformations, referring explicitly to his own relationship to the city: "As a result of demolitions and reconstructions," he writes, "the Paris of [the author's] youth, that Paris he carried with him religiously in his memory, is now a Paris of yesteryear."

Any glimpses of nostalgia for Paris of the past are understandable. The author had begun the book in his Paris home, but abandoned the writing for many years, and it was only during his sad exile on Guernsey, in the closing days of 1860, that he resumed his work on it, and did the lion's share there. The Paris he wrote about, then, was Paris as he remembered it from a distance (though partly fact-checked by his obliging friend Théophile Guérin, who did research on the ground). So it was really Hauteville House in Guernsey that was the unlikely site of this novel's gestation and birth. All the more appropriate, then, that since a 1927 gift this unlikely house of pilgrimage has itself belonged to … the City of Paris.

Previous page: "Cosette was made to run errands, scrub floors, sweep the yard and the pavement, wash the dishes and even carry large burdens." *Cosette Sweeping*, 1862. Illustration by Emile Bayard for the first edition.

TULA OBLAST, RUSSIA

LEO TOLSTOY

ANNA KARENINA (1875–77)

Set in St. Petersburg high society and on the country estate, Tolstoy's great novel of adultery poses unabashedly big questions about the nature of love and the meaning of life. (Both, it turns out, have a fair amount to do with the management of agriculture.)

An early critic of *Anna Karenina* complained that this was "not a novel, but a collection of photographs collected completely at random, without any general idea or plan." As the serialized instalments appeared, readers' letters echoed the charge, reacting to the apparent lack of structure or design of the novel. What these readers found was two stories that seemingly did not intersect: one about Anna and her adulterous affair with the officer Vronsky and another about a landowner, Konstantin Levin, and his vexed searching for answers to questions about faith, family life, and agricultural reform. Tolstoy famously defended the "architecture" of his novel, claiming that its meaning lay in a "labyrinth of linkages," and could be conveyed only by "writing the same novel over again from the beginning."

The landowner Konstantin Levin, is a semi-autobiographical incarnation of his creator, who was known as Lev as well as Leo Tolstoy, sharing a metaphysical searching and crisis of faith.

Anna Karenina started life as monthly installments in the *Russian Herald* in January 1875. They continued until April 1877, when the editor refused to publish the final installment due to its politically sensitive treatment of the Balkan war. Enraged, Tolstoy issued the epilogue as a separate brochure. A complete edition, with the epilogue as Part Eight, was published in 1878.

Tolstoy's novel opens with one of the most famous first lines of world literature: "All happy families are alike; each unhappy family is unhappy in its own way." The paragraph that follows contains forms of the Russian word for "house" or "home" six times. The principle of comparison set forth in that first line offers a powerful interpretative tool for the novel—even if readers may, in the end, refrain from drawing such clear-cut conclusions as this authoritative voice proclaims. And the prominence of "home" declares the novel's most highly valued setting. Following the novel's characters and moving between plotlines, readers are asked to compare its forms of love and family life—and its settings, the places where homes are made: Moscow and St. Petersburg; city and countryside; Russia and Italy; Pokrovskoe and Vozdvizhenskoe (the country estates of the Levins and of Anna and Vronsky, respectively).

In contrast to the falsity and modernity of the city stands the countryside. If Anna is most often depicted in interiors, then Levin is to be found (at his most comfortable) outside and in the country. He finds solace—and, eventually, faith—in these open spaces: mowing in the meadow alongside peasants, contemplating the wide sky, striding out along a road.

Levin's estate, Pokrovskoe, is as beloved to Levin as Tolstoy's own estate, Yasnaya Polyana, was to him. It appears in the novel as something of an ideal, especially when, in Part Six, it is juxtaposed to Vozdvizhenskoe, where

Mashkin Heights were mown, and the peasants, having completed their last swaths, put on their coats and went home in high spirits ... [Levin] looked back from the top of the hill. He could not see the men, for the mist rising from the hollow hid them; but he heard their merry rough voices, laughter, and the clanking of the scythes.

Anna and Vronsky have set up their troublingly inauthentic household. Its name is derived from the Russian root *pokrov*, meaning "protection" or "sanctuary." By the end of the novel, Pokrovskoe is a world unto itself, a place where all the parts of his life Levin most cares for have come into holistic alignment: we leave Levin with his wife, baby, and extended family, engaged in daily interactions with the peasants, tending to the duties of family life and estate management.

One of the world's great realist novels, *Anna Karenina* impresses on us the solidity of its setting, the apparent objectivity of its world. But, rather than a backcloth painted in by an omnisicent narrator who is given to description, the setting of *Anna Karenina* is almost always allied to the experience or point of view of a particular character.

Take, for example, the scything in the fields. As he mows, Levin sheds all conscious thought, all sense of time, and experiences only blissful "moments of oblivion," a pure present in which he is fully immersed in the rhythmic physicality of the scything. The description of the surroundings comes only when Levin wakes from a nap after lunch and looks around to find that he

> hardly recognized the place, it had changed so much. An immense expanse of the meadow had been mown, and with its already fragrant swaths, shone with a special new gleam in the slanting rays of the evening sun... [T]he sheer wall of grass in the unmowed part of the meadow, and the hawks circling above the stripped meadow—all this was completely new.

His previous experience and all the sensations of mowing are understood anew, integrated with a broader perspective on space and time that sees the entirety of what has been accomplished. *How* Levin sees is as important as *what* he sees: he looks onto the meadow with a sense of wonder.

In *Anna Karenina* movement is as important as the stasis of setting. The plot relies on the movement of characters from one place to another; interpretation relies on the movement of the reader between strands of the multiplot novel. Above all, perhaps, the achievement of Tolstoy's psychological realism lies in its depiction of movements of consciousness: how thoughts and feelings take shape, how changes happen. In this, its literary landscape is indissoluble from character experience.

Leo Tolstoy photographed on his estate at Yasnaya Polyana, c.1900. Tolstoy focused a lot of his attention on farming, expanding the apple orchard from 25 to over 100 acres, and growing a stud farm of over 4,000 horses.

DORSET, ENGLAND

THOMAS HARDY

The Return of the Native (1878)

Hardy's darkly imagined Edgon Heath in Wessex provides a fulcrum for this tragic love story between the 'native' Clym Yeobright and the outsider Eustacia Vye.

Thomas Hardy (1840–1928), was the son of a stone-mason and originally trained as an architect; he became familiar with the classics mainly through his friendship with Horace Moule.

The Return of the Native was initially serialized, published in twelve monthly installments in *Belgravia* magazine in 1878. Its reception was generally positive, and, despite Hardy's initial problems finding a publisher, it was published in volume form later that same year.

The place-word "Wessex" is indivisible from Hardy's fiction. It is an Anglo-Saxon name for what weather forecasters blandly nowadays call the 'south west', but Hardy exhumed the word and made it entirely his own to describe the place he was born, lived most of his life, and revered.

In *The Return of the Native,* his sixth published novel, Hardy sets out to stress that we all come from somewhere—our "birthplace"—and that most of us lose our connection to it. We "transplant." Mobility has obvious life-advantages, but something is lost.Where Thomas Wolfe's most famous novel asserts *You Can't Go Home Again*, Hardy's *The Return of the Native* counters "yes you can." But there's a catch. Will it be the same place (for you)? Tragically no, as the novel chronicles.

The narrative centres on Clym Yeobright, the "native" of the title. He returns from Paris, where he had done well as a gem merchant. But he needs to find himself in the place he was born. He falls in love and marries Eustacia. She wants them to return to Paris and the high life. He resolves to stay. Things go from bad to worse (they always do in Hardy's fiction) and Clym ends up a humble furzecutter, or "cropper," on Egdon Heath. This "vast tract of unenclosed wild" is a composite of the heaths around Dorchester where Hardy grew up, and arguably the novel's lead character. No one could forget Hardy's opening description of the Heath, or not feel a chill reading it:

> A Saturday afternoon in November was approaching the time of twilight, and the vast tract of unenclosed wild known as Egdon Heath embrowned itself moment by moment. Overhead the hollow stretch of whitish cloud shutting out the sky was as a tent which had the whole heath for its floor.
>
> The heaven being spread with this pallid screen and the earth with the darkest vegetation, their meeting-line at the horizon was clearly marked. In such contrast the heath wore the appearance of an instalment of night which had taken up its place before its astronomical hour was come: darkness had to a great extent arrived hereon, while day stood distinct in the sky.

The watercolour artist Walter Tyndale produced a number of paintings of landscapes in the south-west of England. A contemporary of Hardy, he was praised by the writer for his "fidelity, both in form and colour." This is Tyndale's painting of Bere Heath in Dorset (1906), which in part inspired the Egdon Heath of Wessex.

One of the phenomena of landscape described in this grand way is that it dwarfs humanity. Even as majestic a character as Eustacia Vye, who glows with "the raw material of a divinity," has to fight against Egdon's overwhelmingness. Others, like the "native" of the title, are crushed by it.

What, one may go on to ask, is a "heath"? Hardy admitted that he was influenced, in setting and story, by the "blasted" heath in King Lear—a place wholly inhospitable to man. What the returned native Clym discovers is that the heath is not an "unenclosed wild," a wasteland. It is, when one is close to it as Clym is with his scythe, rich and alive. It is something unspoiled:

> Tribes of emerald-green grasshoppers leaped over his feet, falling awkwardly on their backs, heads, or hips, like unskilful acrobats … Huge flies, ignorant of larders and wire-netting, and quite in a savage state, buzzed about him without knowing that he was a man. In and out of the fern-dells snakes glided in their most brilliant blue and yellow guise … Litters of young rabbits came out from their forms to sun themselves upon hillocks, the hot beams blazing through the delicate tissue … None of them feared him.

What the native has discovered is not simply "nature"—in the Wordsworthian sense—but Eden in the Miltonic sense, complete with its own serpent (one of them kills Clym's mother). It is hard to think of a writer who paints landscape, verbally, as feelingly as Hardy. Even by his unmatched standards, the creation of Egdon is a topographic masterpiece.

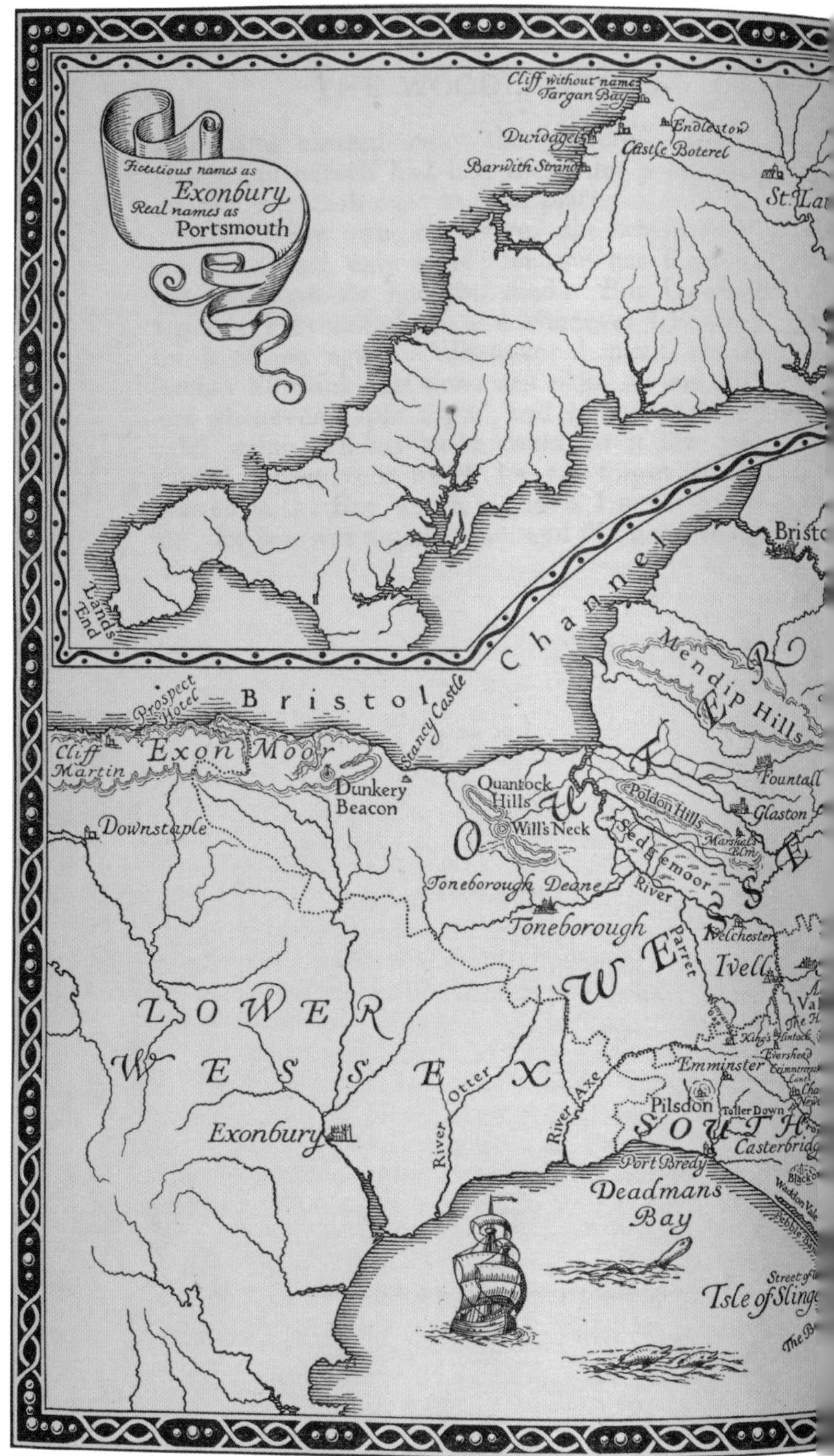

Map of Thomas Hardy's Wessex, 1912, the fictional setting of all Hardy's major novels, described by him as "a partly-real, partly dream-country."

Map of the
WESSEX
of the
Novels and Poems
Scale of Miles
5 0 5 10 15
Septentrio
Occidens
Oriens
Meridies
Lumsdon
Christminster
R. Thames
NORTH
The Brown House
Alfredston
Cresscombe
Marygreen
River Thames
MID
WESSEX
Marlbury Downs
Castle Royal
Gaymead
Kennetbridge
Aldbrickham
Inkpen Beacon
Stoke Barehills
Quartershot
Weydon Priors
Icenway House
The Great Plain
Stonehenge
UPPER
Wintoncester
Melchester
Fernel Hall
WESSEX
Wingreen
Deansleigh Park
The Slopes
Chaseborough
Southampton
Portsmouth
Knollingwood Hall
Lornton Inn
The Great Bramshurst Forest
Warborne
Chene Manor
Solentsea
Havenpool
Sandbourne
The Island
Anglebury
Corvesgate
Knollsea
The Channel
Emery Walker sc.

MISSISSIPPI RIVER, USA

MARK TWAIN

THE ADVENTURES OF HUCKLEBERRY FINN (1884)

A meandering tale that traverses the American South, Twain's classic tries to do the impossible and capture the essence of the mighty Mississippi River on the page.

Mark Twain, born Samuel Clemens, worked as a riverboat pilot in his youth and St Petersburg, the home of Huck Finn and Tom Sawyer, was inspired by Twain's own childhood home, Hannibal, Missouri.

Since the first edition in 1884, the novel has appeared in over 150 American editions alone and 200,000 copies are sold each year.

The Mississippi River s 2,320 miles long. By comparison, the distance between Ireland and Ukraine—the entire breadth of Europe—is 1,700 miles, and between Brazil and Sierra Leone—the width of the Atlantic—is 1,770 miles.

Twain grew up, worked, and lived much of his life on the Mississippi. As a child, he saw it as an opportunity: the privileged, glamorous life of the riverboat pilot. As a young man, he worked on the river, gathering stories, having adventures—also seeing it claim the life of his brother. Twain developed an appreciation and an awe for the river's power.

Huckleberry Finn is a rambling tale of a young man reaching maturity. Young Huck is often a proxy for Twain himself: his youth allows him a naïve appreciation of the river, generous with praise, filled with awe and free to make all the sentimental observations that the vehemently unromantic Twain could not.

Some of its sense of place stems from the way that it directly addressed issues in American society: this is, ultimately, a book railing against slavery, and attempting to explain the cultural divides that led to the Civil War. Twain also uses aesthetic elements to convey geography: the typographical assault on various Midwestern and Southern accents is similar to Sir Walter Scott's attempts to capture the Scottish burr. It can be difficult for modern readers, but still aids in capturing the novel's setting. But, above all, *Huck Finn*'s underpinning Americanness—its indisputable sense of place—comes from the Mississippi River.

The American river has its physical peers only in the Amazon, the Yangtze, and the Nile, and, to Twain's contemporary reader, was as exotic and remote as any of those three. The Nile, with its deeply mythic presence, is perhaps the best comparison: Twain's Mississippi represents not only an untameable natural power, but holds the power of life and death for the people clinging to its banks. Huck's descriptions of the towns clinging to the Mississippi's banks sound like lessons in prehistory: settlements of scavengers, living on what the river provides, completely at its mercy, with their fragile homes slowly eroding away into the water.

As if to further emphasize the Mississippi's incomparable nature, *Huckleberry Finn* freely taps into the rivers of myth. At times, the Mississippi is Styx, Lethe, or even the Acheron of the *Inferno*. It is as if Twain knows his

readers cannot visualize the magnificence of the river in life, and that he needs to draw on legends to help visualize it.

"I got a good place amongst the leaves, and set there on a log, munching the bread and watching the ferry-boat, and very well satisfied." *Watching the Boat*, 1855. Illustration by E. W. Kemble.

Throughout the book, the river provides Huck and Jim with means of rescue and survival—but also claims the lives of others. Huck, throughout his titular book, keeps "dying." In a trick borrowed from Tom Sawyer, Huck fakes his own death to escape from his abusive father: after creating a false trail, he steps into the river, and floats away into the unknown. Huck comes "back to life" when he encounters Jim on an island—a patch of earth totally surrounded by the flowing waters. For the rest of the book, Huck shifts between the two

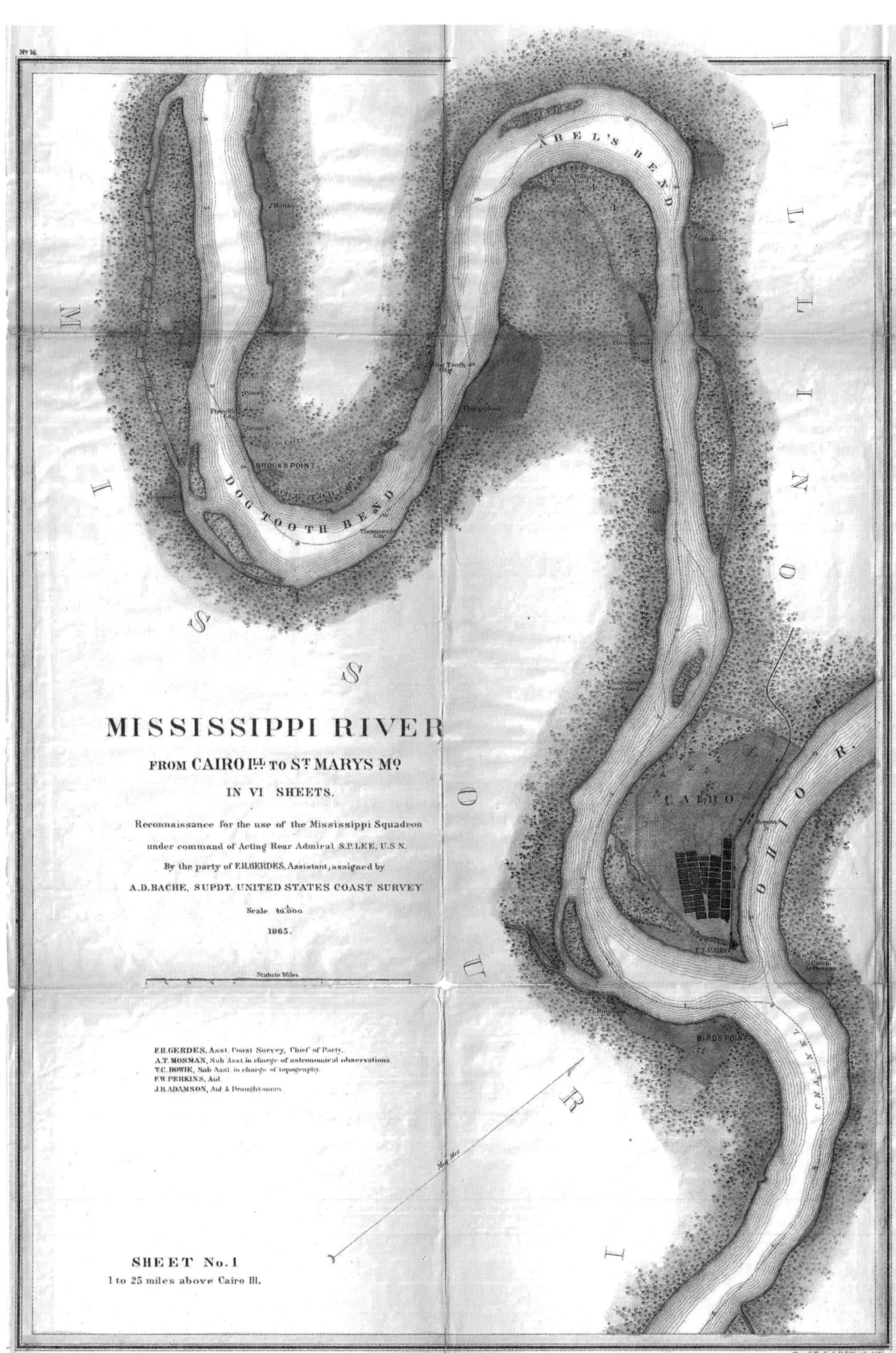
No 16.
MISSISSIPPI RIVER
FROM CAIRO ILL. TO ST MARYS MO.
IN VI SHEETS.
Reconnaissance for the use of the Mississippi Squadron
under command of Acting Rear Admiral S.P.LEE, U.S.N.
By the party of F.H.GERDES, Assistant, assigned by
A.D.BACHE, SUPDT. UNITED STATES COAST SURVEY
Scale 1/40.000
1865.
Statute Miles
F.H.GERDES, Asst. Coast Survey, Chief of Party.
A.T. MOSMAN, Sub Asst. in charge of astronomical observations.
T.C. BOWIE, Sub Asst. in charge of topography.
F.W. PERKINS, Aid.
J.R. ADAMSON, Aid & Draughtsman.
SHEET No. 1
1 to 25 miles above Cairo Ill.
ABEL'S BEND
DOG TOOTH BEND
BROOKS POINT
CAIRO
FT. CAIRO
BIRDS POINT
OHIO R.
CHANNEL
Mag. Mer.
M I S S O U R I
I L L I N O I S
Chas. G. Krebs & E. F. Bartle Lith.

> Two or three days and nights went by; I reckon I might say they swum by, they slid along so quiet and smooth and lovely. Here is the way we put in the time. It was a monstrous big river down there– sometimes a mile and a half wide; we run nights, and laid up and hid daytimes

states. While on the river, Huck remains 'dead'. But whenever he touches its shores, he is forced back to life. He must either be reincarnated (in one of his many ridiculous false identities) or be reborn (as when he encounters Tom Sawyer).

Huck and Jim are not merely using the Mississippi to "die," they are using it to be *forgotten*—drawing from the river Lethe. The Widow Douglas, from whom both Huck and Jim are fleeing, is a "civilizing" influence—and there's nothing Huck fears more. On the shores, he must remember to wear clothes, remember his manners, remember all the arcane edicts around religion and honor. Here, Twain is at his most scathing, and the book is littered with peripatetic asides where Huck encounters strange cultures and societies: two feuding families, killing one another for reasons that no one recalls; an angry lynch mob, unable to complete their bloody mission because no one can "remember how to be a man." These are the evils of memory, the rituals of behavior without sense or meaning behind them. There are entire towns behaving as foolishly as Tom Sawyer planning a jailbreak: doing what they remember they're "supposed to" without ever considering why.

Huck hopes the Widow doesn't mourn him. Jim hopes he's not caught and recaptured. To them, memory is a burden, freedom is in the forgetting. On the river itself, memory holds no sway: they make up their own stories, and are free to enjoy an unencumbered present. While on the river, Huck is free from decision: he can float, neutral, without worrying about his mortal affairs or immortal soul. But, again, when he steps to the *riva malvagia* ("evil shore"), he's forced into action: to ally with or betray con men, to aid or deceive runaway lovers, to help or hinder Jim's escape.

At the start of his adventures, Huck believes what his father told him: "the best way to get along with [evil] people is to let them have their own way." But his time on the river teaches him to trust himself.

Huckleberry Finn is the first truly American classic. The previous canon of American literature was, at best, transatlantic. It all still had a distinctly British feel. With Twain, the fruits of the Revolution had finally ripened. No more backward-facing epics of pre-Colonial adventure. Twain's work was uniquely, boldly, and wonderfully American. His work opened up the West and Midwest, introducing America to itself.

Opposite: The Mississippi River from Cairo, Illinois, to St Mary's, Missouri, US Coast Survey Map, 1865.

HIGHLANDS, SCOTLAND

ROBERT LOUIS STEVENSON

KIDNAPPED (1886)

Entangling eighteenth-century history with adventure fiction, Stevenson's story follows a teenage boy, David Balfour, in his attempts to escape his kidnapper. The craggy Scottish Highlands and imminent Jacobite rebellion provide a powerful backdrop to the drama.

Robert (Lewis) "Louis" Stevenson, born in Edinburgh in 1850, first published *Kidnapped* in serialized form in the magazine *Young Folks* in 1886 under the title "Kidnapped: or, The Lad with the Silver Button."

Stevenson wrote *Kidnapped* whilst he was living in Bournemouth, England, in a house called Skerryvore, named after a lighthouse designed and built by his uncle and father.

Louis Rhead drew more than one hundred illustrations for *Kidnapped*, to convey the majestic countryside of the Highlands represented in the "word-pictures" drawn by Stevenson.

Kidnapped begins and ends in the Scottish Lowlands in and around Edinburgh. It is here that our fictional narrator, adolescent, orphaned David Balfour, narrowly avoids an attempted nepoticide. It is here at the behest of his sly uncle Ebenezer that David is press-ganged and taken on board the brig *Covenant*. Ebenezer's intent is for David to be sold into slavery in the Carolinas. But David Balfour never reaches America.

Mid-novel our tale takes a dramatic twist. Whilst navigating the foggy west coast of Scotland, the *Covenant* scuttles a mysterious rowboat from which the sole survivor, Highlander Alan Breck-Stewart, manages to board the *Covenant*.

Contemporary readers with an interest in Scottish history will have recognized Alan Breck-Stewart as a real person: the supposed vanished assassin in the famous 1752 Appin murder case when the king's factor, Colin Campbell, was ambushed and murdered in the forest of Lettermore.

Kidnapped would somehow have to take a journey through the Highlands. Whilst training to become a civil engineer, Stevenson often accompanied his father in surveying trips around the remote Scottish seashores. One summer he spent three weeks on the islet of Erraid, and perhaps readers should not be surprised when the *Covenant* sinks off the islet of Earraid adjacent to Mull, and David Balfour and Alan Breck-Stewart make their escape toward the Highlands.

Not since James Macpherson's translations of *Ossian's Cycle of Gaelic Poems* and Walter Scott's turn-of-the-century Waverley novels had those landscapes been so vividly drawn. One may expect dazzling mountains, glens, and lochs, and we get that and more. The quietly desolate moors take on a visceral beauty when described by the narrator, David Balfour:

> The mist rose and died away, and showed us that country lying as waste as the sea; only the moorfowl and the peewees crying upon it, and far over to the east, a herd of deer, moving like dots.

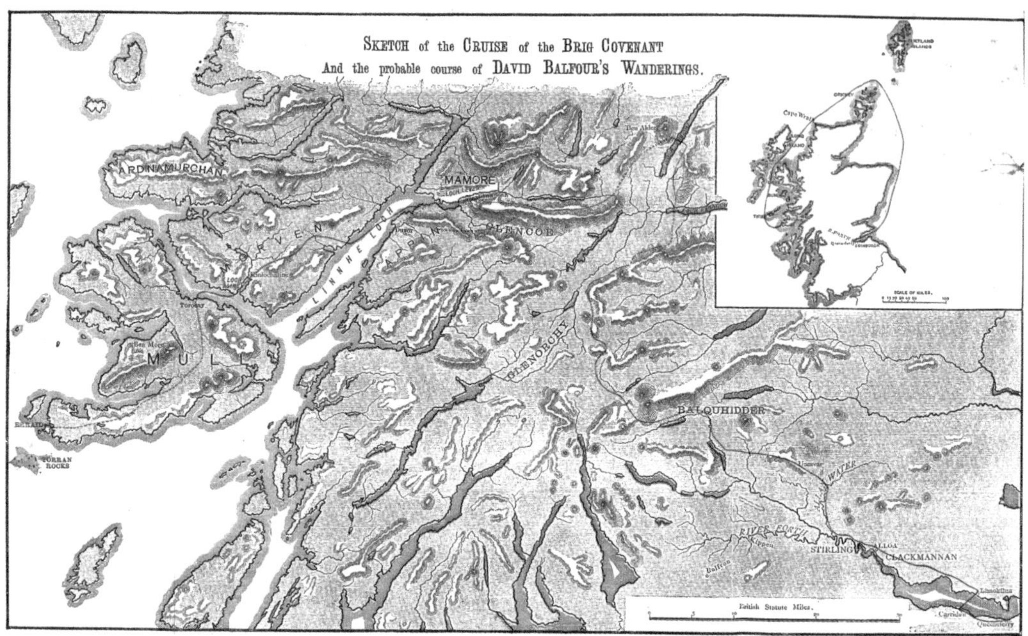

Previous page: "There is a pretty high rock on the northwest of Earraid, which (because it had a flat top and overlooked the Sound) I was much in the habit of frequenting." *On the Island of Earraid*, 1913. Illustration by N. C. Wyeth.

Above: A sketch mapping the cruise of the *Brig Covenant*, tracking the probable route of David Balfour through the landscape of the Scottish Highlands, from the first edition of *Kidnapped*, 1886.

Previously, Stevenson had garnered acclaim for potent characterization with his breakthrough serialized adventure novel *Treasure Island*, and his gothic-novella *The Strange Case of Doctor Jekyll and Mr Hyde*. But it is for *Kidnapped*, and in particular for its evocation of the Scottish Highlands, that Stevenson's reputation for depicting landscapes was forged. Crucially, it was *Kidnapped* that won him the comparison that he most appreciated: with his revered Sir Walter Scott.

Thanks to the many radio, television and film adaptations of *Kidnapped* and its sequels, the Scottish Highlands retain a mystical Stevensonian charm and a hold on our imagination. Modern readers can still follow the breathtaking 230-mile circuit, Stevenson Way, a copy of *Kidnapped* in their rain-proofed rucksacks, marking off the exotic Gaelic names of the mountains, moors, and lochs en route. And who better to travel through that region with than Stevenson? Although Lowland born, this much-traveled polyvalent writer of travel memoirs, poetry, and fiction had excellent credentials to write this particular story.

Stevenson knew the country, the people, and the history, so when David Balfour narrates that the moors were "red with heather; broken up with bogs and hags and peaty pools... a forest of dead firs, standing like skeletons," he sees it with Stevenson's eyes, Stevenson's years of experience of accompanying his lighthouse builder father through the Highlands, of summer holidays spent in the region, of walking those tracks. But most importantly he speaks with an insight into the Highlander's heart and feeling for the landscapes.

KYMMENDÖ, STOCKHOLM ARCHIPELAGO, SWEDEN

AUGUST STRINDBERG

The People of Hemsö

(HEMSÖBORNA) (1887)

Comic, sensuous and distinctly lacking in Strindberg's customary tragedy, The People of Hemsö *tells the story of an interloper, Carlsson, who inveigles himself into a small island fishing community and the affections of a vulnerable widow, yet whose very overconfidence brings about his own downfall.*

> Sad and tired, harassed, hunted like a wild animal, last August I sat down at my writing desk to amuse myself. Wrote: the story of a farmhand, my summer memories of unforgettable days in the Stockholm archipelago (since I have had a lot of fun in my life, too). Banished the woman question, outlawed socialism, politics, all drivel, and decided to make a Swedish and an amusing and a broad, droll book, showing how a farmhand with sound nerves and a good temper, without gall, moves through life, taking what is offered, letting go without tears what he was unable to keep.

August Strindberg (1849–1912) was a Swedish playwright, poet, novelist, essayist, and painter, whose blend of psychology and naturalism in his works created a new form of European drama in the late nineteenth century, that of Expressionism.

Strindberg is famed for the darkness of his style, which often drew on personal experiences. *The People of Hemsö* (1887) was based on his deep knowledge of the landscape and people of an island in the Stockholm archipelago. Its original Swedish title is *Hemsoborna*.

This letter from August Strindberg, from the autumn of 1887, reveals the backbone of *The People of Hemsö,* a novel hailed as a comic masterpiece. Its tone may come as a surprise to those who know him primarily as Strindberg the dramatist of dark, naturalistic plays such as *The Dance of Death* and *Miss Julie*. Writing during a long and difficult period when he was living in virtual exile in Germany and France, Strindberg used the island of Kymmendo as a model for Hemsö. Situated in the south of the Stockholm archipelago, it is an area comprising smaller scatterings of islands, or skerries (Swedish: *skargard*), where Strindberg had spent summers since boyhood. So realistic were the characters, however, and the inhabitants so outraged by his barely fictional treatment, that he was unable to return to this island sanctuary. "Bays and islands, bays and islands stretching far out to infinity," Strindberg recalled in his autobiography. In a series of articles written in 1884, looking out over the Mediterranean Sea (Strindberg's last visit to Kymmendo had been with his wife and children in 1883), he longed not for the scene before him "but small rough gneiss hillocks with thorny spruce firs and red cottages."

Straightforwardly written as entertainment and without the tragic symbolism that constitutes so many of his other works, *The People of Hemsö* is the story of an outsider, Carlsson, who is hired by a relatively well-off, middle-aged widow, Anna Eva Flod, to run her failing farm near a fishing village on the island. Her son and heir, Gusten, suspicious and contemptuous of mainlander Carlsson's lack of experience, prefers to neglect the farm and

A fire was burning in the cottage parlour, and the white deal table was covered with a clean cloth. On the cloth stood a bottle of schnapps, waisted in the middle like an hourglass, and around it a coffee service of Gustavberg china in a pattern of roses and forget-me-nots. A newly baked loaf, crisp rusks, a butter dish, sugar basin and cream jug completed the table arrangements, which, to Carlsson, had a look of prosperity about it that he had not expected, here at the back of beyond.

fish for his own pleasure; the locals, all sailors and fishermen themselves, are naturally hostile toward the newcomer. Is he a confidence trickster, or genuine? Carlsson quickly makes himself indispensable to Mrs. Flod, both practically and in her affections, and also attracts the attention of Ida, a young cook who is part of the retinue of a professor's family staying as paying guests at the farm over one summer.

The People of Hemsö is the most conventional, and, in its delivery, perhaps the most impersonal among Strindberg's writings. It is comic, burlesque, packed with vivid instances of life on the archipelago, as familiar to Strindberg's audience—many of whom would have vacationed for three months each summer on islands similar to "Hemsö"—as it was to Strindberg himself. (He described it as his "sanest" book.) Thematically it is a portrayal of rural, isolated life and nature, and those from the mainland and the big city who seek to infiltrate and exploit it. It is set over three years, and its flora and fauna are beautifully rendered. The icefields of the midwinter season thaw quickly; the white nights of the July haymaking and dancing festivities, where Carlsson takes Ida's hand for the first time, are foregrounded. The language is attentive, and precise; whether in describing the particular landscape, or the composition of an interior, all is fertile and abundant: "Bream spawned, juniper shed its smoky pollen, bird cherry blossomed, and Carlsson sowed spring rye above the frozen autumn grain."

Seglare (Sailors), painting by August Strindberg, 1873. The painting takes a stormy seascape as its subject, much like that which challenges Carlsson in the novel.

Carlsson is pragmatic; something of a rogue. Strindberg describes him as "an enterprising fellow. He came to Hemsö like a snow squall on an April evening...unreliable, but exceedingly spirited." At the novel's close we see that he has aimed too high in his quest for property and stability, and failed. His attempt and fall are chronicled cyclically: arriving in spring, flourishing in summer, chaos in autumn and fatal defeat in winter, as the sea he has never understood gets the better of him. But life goes on. "He got no more than he deserved," says Gusten, as Strindberg closes the novel with his rightful homecoming. "And at the helm of his boat, the new master of Hemsö was rowed home by his men, to pilot his own craft across life's windy bays, and through its green and sheltered narrows."

SURREY, ENGLAND

H. G. WELLS

THE WAR OF THE WORLDS (1898)

Martians invade Victorian Surrey, destroy Woking, work their way along the Thames to central London spreading red weed across the landscape, and finally perish from their exposure to earthly pathogens.

Herbert George Wells (1866–1946) was a highly prolific writer and published over one hundred books. In addition to his writing, he was a passionate social reformer and pacifist. In the aftermath of World War Two, his advocacy of human rights played a significant role in the formation of the United Nations.

The War of the Worlds was first published by Heinemann in 1898 and since then has never been out of print.

The town of Woking memorializes Wells's novel with a 25-foot high silver sculpture of a Martian tripod in Crown Passage near the railway station, designed and built by artist Michael Condron.

Newly married, Wells and his wife Jane moved in 1895 to a small house in Woking, Surrey, 20 miles south-west of London. Wells, not yet famous, was scratching a living writing reviews and essays for the London newspapers while incubating the idea for a novel: alien invaders from Mars laying waste to the cozy bourgeois landscape of south-east England. Not rich enough to own a car, Wells could just about afford a bicycle; he cycled around the countryside as he planned the novel that was to make his fortune. "I wheeled about the district," he later recalled, 'marking down suitable places and people for destruction by my Martians."

The War of the Worlds proved an immediate hit, and remains one of the most famous science-fiction novels ever published. The story starts when Martian spacecraft crash to Earth on Horshell Common, a mile outside Woking: a place of mixed woodland, heath, and sandpits—and now the site of pilgrimage for science-fiction fans. For a while the fleshy octopoid aliens lurk in the craters made by their landing, constructing their war machines, but soon enough the iconic Martian tripods rise up: giant metal machines taller than the trees, each piloted by a Martian. They stride about the countryside on three legs, blasting human resistance with a laser-like "heat ray," or poisoning larger areas with "black smoke." They quickly defeat the British army and march northeast into the center of London.

Wells is precise as to the path this mechanized Martian army takes. It is easy to follow on a map, and not hard to retrace their progress on the ground. The landscape has, since Wells's day, been overwritten by three major motorways (the M3, M4, and M25) but is otherwise remarkably unchanged. You can drive, or cycle, the invaders' route, from Woking to Weybridge and then along the Thames past Hampton Court, Kingston, and Richmond to the location of the novel's plangent climax in central London.

These Surrey villages retain a high proportion of nineteenth-century architecture of the kind upon which the Martians wreak devastation. Cobham (Wells's narrator reports the striking detail that "the Heat-Ray had shaved the chimney tops and passed") is much as it was, and the path along the Thames past Hampton Court to Hampton and Richmond is both eminently walkable today, and rather more pleasant than as described in the novel:

> we went along the blackened road to Sunbury, [passing] dead bodies lying in contorted attitudes, horses as well as men, overturned carts and luggage, all covered thickly with black dust. At Hampton Court our eyes were relieved to find a patch of green that had escaped the suffocating drift. We went through Bushey Park, with its deer going to and fro under the chestnuts, and some men and women hurrying in the distance towards Hampton.

Primrose Hill—where Wells's story ends and where his narrator finds a motionless tripod, its pilot killed by earthly bacteria gives as good a view across central London today as it did then.

One of the things that makes the novel so powerful is the way Wells understood that the strange and alien come most fully alive if placed in a context that is known, familiar, and comfortable. Human life in Wells's South Downs is small-scale and cozy. The Martians who erupt into it are towering, pitiless, and strange. That dramatic contrast powers the novel, and it is rendered through the landscape.

We are never given the narrator's name; he is more a point-of-view (albeit an unusually perceptive one) than a fully realized character. What he sees are invaders who not only dominate the landscape but exist on the scale of it. The Martian tripods tower over houses and trees: "a monstrous tripod, higher than many houses, striding over the young pine trees, and smashing them aside in its career ... suddenly the trees in the pine wood ahead of me were parted, as brittle reeds are parted by a man thrusting through them; they were snapped off and driven headlong, and a second huge tripod appeared, rushing, as it seemed, headlong towards me."

The Martians do more than invade Surrey; they *remake* it. Wells took from the scientific consensus of the day the erroneous but dramatically potent idea that Mars's red color was a consequence of a pervasive red weed growing across the planet's surface (in fact Mars is arid, its red color deriving from the exodized dust of its global desert). In Well's story the invaders bring this weed with them. So over the course of the novel, the green fields and copses of Surrey gradually change to an alien, bright-red territory, and the Thames becomes choked with scarlet reeds. Walk the invader's path today and it's easy to imagine the familiar low-rise green hills and small villages ruined and remade in red. This is a novel that takes the known landscape and, brilliantly, estranges it.

Overleaf, left: *Abandoned London*, Henrique Alvim Corrêa's (1906) illustration for the Belgian edition.

Overleaf, right: The narrator travels to London after the death of the Martian invaders, to find the Londoners examining the leftover debris. Illustration by H. A. Corrêa, 1898.

CAVENDISH, PRINCE EDWARD ISLAND, CANADA

LUCY MAUD MONTGOMERY

ANNE OF GREEN GABLES (1908)

An orphaned girl transforms the lives of siblings Matthew and Marilla Cuthbert through her exuberant personality and love of the island landscape that becomes her home.

Since its publication, *Anne of Green Gables* has sold more than 50 million copies and has been translated into at least thirty-six languages.

Anne of Green Gables was first published in 1908, and was followed by 10 sequels featuring Anne, the last of which was published in 2009, sixty-seven years after Montgomery's death.

Montgomery's novel has been adapted into multiple film, stage, radio, and television productions, including a Japanese animé directed by Isao Takahata.

Anne of Green Gables's famed red-headed heroine, whom generations of readers have loved for her loquacious big-heartedness, is slow to make an appearance in the novel that bears her name. Rather than beginning with Anne, this famous Canadian novel begins with an intricate, tripping sentence that focuses on the perspective not of a person, but a place—a *brook*, making its way through the local village. "Mrs. Rachel Lynde lived just where the Avonlea main road dipped down into a little hollow, fringed with alders and ladies' eardrops," we read, "and traversed by a brook that had its source away back in the woods of the old Cuthbert place." The sentence goes on:

> it was reputed to be an intricate, headlong brook in its earlier course through those woods, with dark secrets of pool and cascade; but by the time it reached Lynde's Hollow it was a quiet, well-conducted little stream, for not even a brook could run past Mrs. Rachel Lynde's door without due regard for decency and decorum; it probably was conscious that Mrs. Rachel was sitting at her window, keeping a sharp eye on everything that passed, from brooks and children up, and that if she noticed anything odd or out of place she would never rest until she had ferreted out the whys and wherefores thereof.

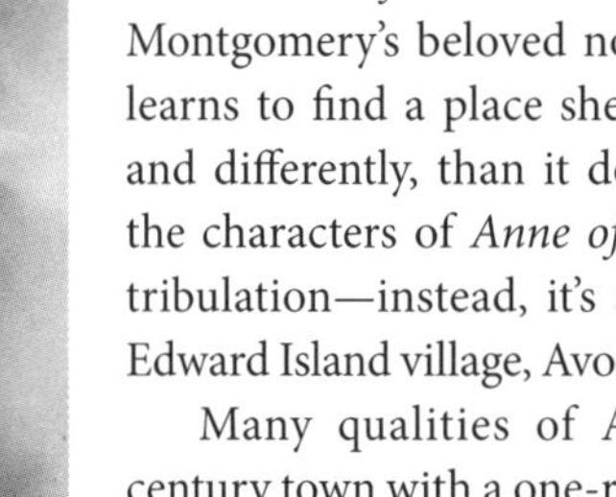

In *Anne of Green Gables* place is a character, but it is also the plot. L. M. Montgomery's beloved novel tells a story—of a young orphaned girl, who learns to find a place she could call home—but the setting matters more, and differently, than it does in most other children's fiction. What unites the characters of *Anne of Green Gables* is not any kind of quest, hope, or tribulation—instead, it's simply sharing the place of their distinct Prince Edward Island village, Avonlea.

Many qualities of Avonlea may sound like any late nineteenth-century town with a one-room schoolhouse, village hall, and a church to visit on Sundays. But Avonlea's textures and temperaments render it distinctly Canadian. The villagers of Avonlea have no interest in the American

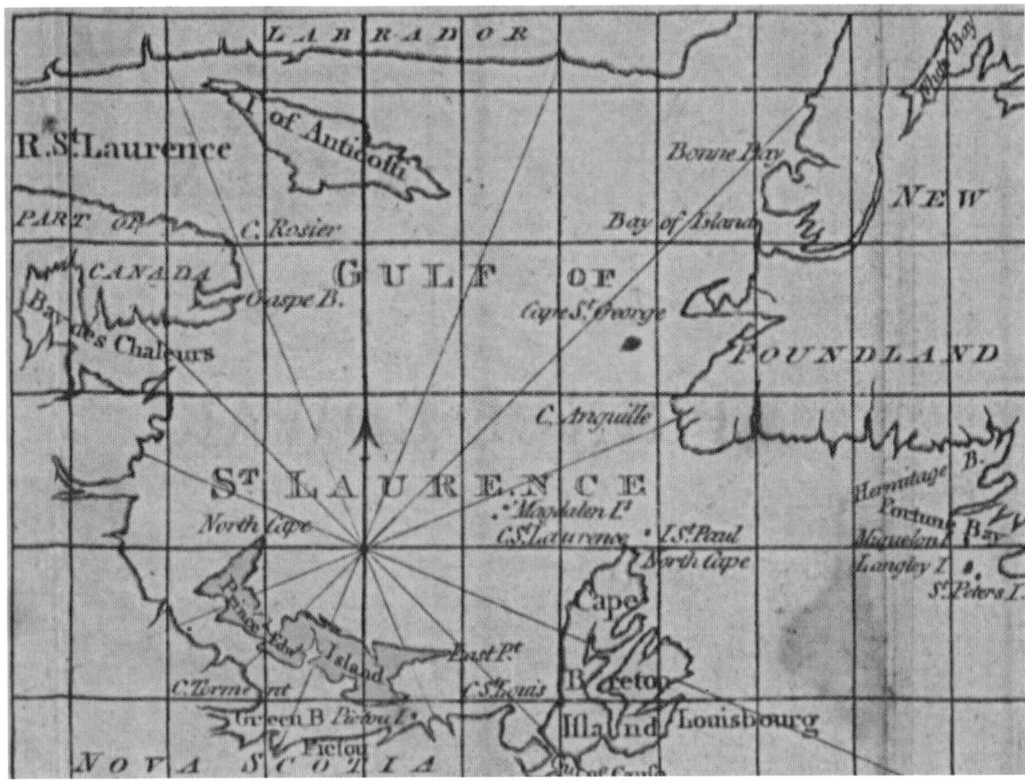

Map of Prince Edward Island, Canada, the location of the fictional community of Avonlea. Montgomery based Avonlea on her childhood experiences in communities around the island.

pioneer-like roaming that drives Laura and Pa onward throughout the *Little House* books—but, on the other side, there's none of the British manor house aristocracy of books like *A Little Princess* or even *Pride and Prejudice*. Montgomery's *Anne* novels describe a social world that's democratic but deeply rooted, and profoundly concerned, like the brook is, with "decency, and decorum." And, not only is Avonlea Canadian, but it is also an island town. The provincial Maritime feel of Prince Edward Island—on the fringes of the world, detached from the sweep of history—allow small events to flourish into meaningfulness. The attentively described seasonal landscape of sea views and verdant gardens takes the place of epic events.

And in this simple world of ice cream socials, spelling bees, and may flowers, brooks and children are equally fascinating occurrences, worthy of our richest attention. In fact, the novel's opening sentence tells us something about how the story will go—for though she will always keep her "pool and cascade," "headlong" Anne, too, will come to be a "well-conducted little stream" as she courses through the narrative landscape that embraces her.

Children's literature is full of magical destinations—in most so-called "chosen one" narratives a child, often an orphan like Anne is whisked away to a place where her potential can be mentored toward some final heroic accomplishment. Think Oz, think Wonderland, think Narnia, think Hogwarts, think even Treasure Island (you could even consider, in a darker iteration, Katniss's Hunger Games arena in this view). What's remarkable about the place is that only chosen people might go there—and what's remarkable about the child is that only she can set it right. In these exceptional places, unusual abilities within the child are unleashed—and villains are vanquished, a right order restored. It's only at the end that the child might whisper, like Dorothy, "there's no place like home."

Anne of Green Gables shares some kinship with these stories. Although Anne Shirley pines for romances, not heroic adventures, she begins the novel named after her yearning for drama, and certainly no one around her finds her—with her sparkling imagination, warm heart, and quick temper—anything less than remarkable.

> ... the Avonlea hills came out darkly against the saffron sky. Behind them the moon was rising out of the sea that grew all radiant and transfigured in her light. Every little cove along the curving road was a marvel of dancing ripples.

But Green Gables is not a magical kingdom. Prince Edward Island is an island like Neverland, but there are no pirates or crocodiles, and the heroism that happens there revolves not around any terrible antagonist, but rather the more simple, if not less impressive, acts of building a community, and a family, out of people whose hearts, before, had not known how to be opened. The lonely brother and sister, Matthew and Marilla Cuthburt, who adopt Anne live an orderly life before she arrives. But they are cold, fearful, closed down—they have spent their lives shying away from any personal intimacy—and it is only after Anne arrives that the beauty of their home becomes luminously able to awaken a sense of love within them. They learn that decency can include joyfulness and imagination. And Anne knows from the beginning that home makes love possible.

The deep-heartedness of L. M. Montgomery's story perhaps blooms from her personal connection to it. Like Anne, Montgomery grew up on a small Prince Edward Island farm. The village of Cavendish, where she grew up, is clearly a model for Anne's Avonlea. And like Anne, Montgomery was adopted—not by strangers, but rather by her grandmother. Montgomery's biography illustrates that her home was not a loving one. Signs of her grandmother's love were withheld, even if they were present.

So perhaps it's not surprising that Montgomery crafted a novel where the world works differently. Over the course of the novel, Anne grows from a neglected girl to a confident young woman, secure in the love of her adopted family. She realizes that her bitter school rival, Gilbert Blythe, deserves to be her friend; she learns particularly that Marilla, the woman who adopted her, loves her abidingly.

These transformations begin at the novel's opening, when, over the course of the first three chapters, Anne is introduced to Avonlea. But it might be more accurate to say that Anne introduces Avonlea to the adopted family who has always lived there without fully appreciating it. Dazzled with the beauty of her new home, Anne immediately offers up names—the White Way of Delight, the Lake of Shining Waters, the Snow Queen—for paths and ponds and cherry trees that amplify the magical capacity of these seemingly ordinary places. They are not "magical" in the sense that they have an otherworldy power. But when they are fully loved, as Anne loves them, they encourage a full engagement with daily life—an engagement that is sustaining, entertaining, and even ennobling.

Certainly this is the case for Anne, as well as for Matthew and Marilla Cuthbert. While Matthew warms to Anne immediately, Marilla's path forward is different, slower. She remains afraid of her growing love for Anne; she's hesitant to share affection with the child who craves it.

But home saves them. At the novel's ending, Matthew suddenly dies. Montgomery describes mourning him in a way predictably attentive to the emotional experience of place. We read:

> Two days afterwards they carried Matthew Cuthbert over his homestead threshold and away from the fields he had tilled and the orchards he had loved and the trees he had planted; and then Avonlea settled back to its usual placidity and even at Green Gables affairs slipped into their old groove and work was done and duties fulfilled with regularity as before, although always with the aching sense of "loss in all familiar things."

Loss aches, but in that hurt blossoms a kind of hope. Mourning her brother, Marilla opens her heart to Anne for the first time—and their openness to each other is sealed by mutually committing to maintain Green Gables as their home. "You can't sell Green Gables," Anne tells Marilla. "No one will love it like we do."

In the later volumes of the *Anne* series, Green Gables remains a transformative place. In *Anne of Avonlea,* two "harum-scarum" twins, Davey and Dora, fall under its pacifying influence; in *Anne of Windy Poplars,* the bitter and hopeless school vice-principle Katherine warms to human connection for the first time.

Anne is a part of these transformations too. But what all eight novels show, and why so many readers love them, is an almost alchemical reaction between character and setting that make story possible where it wasn't before. There was a Green Gables, a farmhouse in the small town of Avonlea, before the orphan Anne Shirley arrived there. But it is only after Green Gables shines in Anne's love that it becomes a place where character's lives and hearts—not only Anne's, but certainly hers—could be transformed. And it's this central lesson, that there can be magic in our home places if we love it into being, that transforms not only Montgomery's characters but also her readers.

NEBRASKA, USA

WILLA CATHER

O PIONEERS! (1913)

Alexandra Bergson, daughter of Swedish immigrants, successfully tames and prospers in the severe but eventually bountiful Nebraska plains despite the difficulties and tragedies posed by her younger brothers.

Willa Cather (1873–1947) spent part of her youth in Nebraska, but in 1896 as a twenty-three-year-old, moved to Pittsburgh and lived there, Washington DC, and New York, never returning to the Midwest.

O Pioneers! is the first in Cather's Great Plains trilogy; the later books are *The Song of the Lark* (1915) and *My Antonia* (1918).

The title is from a Walt Whitman poem, which celebrates the broad range of settlers and explorers who made the American West their conquest.

We think we know what the word "pioneer" means: it conjures up visions of open prairies and wagon trains, and suggests the Manifest Destiny of European immigrants working their way across the American West. However, the word, from Old French, originated in military usage and was used through World War II: they were the engineers who built camps, bridges, roads, and railroads, and constructed mines. In 1779 British Captain George Smith's military dictionary noted that they were "provided with aprons, hatchets, saws, spades, and pickaxes." The tools make the connection clear: these were the people, leaving their own homes to make another, who battled the hard, bare land, the relentless weather, and the loneliness of a new land to make homes and communities in the prairies and plains.

Willa Cather experienced the shock of the wide open land as she moved with her extended family from Virginia to Nebraska as a ten-year-old after her family farm burned down. Despite living most of her adult life in Eastern cities, Cather's values were shaped by the hard physical work and unflinching perseverance demanded by the land of the upper Great Plains. Southern Nebraska, like most of the high plains, is not lush or green or gently rolling; its beauty is austere but elegant, huge but exhilarating. One hundred and eighty degree horizons and undulating grasslands are punctuated by tree-rimmed waterways. Skies glory in shades of blue, gold, and pink when not besieged by livewire thunderstorms or blizzards that rival those of the home countries of many immigrants. Snow creates its own bold architecture in drifts and hollows. High summer heat raises shimmering waves over miles of browned grass. The animals of this environment do not require tree cover or large bodies of water; the prairie dogs, quail, bison, and coyotes rely on color camouflage, speed, or size for protection.

The people pioneering this country must be absorbed in it to survive in it. After her father's death Alexandra does not become a farmer, but a skilled, progressive manager of the farmlands she inherits and buys. Where her father and brothers give up or depend on old ways, Alexandra assesses her environment and obliges the demands of the land rather than trying to force

Photograph of buggies in front of the Miner Bros. store, Red Cloud, Nebraska, 1880. Cather described her writing process in an interview as "recapturing in memory people and places I'd forgotten."

Old World ways on it. The earth responds with unforeseen generosity after a couple of decades of tilling: "The rich soil yields heavy harvests; the dry, bracing climate and the smoothness of the land make labor easy for men and beasts." Now, the beauty of the land does not inhere in an alien remoteness, but wealth in harvest and hence in financial prosperity. Herds and colonies of animals no longer dot the prairie as telephone wires and fences define space and human control.

The real story of *O Pioneers!*, however, is not how the immigrants domesticate the terrain, but how it shapes—or breaks—those who try. Alexandra's brothers dislike farm life and do not share their sister's prescient relationship with the earth, but her principle seems to be her oneness with her land: "For the first time, perhaps, since that land emerged from the waters of geologic ages, a human face was set towards it with love and yearning. It seemed beautiful to her, rich and strong and glorious." The concept of natural beauty was redefined by the American prairie, which in turn redefined those who learned to live in and with it. While this novel is in no way a statement of Leopoldian environmentalism, the love of something wild and an appreciation of its power and abundance can make the spades and pickaxes of these pioneers the creative tools of a sculptor rather than instruments of destruction.

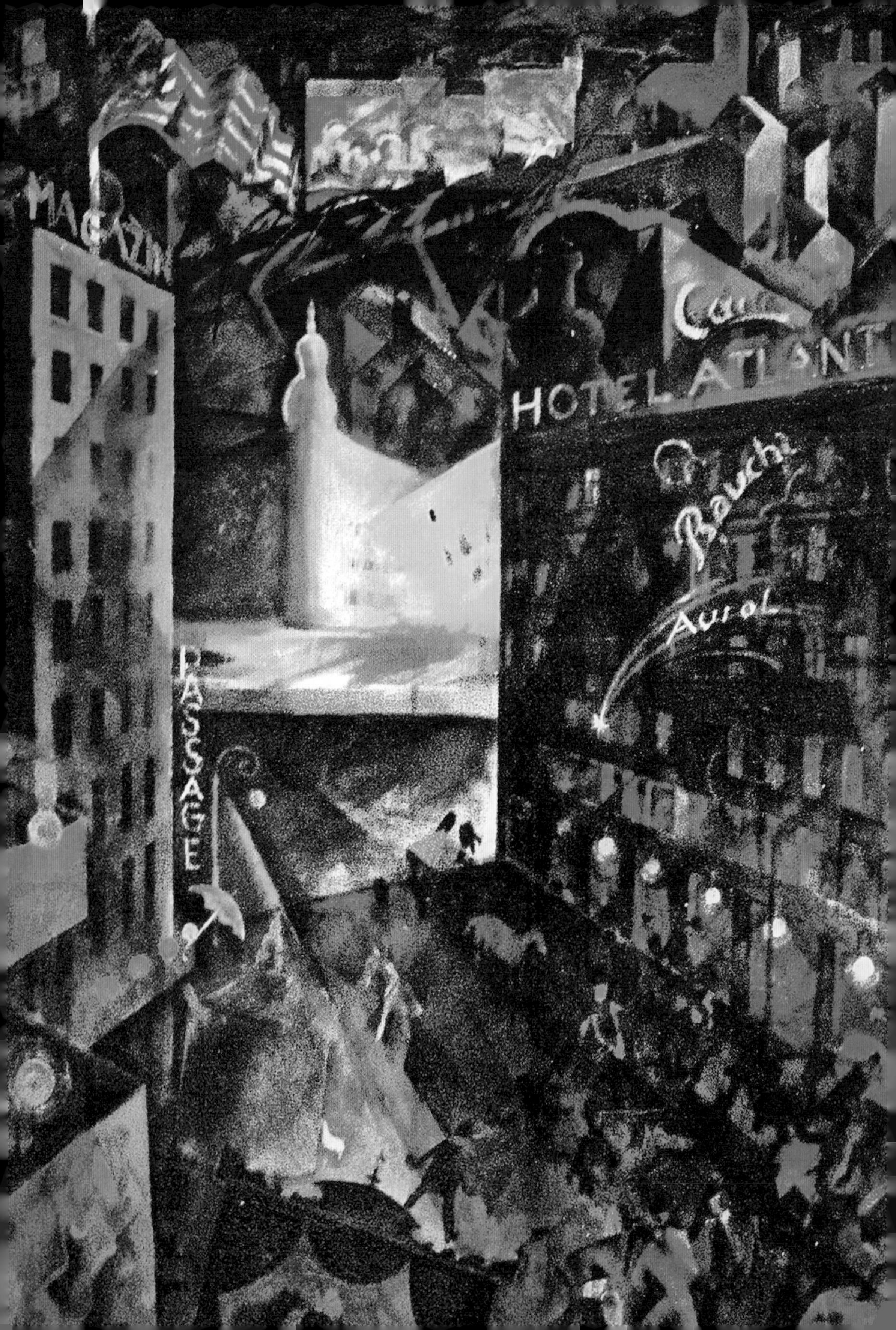
MAGAZIN
HOTEL
PASSAGE

1915–1945

2 Mapping Modernism

As successive World Wars began to redefine the geographical boundaries of the familiar world, the modernist movement emulated the new chaos of experience. In fragmentary, experimental prose, their unravelling topographies pressurized notions of belonging and identity.

NOTTINGHAMSHIRE, ENGLAND

D. H. LAWRENCE

THE RAINBOW (1915)

The Rainbow *is a rich evocation of rural Midlands life from the mid-Victorian period to the decade just before the First World War, seen through the eyes of three generations of the Brangwen family.*

David Herbert Lawrence was born in Nottinghamshire in 1885, the son of a working-class miner father and a middle class mother, he wove this tension into his writings as much as he attracted scandal into his own life.

Lawrence's frank treatment of human relationships, sex, the natural world, and his objection to mass industrialization and militarism made him a constant target for the authorities.

He published twelve novels, many of which were banned in his lifetime, including, on publication, *The Rainbow*.

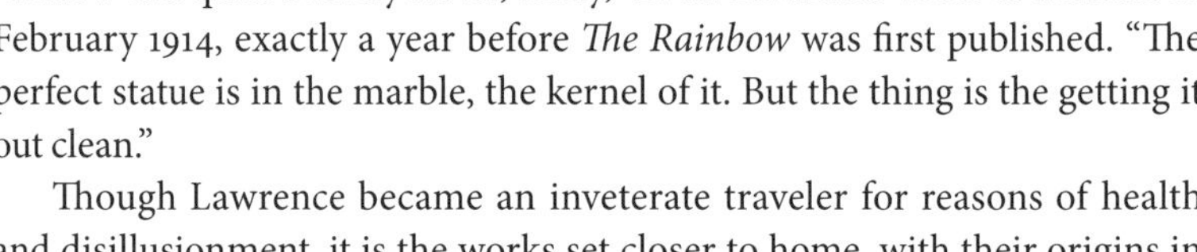

"I know it is quite a lovely novel, really," D. H. Lawrence wrote to a friend in February 1914, exactly a year before *The Rainbow* was first published. "The perfect statue is in the marble, the kernel of it. But the thing is the getting it out clean."

Though Lawrence became an inveterate traveler for reasons of health and disillusionment, it is the works set closer to home, with their origins in the shackles of Victorian society and English rural working-class life, which remain his best known, and best loved. Written before he embarked on his self-proclaimed "savage pilgrimage," these early autobiographical novels are based on Lawrence's own background.

The Rainbow is Lawrence's epic story of three generations of the Brangwen family and their farm on the Nottinghamshire-Derbyshire borders from around the 1840s to 1905, a frank study of individual quest for self-fulfilment against the backdrop of a countryside, unchanged for centuries, moving into the industrial age, and soon to be forever altered by war. The Erewash Valley, where the novel is set, is known for that industry—deep coal mining in the mineral-rich earth, and lace-making in its mills. Lawrence mainly focuses, however, on an almost prelapsarian state: the countryside, its challenges, consolations, and the endless rhythm of birth and death, amid a close-knit farming community who have preserved traditional ways for centuries, where even the familiar can seem miraculous.

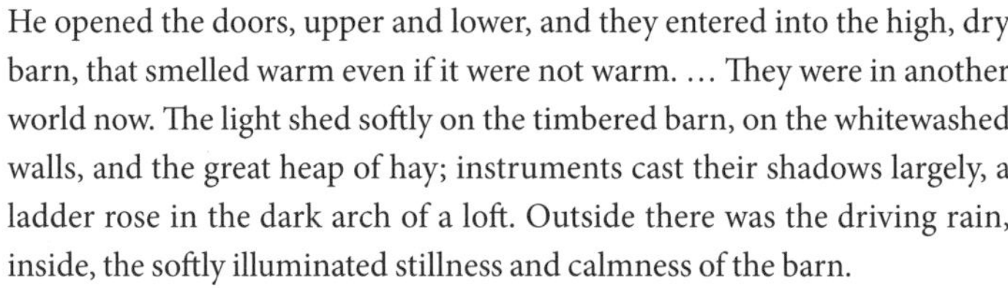

> He opened the doors, upper and lower, and they entered into the high, dry barn, that smelled warm even if it were not warm. ... They were in another world now. The light shed softly on the timbered barn, on the whitewashed walls, and the great heap of hay; instruments cast their shadows largely, a ladder rose in the dark arch of a loft. Outside there was the driving rain, inside, the softly illuminated stillness and calmness of the barn.

Muscular in style, deeply sensual, with an almost dizzying evocation of the natural world, yet a rigorous command of plot, Lawrence depicts a

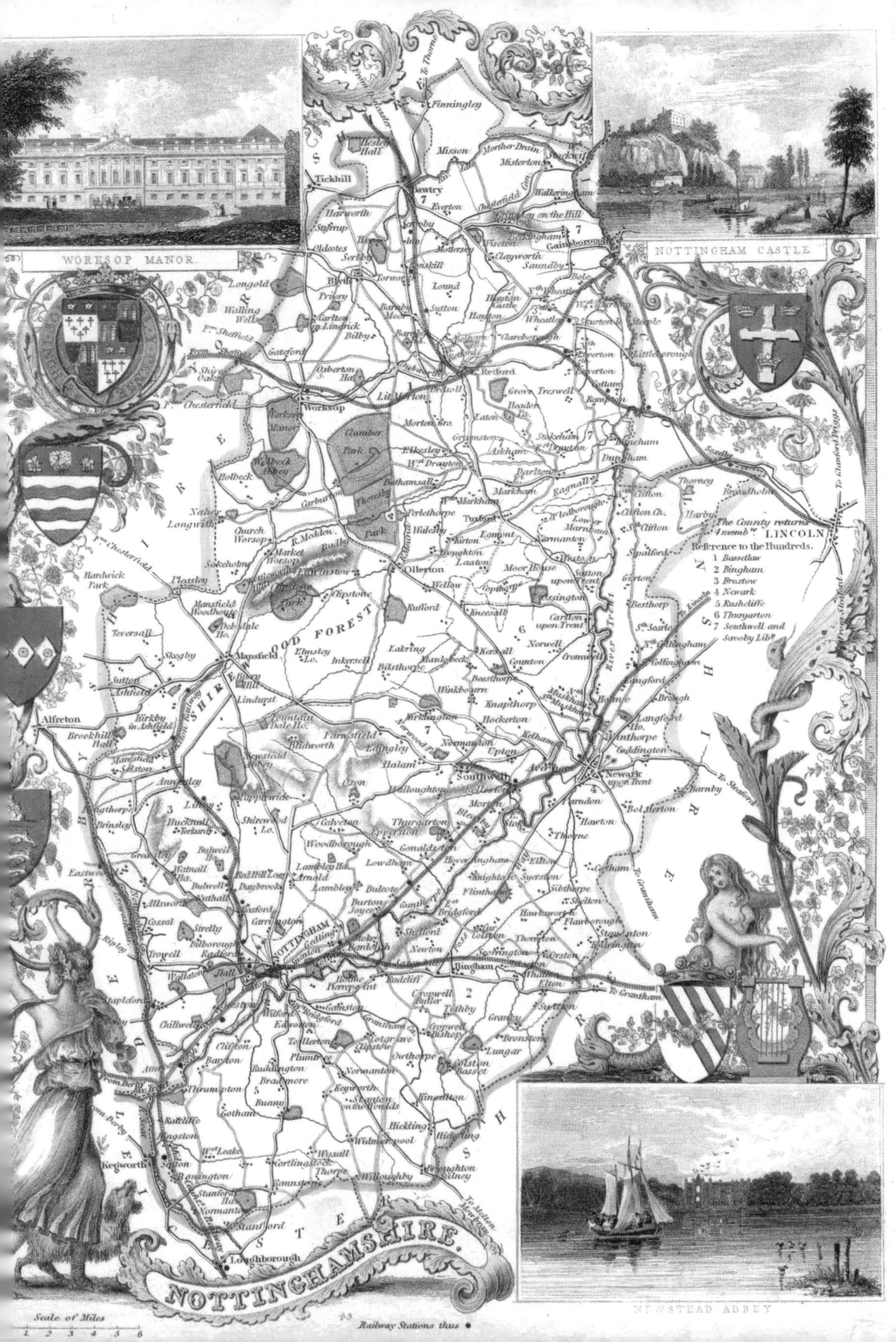
NOTTINGHAMSHIRE.
WORKSOP MANOR.
NOTTINGHAM CASTLE
NEWSTEAD ABBEY
The County returns 4 memb.rs
Reference to the Hundreds.
1 Bassetlaw
2 Bingham
3 Broxtow
4 Newark
5 Rushcliffe
6 Thurgarton
7 Southwell and Scooby Lib.ty
Scale of Miles
1 2 3 4 5 6
Railway Stations thus
River Trent
SHIREWOOD FOREST
LINCOLN
Finningley
Tickhill
Bawtry
Misson
Misterton
Gainsborough
Blyth
Worksop
Retford
Clumber Park
Thoresby Park
Welbeck Abbey
Mansfield
Ollerton
Rufford
Southwell
Newark upon Trent
Nottingham
Bingham
Alfreton
Loughborough
Kegworth
To Grantham
To Stamford
To Lincoln

timeless landscape of shifting seasons and personal internal commotion, with an unashamed earnestness which, over 100 years after the book first appeared, is still as fresh in approach and radical in intent as it must have seemed in 1915.

From the very start of the novel, which opens with the specific placing of a family and their home, steeped in unending tradition, the seed of something other, something possible is planted:

> The Brangwens had lived for generations on the Marsh Farm, in the meadows where the Erewash twisted sluggishly through alder trees, separating Derbyshire from Nottinghamshire. Two miles away, a church-tower stood on a hill, the houses of the little country town climbing assiduously up to it. Whenever one of the Brangwens in the fields lifted his head from his work, he saw the church-tower at Ilkeston in the empty sky. So that as he turned again to the horizontal land, he was aware of something standing above him and beyond him in the distance.

Tom Brangwen, the son of the Marsh Farm, is the powerful central character in the first third of the book; his marriage to a young Polish widow, whose daughter Anna grows up to marry his nephew Will and in turn has a daughter of her own, Ursula, strong-willed and restless, forms a chain of events each connected yet different in their own complexity.

> Odd little bits of information stirred unfathomable passion in her. When she knew that in the tiny brown buds of autumn were folded, minute and complete, the finished flowers of the summer nine months hence, tiny, folded up, and left there waiting, a flash of triumph and love went over her. "I could never die while there was a tree," she said passionately, sententiously, standing before a great ash in worship.

In Ursula we see the young Lawrence fictionalized in the form of a woman seeking emancipation, in her case through love affairs with both a woman and man, a hellish baptism as a teacher, university, and the promise of a world beyond her Midlands backwater. The novel is heavily symbolic: years before, Ursula's mother Anna has had a half-vision of a rainbow: "...she saw the hope, the promise. Why should she travel any farther?" it is for the next generation, through Ursula, to take that hope forward, the "getting it out clean" to create her own version of art, and life.

Previous page: Set at the western edge of Nottinghamshire, Lawrence's birthplace of Eastwood provided the inspiration for most of the locations in his novels. The tiny village of Cossall can be seen on this map of 1840 on the banks of the River Erewash, representing the location for the Brangwen's Marsh Farm.

GUDBRAND VALLEY, NORWAY

SIGRID UNDSET

KRISTIN LAVRANSDATTER (1920–22)

This trilogy of religiously attuned historical novels follows a medieval Norwegian woman from childhood through marriage, motherhood, and old age.

The fourteenth-century Scandinavia of the *Kristin Lavransdatter* series can seem like an ever-so-slightly enchanted place. Christianity arrived relatively late in Norway, just about 300 years before the heroine's birth, and the Norse myths linger around the series' edges. Early in the first volume, young Kristin wakes up groggy from a nap on a grassy plateau and follows her father's horse to a mountain stream. When she looks up across the water, she sees a woman with long blonde hair, covered in gleaming jewelry—a "dwarf maiden," Kristin believes. The woman silently beckons to the child, who flees back to her father.

The scene is something of a red herring, however: the mystical apparition is a hint at Kristin's psychological and spiritual life, and her people's haunted memories, not the world around her. Kristin's Norway proves to be both a "perilous and beautiful world," as one passage puts it. And Undset's portrait of the medieval North is as complex a feat of world-building as any science-fiction series.

Though it spans only one woman's lifetime, the trilogy has the feel of an epic. The first volume, *The Wreath*, follows Kristin's childhood in a loving and prosperous farm family, and her scandalous romance with the dashing Erlend Nikulaussøn. In the second volume, *The Wife*, Kristin bears Erlend seven sons, and struggles through periods of financial, political, and spiritual heartbreak. The final installment, *The Cross,* finds the couple watching their sons grow up and reckoning with their own passion, impulsivity, and regrets. (To say much more would spoil the pleasures of the plot, but suffice to say the series includes sex, violence, drunkenness, infidelity, natural disaster, and deathbed confessions, to name a few. Undset is interested in virtue but does not shy away from vice.)

Most of the series takes place on several large estates, including Jørundgaard, the valley manor where Kristin grows up and later returns to run, and Husaby, her husband's grand property on a mountain slope. Undset captures the daily and yearly rhythms of sustaining life and maintaining traditions, from summer bounty to long winters, from banquets to religious fasts. She also describes the particular architecture and furniture of the era: open courtyards ringed with simple wood buildings; open hearths and bridal

Sigrid Undset (1882–1949) is the author of thirteen novels, which have been translated into almost all major languages. She won the Nobel Prize for Literature in 1928 for "her powerful descriptions of Northern life during the Middle Ages". She was also a translator of various Icelandic sagas into Norwegian.

Kristin Lavransdatter, an international bestseller, is a trilogy consisting of *Kransen (The Wreath*, 1920), *Husfrue (The Wife*, 1921), and *Korset (The Cross*, 1922).

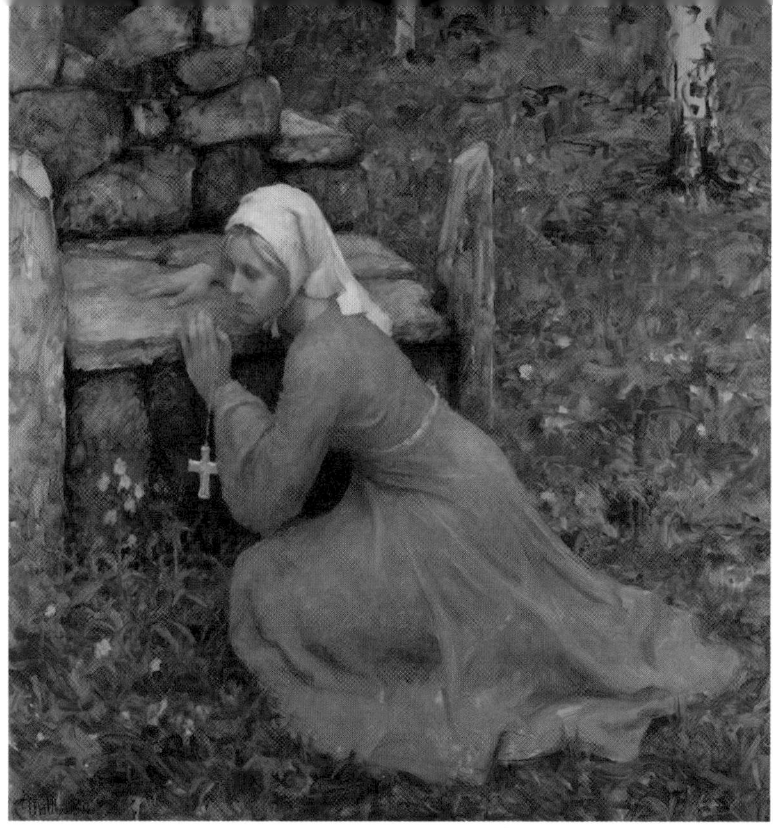

Penguin Classics cover artwork by painter Matthew Peak for the final instalment of *Kristin Lavransdatter III: The Cross.*

lofts; the "high seat" in the middle of the long dining table, reserved for honored guests. Contemporary readers who take car and air travel for granted will also be struck by the enormous effort it took to travel from estate to estate, or from home to town to city.

The action veers to other settings, too, from castles to cathedrals to quiet country churches. There's the convent where Kristin is educated; the bustling city fair where she first encounters her rakish future husband, and the decrepit farm where they spend an indelible romantic interlude years into their marriage. And near the end of her life, she makes a final pilgrimage to the city of Nidaros, now known as Trondheim, a port city where she devotes herself to caring for victims of the Bubonic Plague.

Undset often compares her heroine's rich internal life to the natural world; Kristin's simultaneous tenderness and bitterness toward her soon-to-be-husband is "like a glittering river over stones". The series' depiction of the crystalline beauty of the unspoiled Scandinavian landscape helps explain why fans of the series now flock to "Kristin's" farm, constructed for the filming of a forgettable 1995 film version the story. Thousands of pilgrims also trek to admire a large statue of Kristin in the valley at Gudbrandsdal. They are understandably eager to step into Kristin's domain, if only for an afternoon:

> Kristin came home during the loveliest time of the spring. The Laag River raced in torrents around the farm and the fields; through the young leaves of the alder thickets the stream glittered and sparkled white with silver flashes. The glints of light seemed to have voices, singing along with the rush of the currents; when dusk fell, the water seemed to flow with a more muted roar. The thunder of the river filled the air of Jørengaard day and night, so that Kristin thought she could feel the very timbers of the walls quivering

Kristin's interior and exterior worlds are so convincing that it can be hard to remember that her creator was a thoroughly modern woman. Undset was born in Denmark in 1882, and the family moved to Norway when she was a toddler. Her father was an archaeologist specializing in the Iron Age, and he encouraged the young girl to handle ancient relics at the Oslo museum where he worked. But he died when Sigrid was just 11, and the family's fortunes declined. Instead of going to college, Sigrid took a secretarial course as a teenager, and began working as a secretary at an engineering firm when she was just sixteen to support her mother and her two younger sisters.

In her late twenties, Undset fell in love with a painter, a married father of three children. They eventually married and had children of their own, and the large household kept Undset busy and financially strained. Pregnant with her third child, she moved with her children to the hamlet of Lillehammer for what was meant to be a temporary break. Instead, the marriage deteriorated and the couple separated permanently. Undset built a compound of timber houses with a large garden in Lillehammer, and settled in to write.

Undset converted to Catholicism in 1924, when she was forty-two years old. She was a public figure by then—the *Lavransdatter* series was becoming an international sensation—and the conversion caused something of a scandal in her home country. Norway was an overwhelmingly Protestant nation, and Catholicism was highly suspect, in both conservative and progressive circles. Undset was a natural contrarian who bristled at the conventional wisdom of the time, including the growing movement for women's rights; she happily joined the fray to defend her adopted faith. She fled Norway when the Germans invaded, returning after the liberation but never writing again.

Undset's biography provides insight into the real engine of the *Kristin Lavrandsatter* series: the drama of life as a woman who is equally lusty and devout. But Undset maps the landscape of Kristin's rich inner life so convincingly that the reader could take for granted how completely she maps her heroine's unforgettable natural surroundings, too.

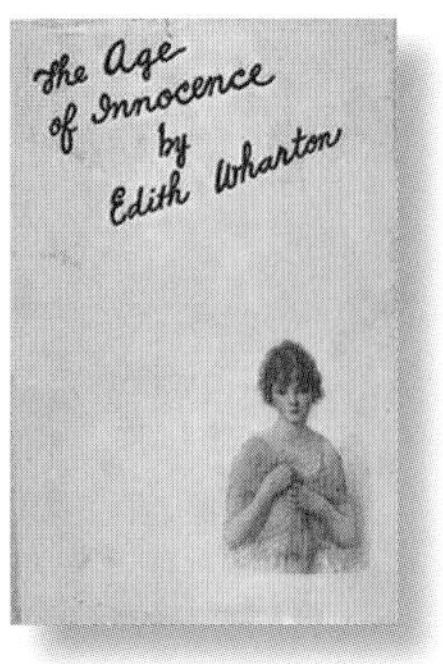

NEW YORK CITY, USA

EDITH WHARTON

THE AGE OF INNOCENCE (1920)

Newland Archer's engagement to May Welland is thrown off course after he meets her exotic, European cousin, Countess Ellen Olenska, who tempts him to rebel against the strict confines of the society he has grown up in.

Edith Wharton, née Edith Newbold Jones (1862–1937), was the first woman to win a Pulitzer Prize for *The Age of Innocence* in 1921. She started writing fiction in her forties, and she was very prolific, writing over forty books in forty years.

The Age of Innocence was Wharton's twelfth novel and was initially serialized in 1920 in four parts in the magazine *Pictorial Review*. When D. Appleton & Company published it in book form later that year, the reception was almost exclusively positive.

Wharton was also an interior designer; her first published work was *The Decoration of Houses* (1897).

Edith Wharton describes 1870s New York as a "small and slippery pyramid," where traditions were "precise and inflexible" and divorce meant social ruin. The confines of the Gilded Age provide Wharton with the perfect backdrop for *The Age of Innocence*, a love story that could never have a happy ending.

Countess Ellen Olenska, the naïve European newcomer to New York, wonders why the city is such a "labyrinth," hinting at a society of unspoken words and suffocating customs. "I thought it so straight up and down—like Fifth Avenue! And with all the cross streets numbered!"

Protagonist Newland Archer, who is engaged to the Countess' cousin, replies: "Everything may be labelled—but everybody is not."

Archer, a restless lawyer, warns the Countess against divorcing her husband, but soon realizes he has devised his own trap. He feels a growing attraction toward her exotic dress, her questioning of society, and her "faded and shadowy charm of a room" on West 23rd Street.

While the Countess' bohemian décor emphasizes her efforts to be free, the stuffy, oppressive interiors of Gilded Age homes encapsulate the strict confines of the other inhabitants. Within days of meeting the Countess, Archer sits in his "Gothic library with glazed black-walnut bookcases" and realizes his fiancée, doll-like May Welland, is a "terrifying product of the social system he belonged to and believed in."

As Archer spends more time with the Countess, he fears the "green mould of the perfunctory" spreading over his life, in a city of brownstones "of which the uniform hue coated New York like a cold chocolate sauce." Archer and Welland plan to move into their new home on East 39th Street: he predicts that his betrothed will want the same marriage, and interior design, as her parents:

> The young man felt that his fate was sealed: for the rest of his life he would go up every evening between the cast-iron railings of that greenish-yellow doorstep, and pass through a Pompeian vestibule into a hall with a wainscoting of varnished yellow wood.

Newland Archer (Daniel Day Lewis) and May Welland (Winona Ryder) stand in front of matriarch Mrs Mingott (Miriam Margolyes) in the 1993 film adaptation directed by Martin Scorsese.

Overleaf: Aerial view of New York City, 1870. Currier & Ives hand colored lithograph print.

Archer and his set were destined to conduct their lives within a small terrain, which spanned from Wall Street to a few blocks north of Madison Square Garden. Countess Olenka lives five blocks south from Archer; where her neighborhood adds to her reputational damage, his townhouse, which he shares with his mother and sister before marriage, is perfectly respectable. There are small rebellions, but only "within Fifth Avenue's limits."

Outside of Manhattan, characters are allowed to confront more unpleasant realities. At their holiday home in Florida, Welland asks her fiancé why he is so keen to advance their wedding date. Does he love another woman? Archer denies it. Not long after marrying her in a traditional ceremony at Grace Church on Broadway, he plans to elope with the Countess. His plans are thwarted when the Countess is called on to aid her ailing grandmother, and she then flees to Europe. Archer must accept his life as it is.

When Wharton wrote her Pulitzer Prize-winning novel, the era of New York she was describing had long gone; but although Wharton knew how quickly society was to change in New York, she also knew it would not be fast enough to accept the love between Archer and Countess Olenska.

The novel ends in Paris, where Archer and his son Dallas plan to visit the Countess. Archer sits on a bench outside and looks up at her window: "What is left of the little world where he had grown up in, and whose standards had bent and bound him?" Archer's wife is dead and he is a free man, but he still cannot escape the suffocating customs of old New York, the only world he has ever known.

CITY of NEW YORK

DUBLIN, IRELAND

JAMES JOYCE

ULYSSES (1922)

Homeric in structure, Ulysses *follows Leopold Bloom through the streets of Dublin over the course of one day. Joyce produced an ambitious novel that has become the quintessential modernist work.*

James Joyce (1882–1941) was born and raised in Dublin, where he set the majority of his fiction, although he mostly lived elsewhere, in particular Trieste, Paris, and Zurich, moving away to escape the constraints of conservative Irish society.

Ulysses was first published in Paris by the bookshop called Shakespeare and Company.

The novel was banned in the United States and in many other countries on grounds of obscenity, but not in Ireland, where no citizen felt that he or she understood it sufficiently to make a case against it.

Joyce called Dublin "the last of the intimate cities." Its streetscapes lacked the imprint of a singular intelligence, such as Haussmann's Paris. Instead, it was a higgledy-piggledy assemblage of villages, which had somehow been joined together. In much the same way, *Ulysses* (set in 1904) is a collection of short stories and anecdotes in the drag of an experimental novel. Each of Dublin's micro-villages still had a rural feel in those days, with cattle being herded through the streets down to the city docklands for live export.

Many of the 200,000 citizens of the Irish capital had come in from the countryside, bringing with them a love of storytelling and gossip. "What a town Dublin is!", Joyce exclaimed to the English painter Frank Budgen: "I wonder if there is another like it. Everybody has time to hail a friend and start a conversation about a third party." This seemed quite different from London, whose people often expressed a horror of common hallways, in which a person might have to talk with a total stranger. In Dublin there were no ultimate strangers—only friends who one hadn't yet met. *Ulysses* celebrates the chance meeting of a bourgeois adman and a bohemian postgraduate student, suggesting that one of the main functions of a modern city is to connect people with their own inner strangeness. Hence its protagonist, Leopold Bloom, is a wanderer of part-Jewish background, the outsider-insider who takes in more of the city—its sights, smells, and sounds—than any other character in the book.

Dublin was (and still is) a city of walkers. Bloom spends most of 16 June 1904 meandering through its streets. Some readers have understandably wondered whether he is "trying to walk something off"—the troubling knowledge that, back in his home at 7 Eccles Street, his wife Molly has taken to bed a lover named Blazes Boylan. It has even been suggested that Bloom's wanderings, traced on a map, take the form of a question mark, to convey his worry about this betrayal, summed up in his adage "An Irishman's house is his coffin."

At a time of dire overcrowding, with constant evictions of tenants by bailiffs and death rates close to those of the slums of Calcutta, many people

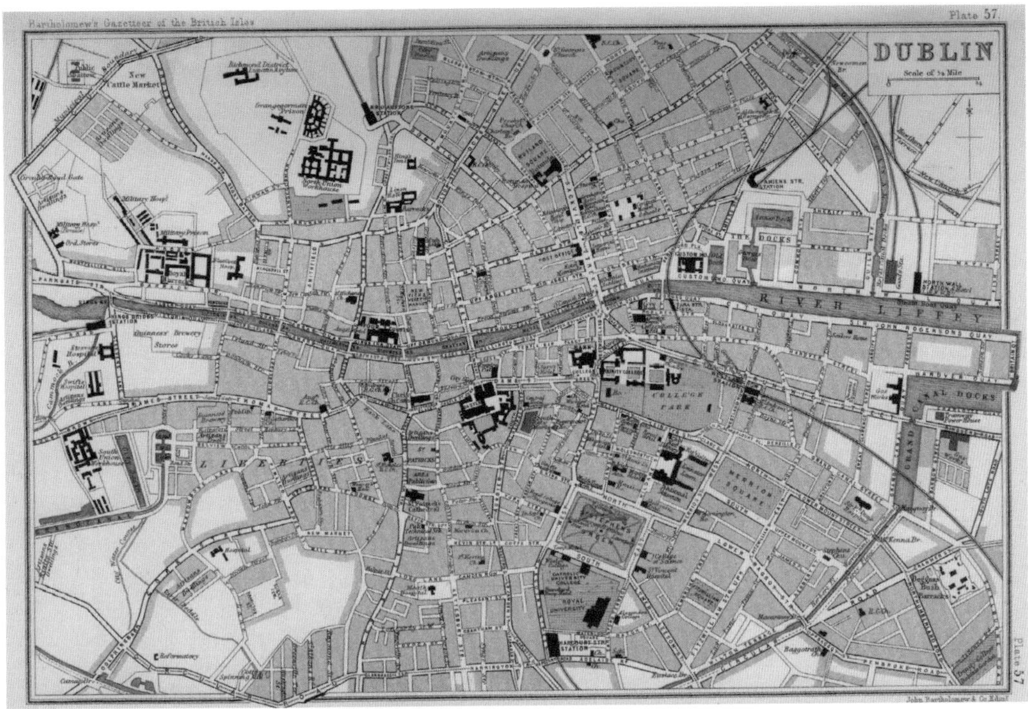

1904 map of Dublin city. Over the course of June 16, 1904, Leopold Bloom wanders from one side of Dublin Bay to the other, passing through the center of the city. The realist geography of the novel has lead to an annual literary pilgrimage known as Bloomsday, retracing the protagonist's route through the city.

preferred the streets as places of glamour and mystery. The pleasures of the flaneur were not known only by those who strolled past the windmill at Montmartre (another producer of village modernism). Joyce believed that the free circulation of bodies in a city's streets was a sign of social health, much like the unimpaired circulation of blood in the hale human body. Each episode of *Ulysses* is dedicated to an organ of the body—lung, heart, kidney, etc. Joyce wished to recognize the human body after decades of its denial by Victorian prudes but also as an image of the restored freedom of the mind. For, Dublin, even as Joyce constructed his masterpiece between 1914 and 1921, was changing in character from a colonial to a liberated city. The restored human body may have been his image of the reconquest of Ireland by its own people, achieved finally in the year of the novel's publication, 1922.

The book is justly famous for its interior monologues, especially those that render the stream of consciousness as experienced by Bloom. It is a narrative in which little enough happens at the level of plot. Instead, the strolling of characters in city thoroughfares provides endless prompts to thought. If, in Renaissance poetry, the rhythm of iambic pentameter recapitulated the movements of a rider on a horse, here the cadences of thought itself are keyed to the rhythm of walking... and of pausing in mid-ambulation. A paradox ensues: a book that is famous for its private ruminations and personal daydreams is largely set in public spaces: streets, beaches, libraries, churches, a maternity hospital, hotels, and—most of all—pubs. In these licensed premises, men seek from the drink purveyed by curates (as bartenders were then called) something of the solace that their women seek from the curates who say Mass and Benediction in the house of prayer.

Joyce lived all of his adult life in exile from this city of his youth. At first, his attitude was caustic: the stories of *Dubliners* (1914) describe the attempts by various characters, young and old, to escape the city as "the centre of paralysis." Where English or French artists might have chronicled the progress of an ambitious young man from the provinces to the revelatory moment when he could look with triumph over the rooftops of London or Paris and say "I have arrived!", the young Joyce could see liberation only in terms of escape from the Irish capital. Even in his first published novel, *A Portrait of the Artist as a Young Man* (1916), the protagonist declares his philosophy to be "silence, exile and cunning." But, by the time he wrote *Ulysses*, Joyce's attitude had softened. Knowledge of life in the other great cities he had come to know—Trieste, Zurich, and Paris—made him more appreciative of the virtues of what he called "the seventh city of Christendom."

Signatures of all things I am here to read, seaspawn and seawrack, the nearing tide, that rusty boot. Snotgreen, bluesilver, rust: coloured signs. Limits of the diaphane.

Ulysses celebrates Dublin's friendliness, musicality, and expressiveness of language (the rainy weather being "as uncertain as a child's bottom"). In the course of his long day, Bloom moves from the cemetery, through pub and beach, to the maternity hospital, as if to echo Joyce's notion of literature as an affirmation of life against death. Even in the graveyard, he is witty, suggesting that, instead of maudlin pieties, tombstones should simply describe the useful work done by the persons buried beneath them: "I cooked good Irish stew," "I travelled for Cork lino." In a city church, this sardonic rationalist likens the repeated ritual "pray for us and pray for us" to his own mantras as an ad canvasser—"buy from us and buy from us." Yet, despite this critical edge, his deepest impulse is empathy for fellow citizens, as for the pain suffered by women in childbirth ("kill me, that would"). Though cuckolded, he rises above all humiliation, offering rescue to a drunken bohemian and evoking a tribute to his own skills as a lover by an already repentant wife.

Though Bloom is one of the most fully realized characters in literature, he remains finally a mystery to himself, his wife, and even the reader. So also ,does Dublin. As with any city, this book can be entered and exited through many routes—the famous psychologist Carl Jung started by reading the final chapter, entering (as it were) by an unofficial route.

Like Proust's Paris or Musil's Vienna, Dublin through this book has become one of the cities of modernism, a place in which premodern poverty and the latest technology exist side by side. Joyce records a gleaming new system of public trams but also the sub-life of people in city sewers. He explores the paradox by which one of the most "backward" places in Western Europe

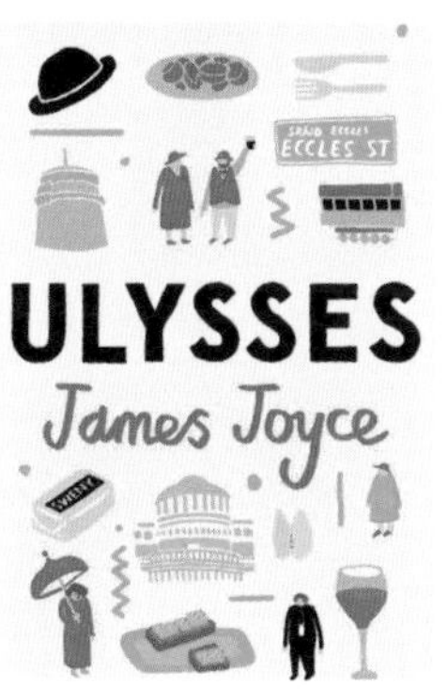

To match the bold modernist style of Joyce's text many publishers featured striking, graphic cover designs, including Penguin Books (top right) and the Gabler Edition (bottom right).

produced some of its most avant-garde, experimental art. If you educate people to high levels but debase their economy, as the British empire had done in late nineteenth-century Ireland, you create the conditions for artistic and political revolution. The Dublin Joyce abandoned was a site of cultural richness and material poverty. But it was a place to which, in the end, he gave unconditional love.

He said that he could think of no higher calling than being mayor of a great city. Every year, when people in Edwardian costume reenact scenes from his book on Bloomsday, Joyce becomes something even better than a mayor: he becomes the inventor of a city, as myth and as matter of fact.

ALPS, SWITZERLAND

THOMAS MANN

THE MAGIC MOUNTAIN

(DER ZAUBERBERG) (1924)

In the decade before the Great War a young man visits his tubercular cousin at a sanatorium in the Swiss Alps for a planned stay of three weeks and ends up staying seven years.

Thomas Mann (1875–1955) won the Nobel Prize for Literature for his novels *Buddenbrooks* (1901) and *The Magic Mountain* (1924) and his various short stories.

The Magic Mountain was intended as a comic reworking of Mann's novella *Death in Venice*. He began work on it in 1912 but was interrupted by the Great War, and didn't complete it until 1924. By then it was over 900 pages long.

Mann drew upon a tradition of enchanted mountains in German folklore. In Goethe's *Faust* the hero is led up the Brocken by Mephistophles in order to partake in the Witches Sabbath; in Wagner's *Tannhäuser* the Venusberg is a place of dire temptation.

"An ordinary young man was on his way from his hometown of Hamburg to Davos-Platz in the canton of Graubunden."

So begins *The Magic Mountain*: Thomas Mann's 900-page meditation on life, love, and death, set in the rarefied confines of a sanatorium for tuberculosis during the years immediately prior to the Great War. The ordinary young man making the journey to the International Sanatorium Berghof is Hans Castorp—the unassuming hero of the novel. Hans is taking a three-week break from his job as a shipping engineer in order to visit his consumptive cousin Joachim. But as the train bears Hans through the Swiss Alps, winding its way ever-upward through ravines and gullies and past "magnificent vistas" of "ineffable, phantasmagoric Alpine peaks," Hans becomes dizzy at the idea that such commonplace things as hardwood forests and songbirds now lie far below him. He has not even arrived at his destination and already the mountain's magic is going to work on his senses; he is journeying—both figuratively and literally—into realms far beyond his ken:

> Two days of travel separate this young man (and young he is, with few firm roots in life) from his everyday world, especially from what he called his duties, interests, worries, and prospects … Space, as it rolls and tumbles away between him and his native soil, proves to have powers normally ascribed to time … Space, like time, gives birth to forgetfulness, but does so by removing an individual from all relationships and placing him in a free and pristine state … Time, they say, is water from the river Lethe, but alien air is a similar drink; and if its effects are less profound, it works all the more quickly.

Although Hans has difficulty acclimatizing to the clear "alien air" of Berghof (he develops a nervous tremor; his cheeks are permanently flushed; his favorite cigar has an unpleasant leathery taste), he finds it much easier to adapt to the milieu of strictly regimented leisure. Life on the mountain is one of "horizontal" rest cures on one's balcony; of prescribed walks in the well-kept gardens or into the scenic valley with its pines, brooks, and waterfalls; of snowcapped peaks and feverish flirtations. And when Hans himself is diagnosed with having a "moist spot" on the lungs and advised to stay a little longer than his allotted three weeks, he only-too-happily complies.

The International Sanatorium Berghof, with its modern facilities and its cosmopolitan clientele, is nothing less than a self-sufficient microcosm of prewar bourgeois Europe. And young Hans, with his impeccable manners and mail-order cigars, is a perfect "petit bourgeois." But, lest we forget the title of the novel and its mythological antecedents, the sanatorium is also a hermetically sealed world of sickness and death. It's over a mile above sea level and so far removed from the day-to-day concerns of the "flatlands" (the inhabitants' derogatory term for home) that even the very notion of the day-to-day is rendered obsolete. Here time exists on the grand scale (the month is considered the smallest unit), so that time itself becomes slippery: snow is eternal and the seasons cease to exist in any ordered fashion. And this sense of timelessness and isolation, and the chilling ambiguity as to just how much of Hans's illness is genuine, give the novel a wonderfully uncanny feel. The setting may be ostensibly that of the Swiss Alps, but *The Magic Mountain* is a novel of otherworldly strangeness *par excellence* (the oft-repeated phrase "we don't feel the cold up here" chimes forebodingly throughout).

And of an evening, when the almost circular moon appeared, the world turned magical and wondrous – flickering crystals and glittering diamonds flung far and wide. The forests stood out black against white. The regions of the sky beyond the reach of moonlight were dark and embroidered with stars.

Inspiration for *The Magic Mountain* came to Mann when he was visiting his wife in a sanatorium at Davos, Switzerland. Like the hero of his novel, Mann was diagnosed as tubercular by one of the doctors and advised to stay on as a patient. "If I had followed his advice," Mann wrote years later in the afterword to the novel, "who knows, I might still be there! I wrote *The Magic Mountain* instead."

A critical and commercial success upon publication, *The Magic Mountain* is now rightly considered a classic of twentieth-century literature. Part Bildungsroman, part allegory, it also is a tender and witty eulogy for a way of life that was about to be swept away by the Great War—and arguably Mann's masterpiece.

During a visit to Davos, Switzerland, to improve his health, Ernst Ludwig Kirchner produced this expressionist piece, *Davos in Winter,* 1923. It shares with Mann's masterpiece the beauty and claustrophobia of the winter mountain-scape.

LONDON, ENGLAND

VIRGINIA WOOLF

MRS DALLOWAY (1925)

A novel of London taking place over the course of a single day in June, Virginia Woolf's fourth novel was intended, she noted in her diary, "to give life & death, sanity & insanity; I want to criticize the social system, & to show it at work, at its most intense."

Virginia Woolf (1882–1941) is considered one of the foremost literary figures of the twentieth century. A Londoner born and bred, she innovated the narrative technique of "stream of consciousness" across her novels and short stories.

Mrs Dalloway was first published by the Hogarth Press, and sold more than 1,000 copies in two weeks.

One of Woolf's pleasures was what she called "street-haunting": walking London's paths and parks for inspiration and solace.

Described as "a book whose afterlife continues to inspire new generations of writers and readers," Virginia Woolf's fourth novel, acclaimed as one of the great works of literary modernism, takes place, like her contemporary James Joyce's *Ulysses*, over the course of a single day: in Woolf's case, a summer's day in London, the date of which can be narrowed down to 13 June 1923, a Wednesday. (Woolf's particularities involving the noting of time at pivotal moments in the book inspired its original title, *The Hours*.) Her protagonist, Clarissa Dalloway, is the middle-aged upper-class wife of a politician, preparing for a significant party taking place at their home in Bond Street later that evening.

As the novel opens we are invited to witness something unusual for this society lady with servants: "Mrs Dalloway said she would buy the flowers herself". Thus proceeds her day through the city of London ("the swing, tramp, and trudge; in the bellow and the uproar; the carriages, motor cars, omnibuses, vans, sandwich men shuffling and swinging; brass bands, barrel organs; in the triumph and the jingle and the strange high singing of some aeroplane overhead was what she loved; life; London; this moment of June"), touching not only on the sights, sounds, and impressions around her, but her inchoate, internal longings: the never-enacted possibilities with Peter Walsh, her former suitor, and with Sally Seton, a friend she once kissed. The apotheosis of Woolf's extraordinary writing technique of "stream of consciousness" (eschewing factual realism for a more artistic profundity), *Mrs Dalloway* leads the reader through a densely populated city emerging from the terrible memories of the First World War, into the modern age and the unknowable aloneness of the human mind—that of Clarissa, of Peter, and also of a shell-shocked former soldier, Septimus Warren Smith, who, shut out of university education due to his social class, is an autodidact who went to war to fight for a romanticized view of Shakespeare's England.

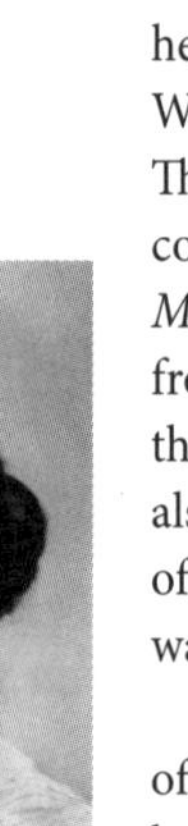

Now he is neglected, wretched, and suicidal. Septimus's London is one of nightmarish visions; he feels engulfed by the city. For Peter, returning home from five years in India, the city is a familiar stranger to which he is happy to succumb, yet he recalls the long shadow of the war, and the solemn

One feels even in the midst of the traffic, or waking at night, Clarissa was positive, a particular hush, or solemnity; an indescribable pause; a suspense before Big Ben strikes. There! Out it boomed. First a warning, musical; then the hour, irrevocable. The leaden circles dissolved in the air. Such fools we are, she thought, crossing Victoria Street.

remembrance ceremonies each autumn at the Cenotaph. For Clarissa, it is a place of security, even of sacrament. The somber tones of Big Ben punctuate the novel and its sections, the cycle of the day, and also the life cycle, as we move through its various scenes.

Sitting in the arboreal haven of Regent's Park paralyzed with fear and grief, Septimus is certain that "leaves were alive, trees were alive ... the leaves being connected by millions of fibres with his own body," with the birds singing to him in "voices prolonged and piercing in Greek words." The circularity of her characters' impressions are woven into Woolf's plot structure, with overlapping scenes and differing sensations and perspectives: Clarissa, Septimus, and his wife Rezia all hear the same motor car backfire in Bond Street from different vantage points; they converge separately in Regent's Park in contrasting states of mind. Peter notes an ambulance rushing down Tottenham Court Road: admiring its efficiency, he is unaware that it is on its futile way to Septimus, who has taken his own life.

Woolf was a walker, and the central London setting of *Mrs Dalloway* was her inspiration and liberation from her stifled Victorian upbringing in Kensington. Years later, in the months before her own suicide in 1941, she would tramp the bombed-out streets and decimated squares in desperation at the destruction caused by a second world war in her lifetime.

Yet for all its preoccupation with death, *Mrs Dalloway* is a celebration of life. As a work of fiction it is dazzling: as a novel of empathy it is deeply humane, placing London at its center and into the heads and hearts of its characters.

Overleaf: Showing the densely packed streets of central London, Bacon's 1903 map was created twenty years before the novel was published. The routes her characters take in the book are traceable in this map.

London: G. W. Bacon & Co., Ltd., 127, Strand. *Copyright.*

22
23
24
25
26
J
K
L
M
N
O
PENTONVILLE ROAD
CITY ROAD
HOLBORN
VIADUCT
NEWGATE ST.
FLEET STR.
CHEAPSIDE
CORNHILL
LEADENHALL ST.
BISHOPSGATE ST.
CHARTERHOUSE ST.
WATERLOO BRIDGE
BLACKFRIARS BRIDGE
SOUTHWARK BRIDGE
LONDON BRIDGE
BLACKFRIARS ROAD
BOROUGH ROAD
WESTMINSTER BRIDGE RD.
LAMBETH ROAD
NEW KENT ROAD
UNION ST.
CHISWELL ST.
WORSHIP ST.
T
H
A
M
E
Bethlem Lunatic Hospital
22
23
24
25
26

NEW YORK CITY AND LONG ISLAND, USA

F. SCOTT FITZGERALD

THE GREAT GATSBY (1925)

In New York during the Jazz Age, Jay Gatsby, a fabulously and mysteriously wealthy young man, attempts to win back the now-married Daisy Fay Buchanan, the lost love of his youth.

Francis Scott Key Fitzgerald (1886–1940) was born in Minnesota to an upper-middle class family. He attended, but never graduated from, Princeton University, leaving college in 1917 to join the army, where he first met his to-be wife Zelda Sayre.

The Great Gatsby is Fitzgerald's third novel; more than 25 million copies have been sold worldwide since 1925. It was not popular when first published: initial sales were less than half that for his first two books.

The last line of *The Great Gatsby* is engraved on Fitzgerald's gravestone.

"Place" is central to *The Great Gatsby*, Fitzgerald's masterpiece often called "the Great American Novel." Occurring 25 times in *Gatsby*'s 174 pages, the word "place" consolidates three notions: geographic location, residential construction, and social position. Place names reflect all three. One notes then a surprising reticence about the narrator, Nick Carraway. He acknowledges, near the end of his tale of "Westerners" in "the East," that "I am part of that ['Middle West' culture], a little solemn with the feel of those long winters, a little complacent from growing up in the Carraway house in a city where dwellings are still called through decades by a family's name." He does not name the city, but it clearly resembles Fitzgerald's own St. Paul, Minnesota.

Fitzgerald studied in the East at Princeton. Nick studied in the East at "New Haven," as he sometimes calls Yale, and afterward went to "Europe," although, in his telling, Nick's easternmost excursion is remarkably bloodless: "I participated in that delayed Teutonic migration known as the Great War. I enjoyed the counter-raid so thoroughly that I came back restless." Although Nick asserts that "I am one of the few honest people that I have ever known," his omissions are many. With a job in New York, he rents a small home on parvenu West Egg, a peninsula on the north shore of Long Island, the fish-shaped island extending far east from Manhattan into the Atlantic. It is, he admits, the "less fashionable of the two."

"Across the courtesy bay the white palaces of fashionable East Egg glittered along the water, and the history of the summer really begins on the evening I drove over there to have dinner with the Tom Buchanans." Tom, a beefy, racist son of Chicago-area wealth and privilege, whom Nick had known at Yale (on the other side of Long Island Sound), has married Nick's cousin, Daisy Fay, whose home in Louisville had the "largest of the lawns" in the city. On Long Island, although Daisy embraces Nick as nearly enough part of her society to urge a dalliance between him and her childhood friend, Jordan Baker, now a celebrity competitive golfer, Daisy does not approve of Nick's residence.

Art deco map showing Long Island in 1933. Fitzgerald's West and East Egg are based on Great Neck and Sands Point, located on the northeastern shore of Long Island.

> She was appalled by West Egg, this unprecedented "place" that Broadway had begotten upon a Long Island fishing village—appalled by its raw vigor that chafed under the old euphemisms and by the too obtrusive fate that herded its inhabitants along a short-cut from nothing to nothing. She saw something awful in the very simplicity she failed to understand.

To Nick, that "simplicity," presumably, was newly won riches, of which Gatsby seemed to have endless amounts, enough to refurbish and fill weekly with lavish parties a mansion in the shadow of which lay Nick's rental. Although Gatsby has bought his mansion in order to glimpse Daisy's and the "green light" at the end of her dock across the bay in East Egg, it is in Nick's rental that Gatsby finally meets Daisy again. They had been brief lovers when he was a young officer stationed near Louisville before shipping out and while she had become his "grail," she somehow couldn't wait and married Tom. Indeed, since Gatsby had no money then, she might never have. While he certainly has money now, he remains a permanently displaced person.

> I would have accepted without question the information that Gatsby sprang from the swamps of Louisiana or from the lower East Side of New York. That was comprehensible. But young men didn't—at least in my provincial inexperience I believed they didn't—drift coolly out of nowhere and buy a palace on Long Island Sound. … The truth was that Jay Gatsby of West Egg, Long Island, sprang from his Platonic conception of himself.

Although place names occur frequently in the novel, the narrative present transpires overwhelmingly in three: New York (meaning fashionable Manhattan), Long Island (meaning only its two eastern counties, Nassau and Suffolk, the former including both West Egg nearer to New York and East Egg), and a place in the Astoria neighbourhood of Queens, one of two counties on the western end of Long Island but a borough of New York. "About half way between West Egg and New York the motor road hastily joins the railroad and runs beside it for a quarter of a mile, so as to shrink away from a certain desolate area of land. This is a valley of ashes—," a soot-covered, hard-scrabble, working-class wasteland over which presides a disused billboard for an optometrist, Dr. T. J. Eckleburg, whose huge eyes see either all or nothing. Unlike the Shadow of the Valley of Death in Psalm 23, in the valley of ashes one should fear evil for nothing, with the possible exception of money, protects anyone.

Movement from place to place is as important as place itself. Gatsby dispatches his limousine to New York to bring wealthy guests to his parties, his station wagon to bring the less wealthy from the railroad. Taxis and hearses abound. The fatal accident that unravels Gatsby's dream occurs on the roadway in the valley of ashes driving from New York to Long Island. Cars (88 times) and other terms for conveyances and conveying (202 times) fill the narrative landscape.

How inspiring that landscape can be. "The city seen from the Queensboro Bridge is always the city seen for the first time, in its first wild promise of all the mystery and the beauty in the world," a promise Nick ultimately finds unfulfilled. Nick notes that West and East Egg "are not perfect ovals—like the egg in the Columbus story, they are both crushed flat at the contact end." Today Great Neck, and particularly its wealthiest neighborhood, Kings Point, still resembles West Egg in class although not in lot size, and Manorhaven across Manhasset Bay, with its even larger estates, recalls East Egg. But Columbus, to find the rich New World, to visualize the journey, "crushed" the egg, as the pursuit of wealth seems to crush almost everyone in *Gatsby*.

Returning again West, dispirited by the summer's tragic events and failures, Nick *Car-away* imagines the first Dutch sailors' view of "the fresh, green breast of the new world," a world always sought, like Daisy or the green light marking her dock, but never attained. "So," Nick writes in the book's last line, "we beat on, boats against the current, borne back ceaselessly into the past."

ASHDOWN FOREST, EAST SUSSEX, ENGLAND

A. A. MILNE

WINNIE-THE-POOH (1926)

Stories of A. A. Milne's son Christopher Robin's adventures in the 100 Acre Woods with his anthropomorphic toys Winnie-the-Pooh, Piglet and Eeyore.

One of the first things you'll find when you open your battered old copy of *Winnie-the-Pooh* is a map. It's a map of a place where many of us grew up, each of the sites marked on it a reminder of an episode that has stayed with us: "Pooh trap for heffalumps," "To North Pole," "Where the woozle wasn't," "Rabbits House," "Bee tree." And of course, the place called "The Hundred Acre Wood."

Sorry—correction: the *100 Aker Wood*.

Just as the characters that animate the books are versions of the Milne family's real toys, so the world in which they live is based on the Milne family's real home, at Ashdown Forest in East Sussex. Cotchford Farm, where the family had a weekend house, is just on the northern edge of the forest—it was here that the real Christopher Robin played with those toys, and here that Milne's most famous books were largely written. And Pooh's illustrator, E. H. Shepard, used views of the same location, with its familiar heather and pines, when creating the visual world of the books. The real forest and the book forest, Christopher Milne would write, "are identical." (The memorial plaque at the top of a footpath commemorates Shepard here as well as Milne.)

If you go to Ashdown Forest today you will also discover, among other things, a bridge over a little stream—newly restored now, and right by the car park—which is just perfect for a game of Pooh-Sticks. And indeed, the real Christopher Robin used to play the game on this same spot, though he couldn't remember which came first: did his playing precede and inspire the story, as his forest adventures sometimes did? Or were his games inspired *by* the stories, since the book world of Pooh and friends would also furnish his imaginary play around Cotchford for years after? (He would get into some trouble when the gardener's wife got her foot caught in his newly dug heffalump trap.)

How precisely certain aspects of the books' topography correspond to specific details still existing in the forest is a matter of debate. Is the old quarry really Roo's sandy pit? What ever happened to the six pines that are supposed to be close to the heffalump trap? Which tree in the 100 Aker Wood is Owl's house? And where exactly should you be heading if you're on an Expotition

Alan Alexander Milne (1882–1956) had a moderately successful career as a humorist and playwright before the phenomenal popularity of *Winnie-the-Pooh* (1926), which sold 35,000 copies in the UK and over 150,000 in the US in the first year.

The toy Winnie-the-Pooh now lives in the New York Public Library. He borrowed his name from "Winnie," an American black bear cub at London Zoo, and a swan called "Pooh," whom the Milnes met on holiday.

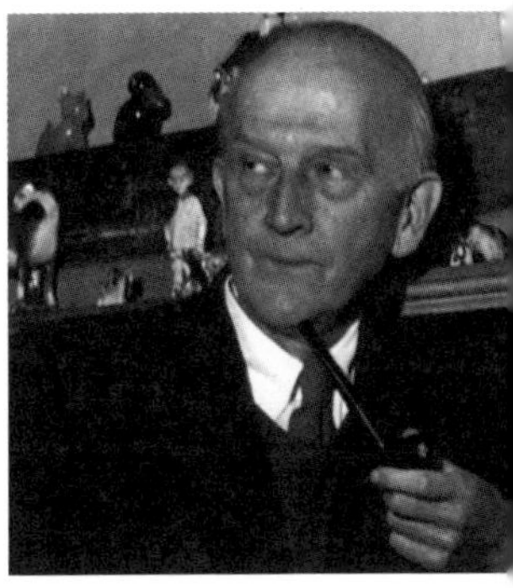

100 Aker Wood map illustration by Ernest Shepard. His illustrations were so integral to the series' success that A. A. Milne arranged for Shepard to receive a share of the royalties.

AND MR SHEPARD HELPD

The Sun was still in bed, but there was a lightness in the sky over the Hundred Acre Wood which seemed to show that it was waking up and would soon be kicking off the clothes. In the half-light the Pine Trees looked cold and lonely, and the Very Deep Pit seemed deeper than it was.

A. A. Milne's son, the "real" Christopher Robin, photographed here with the original Pooh Bear in 1928.

Opposite: Pooh, Piglet ,and Christopher Robin are drawn standing on what was originally called Posingford Bridge. The bridge, which spans a tributary of the River Medway was replaced in 2005 but kept its recognizable form so fans of the books can continue to play Pooh Sticks.

to the North Pole? A helpful local-walks leaflet suggests the Pole is close to Wren's Warren Valley, where you will also find Eeyore's Gloomy Place. (Sigh. If you did ever want to find such a thing. Which I doubt.)

But there is still a "Five Hundred Acre Wood" today (reduced to a mere 100 akers for the books); there are clusters of trees, just where the map tells us there should be clusters of trees; and of course there's the pine-crowned hilltop of Gills Lap, which becomes the books' Galleons Lap, which is at the forest's top, and is its most enchanted place. Galleons Lap had 60-something trees in a circle, "and Christopher Robin knew that it was enchanted because nobody had ever been able to count whether it was sixty-three or sixty-four, not even when he tied a piece of string round each tree after he had counted it".

The Enchanted Places is the name Christopher Robin Milne gave to his memoir of an Ashdown Forest childhood. And this is the place where *The House at Pooh Corner* comes to its tear-jerking conclusion, with chapter 10, "In which Christopher Robin and Pooh come to an enchanted place, and we leave them there." The stories end here, with a boy and a bear. And "wherever they go, and whatever happens to them on the way, in that enchanted place on the top of the Forest, a little boy and his Bear will always be playing." Today's readers flock to Ashdown Forest, in the hope of finding them still there.

ROME, ITALY

ALBERTO MORAVIA

THE TIME OF INDIFFERENCE

(GLI INDIFFERENTE) (1929)

Moravia's first novel, published to immense acclaim (and outrage) in the heyday of Fascism, explored the political indifference and boredom of a feckless, upper middle-class family in Rome.

Alberto Moravia (1907–1990) was scarcely seventeen when, in 1925, he began to write *The Time of Indifference* after recovering in a sanatorium in the Italian Alps from tuberculosis of the bone.

The novel's portrayal of complacency and double-dealing in Mussolini's Rome irked the Fascist authorities; the Duce's brother condemned Moravia as a "destroyer of every human value".

The Time of Indifference is a forerunner of the French existentialist novel. When Moravia visited France in 1946, Jean Paulhan, then the Editor of the *Nouvelle Revue Française*, was reported to have asked him if he had come to see his "sons," Sartre and Camus.

Alberto Moravia was one of *le grandi firme*—big names—of twentieth-century Italian literature. For much of his life he lived in an apartment on the banks of the River Tiber in Rome. Back in the 1960s and 1970s Moravia's views were canvassed on every subject and he routinely spoke about his abiding literary theme: boredom. *The Time of Indifference* (best translated as "The Uncaring Ones") excoriated boredom as a disease corrupting affluent society in Moravia's native Rome. The novel's cynicism and brutally frank attitude to sex turned Moravia overnight into *un scrittore scomodo,* an "unsettling writer." His message was clear: bourgeois Roman society was moribund—like a dirty antimacassar, it was in need of a thorough rinsing.

In pages of emotionally detached prose, *The Time of Indifference* scorns the bourgeois Roman background from which Moravia himself came. Michele, the novel's disgusted antihero, is the first in a long line of distinguished Moravian bourgeois male characters, being a compound of indifference, pusillanimity, and lassitude. His alcoholic father is long dead, while his mother, Mariagrazia, clings pathetically to her lover, Leo Merumeci, who is a sexual predator with designs on Michele's sister, Clara. Clara resignedly prepares to give herself to Leo: sex, typically for Moravia, is seen as the only form of social intercourse available to Clara or else it serves to mollify the "distasteful trivialities of everyday existence." Conjugal love or fidelity has no part at all in *The Time of Indifference.* Clara and her brother Michele have grown up in Rome without the "love of parents, without religion, without moral standards." A fifth character, Lisa, Leo's former lover, longs to take Michele as her lover, but he is bored and disgusted by her vanity and desperation.

Though the word "Rome" is nowhere mentioned in the novel it is clearly set in the Italian capital and the city infuses its almost every page: Moravia, a Roman among generations of Romans, knew the streets, churches, and piazzas intimately. The city's "useless beauty" and the ennui-stricken bourgeoisie that inhabit Rome at the dawn of Italian Fascism are bound up with Benito Mussolini's superficial idealization of Rome's imperial past and the cult of *romanità* ("Romanness"), with its Fascist paraphernalia of stone eagle motifs

A modern view of Rome from the Vittoriano. The view would have largely been the same in the late twenties, when Moravia wrote his novel, for that peculiar characteristic of the city of Rome, "the eternal city," to be indifferent to the fate of humans, unchanged and frozen in its decadent beauty over the centuries.

and suckling she-wolves. In 1919 Mussolini, then an obscure political agitator, had assembled a ragbag of black-shirted followers in Milan, and launched the political movement that was to become, two years later, the National Fascist Party. By the time *The Time of Indifference* appeared in 1929, Rome had served as Fascist headquarters for seven years. The characters' lives are shadowed by the politics of the "divine Caesar" Mussolini, whose balcony ranting and vainglorious sexual antics were known to all.

In chapter seven, Leo takes a taxi to his apartment at 83 Via Boezio (Boethius Street), near Vatican City, where some of the houses were built by Moravia's own architect father. *The Time of Indifference* unfolds in a Rome of rapid social and architectural transformation, when the myth of money and "the good life" pervaded a country that was rushing into war. As a child, Moravia had grown up in grand bourgeois homes on Via Sgambati and Via Donizetti, which were then on the periphery of Rome, but are now in the center. The periphery had begun to grow in 1925, when Mussolini declared that the center must "appear ordered and powerful, as in the days of the first empire of Augustus." Accordingly, the medieval houses and alleys round St. Peter's, the Colosseum and the Forum were demolished in order to make way for "Mussolini modern" buildings with pseudo-Roman insignia.

On the city's crowded pavements, Moravia's existentially bored characters feel inert and leaden. The impossibility of action is a theme that runs like the black line in a lobster through *Gli indifferenti.* Nothing—no inkling of anger, or rage, or hatred—has the power to shake Moravia's unhappy characters. The novel's dissection of neurotic, well-to-do ennui in Fascist-era Rome left a mark on Italian attitudes to sex and marriage.

BERLIN, GERMANY

ALFRED DÖBLIN

BERLIN ALEXANDERPLATZ (1929)

A year in the troubled life of the ex-convict Franz Biberkopf as he tries and fails to go straight, the story is woven together through a panoramic montage of life in 1920s Berlin.

Born in Stettin Germany (now in Poland) to a Jewish family, Doblin moved to Berlin at the age of ten where he lived for the next forty-five years before the rise of the anti-Semitic Nazi party drove him into exile, first in France then the United States. He returned to Europe at the end of the war.

Alexanderplatz is located in the Mitte district of East Berlin. Today it is unrecognizable from the 1920s. Extensively damaged in the battle for Berlin in 1945, it was substantially remodelled by the German Democratic Republic in the 1960s.

In 1980 the director Rainer Werner Fassbinder based a groundbreaking, fifteen-hour television series on the novel.

Alfred Döblin (1878–1957) is today chiefly remembered for *Berlin Alexanderplatz* (1929), his sprawling, modernist novel of life in the German capital in the peak years of the Weimar Republic. It was the author's most commercially and critically successful work. The novel sold around 50,000 copies before it was banned by the Nazis after they seized power in 1933. Döblin was not only a prolific novelist and essayist, but was also a psychiatrist who had practiced in Berlin since 1911. In *Berlin Alexanderplatz* he was able to combine literary experimentation with an intimate knowledge of a milieu drawn from his professional experience.

Berlin Alexanderplatz is one of the key examples of the modernist city novel. It is often compared to (but was not necessarily directly inspired by) Joyce's *Ulysses* (1922) and Dos Passos's *Manhattan Transfer* (1925). As with those works, the novel cannot be summed up by its ostensible "plot." Yet it unquestionably *does* tell a compelling story of thwarted ambitions and human frailties. The hopelessly flawed protagonist is the ex-convict Franz Biberkopf, the setting the area around Alexanderplatz in working-class East Berlin, the year 1928. Franz fails miserably in his attempts to go straight, bouncing from job to job, and relationship to relationship. He loses his arm in a burglary that goes wrong, and his girlfriend, the prostitute "Mieze," is murdered by his nemesis, the sociopathic Reinhold. Plagued by guilt and self-hatred, Franz suffers a total breakdown before, at the conclusion, it seems he has found a path to the light through the "dark avenue" of his life.

Like many other Berlin novels, the novel faithfully reproduces the Berlin dialect spoken by the locals in reported speech and thought. Yet in this novel the location represents more than mere local color. Alexanderplatz is the beating heart of the narrative, both setting and symbol. The district's geography is evoked in extraordinary detail by the omniscient, often playful narrator. At almost every point, the reader knows both where and when things are happening. The characters' negotiation of the network of interconnecting streets and interchanges—Alexanderplatz, Rosenthaler Strasse, Elsasserstrasse, Münzstrasse—can be followed with little difficulty on a

The streets were full of bustle, Seestrasse, people got on and off. Something in him screamed: Watch out, watch out. [...] It was all seething and swarming, but it had nothing going on! It isn't alive. It had complacent facial expressions, it was grinning, it was standing in groups of two or three on the traffic island in front of Aschinger's waiting to cross, smoking cigarettes, browsing in newspapers. Stood there like lamp-post, and getting stiffer all the time. It was just like the paintings, all painted, all wood.

map of Berlin, even a twenty-first-century edition. Local institutions work as additional orientation points, although many of these are now long gone, erased by a century that has taken a heavier toll on Berlin than on many European capitals. We read of the once famous Aschinger restaurant chain, with branches at Alexanderplatz and Rosenthaler Platz; the Tietz department store on Rosenthaler Strasse; the tailor Fabisch on Rosenthaler Platz; the cabaret and restaurant "Neue Welt" (New World) on the edge of the Hasenheide. Bus and tram routes, starting with the 41 tram that Franz takes from the prison in Tegel, are often given in full. Descriptions of the construction of a new underground station, resulting in the removal of the street surface, seem to hint at the nature of the novel itself, which peels back layers to reveal the chaotic simultaneity of the modern city.

Döblin employs a virtuoso narrative style that eschews realist description and linearity in favor of montage and simultaneity. Franz's story runs parallel to a dizzying assortment of statistics, quotations, anecdotes, and almost cinematic sweeps across busy city streets: we are taken on excursions into the private lives of Berliners whose paths momentarily cross; we view shop windows and advertising posters; we hear popular songs; we are given data about Berlin's slaughterhouses, about Berlin's laws and regulations, about science and medicine; we read weather reports and snippets of local, national, and international news. Some of these elements seem to offer an oblique commentary on Franz Biberkopf's tribulations, or to suggest an element of social critique in what could otherwise be viewed as an apolitical work. But they also relate to Döblin's clear desire to recreate the psychological impact of the urban experience. In this respect the ongoing influence of Futurism and Expressionism, formative for the younger Döblin, and of theorists such as Georg Simmel, is very evident.

Previous page: Street Scene by George Grosz, 1923, depicting the inequalities and decadence of Weimar Republic Berlin.

ODESSA, UKRAINE

ISAAC BABEL

ODESSA STORIES

(ODESSKIYE RASSKAZY) (1931)

These are haunting tales of the Jewish community and criminal underground in the busy port city of Odessa leading up to the Bolshevik Revolution in 1917.

Odessa, a commercial port lying on the shores of the Black Sea, was historically a multiethnic and uniquely Jewish city. Its best-known chronicler is Isaac Babel whose hardboiled, fantastical stories of the racketeers, prostitutes, beggars, and rabble rousers of the anarchic Moldavanka district where he was born, from the dying days of the Russian empire through the Russian Revolution of 1917, is one of the great masterpieces of modern Russian literature.

> In Moldavanka, on the corner of Dalnitskaya and Balkovskaya streets, stands the house of Lyubka Shneyveys. In this house you'll find a wine cellar, an inn, a feed store and a dovecote for a hundred pair of Kryukov and Nikolayev doves. All these things, along with plot forty-six at the Odessa quarries, are owned by Lyubka Shneyveys, nicknamed Lyubka the Cossack—all that is, except for the dovecote, which belongs to Yevzel the watchman, a retired soldier with a medal. On Sundays Yevzel heads out to Okhotnitsky Square and sells his doves to city clerks and kids from the neighbourhood.

This vivid snapshot of a thriving, ducking, and diving gig economy in the seaport of Odessa during the waning of the Russian empire and on through the Russian Revolution and its immediate aftermath forms the intense opening paragraph of "Lyubka the Cossack." A story about a woman who neglects her newborn baby for her shady business deals, it is packed with character, incident, violence, and slapstick humor—as well as almost incidentally beautiful imagery. This wild inventiveness is typical of its companion tales in *Odessa Stories*, originally published as magazine pieces in 1923 and 1924, and first collected in book form in 1931. Their author, Isaac Babel, is arguably Odessa's most famous literary export, and certainly its most affectionate, if frequently unflattering chronicler. Babel's tales, pithy, urgent, grimy, and exciting, constitute a guide book, an itemized street map of a vanished city, a time, and—most poignantly—a people, yet such is his

Isaac Babel was born in Odessa in 1894. He began writing short stories in St. Petersburg in 1915, where he met and befriended Maxim Gorky, at that time Russia's most famous author. He died in 1940, shot by a firing squad in a Moscow prison.

First published in magazine form (1923–1924), these stories were collected as *Odessa Tales* in 1931. *The Complete Works of Isaac Babel* first appeared in English translation in 2002. The Pushkin Press edition of *Odessa Stories* (2016), translated by Boris Draluk, is the first standalone collection of the tales that Babel set in his home city.

ВУФКУ
виробництво
держкіно 1 фабрика
одеса
сценарій - Бабеля
режисер - Вільнер
оператор - Калюжний

БЕНЯ
КРИК

boldness of characterization, his piquant use of language (the Russian spoken in this northeastern part of the Black Sea coast is inflected with Yiddish words and grammar; its quickfire modernity bursting through any translation) that we are immediately placed at the center of the action. The impoverished Moldavanka district, where Babel, the son of a Jewish warehouse owner, was born in the summer of 1894, was the equivalent of London's Whitechapel or New York's Lower East Side.

Founded in 1794, by the nineteenth century Odessa had become a significant naval base, port, and Russia's third largest city. Opportunity abounded. Moldavanka district—an area of factories, housing the workers that supplied those factories with labor (today still industrial, but built up with high-rise flats)—was also the principal center for Orthodox Jews in the city, who had been guaranteed right to remain—with restrictions—under Imperial Russia's Pale of Settlement, applicable through Central and Eastern Europe from 1791 to 1917. Following this, Odessa's population had swelled with Jews from the rural *shetls* arriving in the big city to seek their fortunes. Despite this "protection," pogroms were rife; in Babel's shocking semi-autobiographical tale "The Story of my Dovecote" a boy goes to market to buy a pair of red doves he has saved up for, instead becoming unwittingly caught up in anti-Semitic violence.

Moldavanka was Odessa's dark underbelly, run by lawless gangsters of a type recognizable to anyone familiar with the Godfather films of Francis Ford Coppola, the novels of Dashiel Hammett or Raymond Chandler, or the real-life Kray twins of 1960s London. It was this local mythology that fascinated Babel. Following some years in another part of Ukraine, he and his family returned to Odessa in 1906; the young Isaac grew up outside the ghetto, but Babel the writer's affinity with the rich diversity of Moldavanka made it ripe for fictional treatment, and much embellishment ("I was a boy who told lies" begins one of his *Childhood* stories, a formidable salvo for a writer). Throughout the tales, the leader of a notorious criminal gang, Benya Krik, known as Benya the King, takes center stage, his "lightning quick rise and terrible end" (at the hands of Bolsheviks) so gripping public imagination that he became immortalized in a 1926 silent film.

Babel also met a terrible end, one of the millions who fell victim to another thug—Joseph Stalin. Babel was executed by firing squad in Lubyanka prison in Moscow in January 1940 after being convicted on trumped-up charges of espionage. But it is in the tangy sea air of Odessa where Babel's legacy rests. Odessa is the eponymous hero of his barbed, chaotic stories, of which he wrote in 1916: "The literary messiah, for whom we've waited so long and so fruitlessly, will come from there—from the sunny steppes washed by the sea."

Previous page: Poster for the Russian film *Benya Krik* (1926) directed by Vladimir Vilner and based on Babel's collection of short stories. *Opposite:* A 1911 city plan of Odessa, a busy port city on the northwestern shore of the Black Sea. The city's Jewish community grew throughout the nineteenth century despite repeated pogroms.

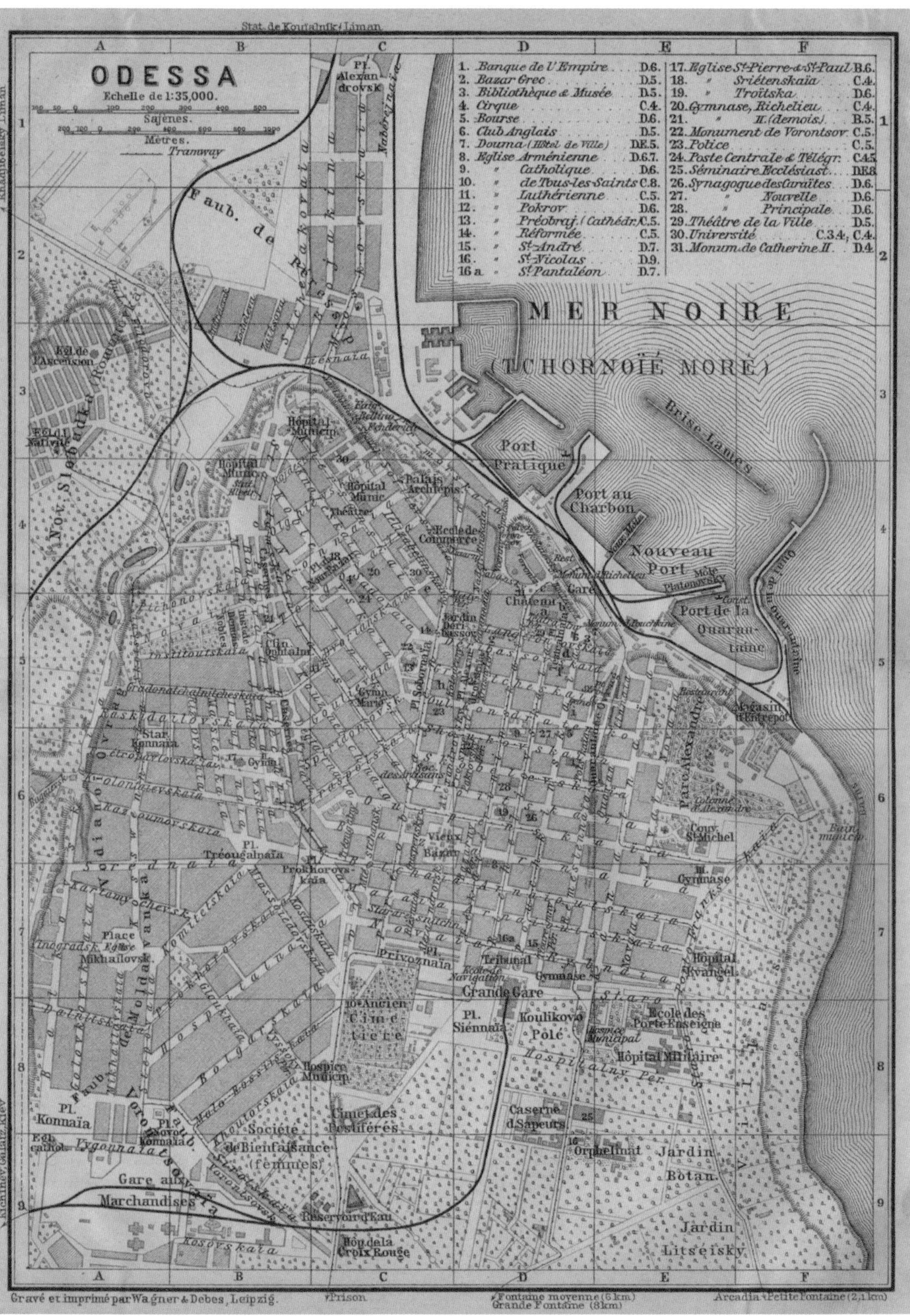
ODESSA
Echelle de 1:35,000.
Sajènes.
Mètres.
Tramway
1. Banque de l'Empire D.6.
2. Bazar Grec D.5.
3. Bibliothèque & Musée D.5.
4. Cirque C.4.
5. Bourse D.6.
6. Club Anglais D.5.
7. Douma (Hôtel de Ville) D.E.5.
8. Eglise Arménienne D.6.7.
9. " Catholique D.6.
10. " de Tous-les-Saints C.8.
11. " Luthérienne C.5.
12. " Pokrov D.6.
13. " Préobraj. (Cathédr.) C.5.
14. " Réformée C.5.
15. " St. André D.7.
16. " St. Nicolas D.9.
16 a. " St. Pantaléon D.7.
17. Eglise St. Pierre & St. Paul B.6.
18. " Sriétenskaïa C.4.
19. " Troïtska D.6.
20. Gymnase, Richelieu C.4.
21. " II. (demois.) B.5.
22. Monument de Vorontsov C.5.
23. Police C.5.
24. Poste Centrale & Télégr. C.4.5.
25. Séminaire Ecclésiast. D.E.8.
26. Synagogue des Caraïtes D.6.
27. " Nouvelle D.6.
28. " Principale D.6.
29. Théâtre de la Ville D.5.
30. Université C.3.4; C.4.
31. Monum. de Catherine II. D.4.
MER NOIRE
(TCHORNOÏÉ MORÉ)
Port Pratique
Port au Charbon
Nouveau Port
Port de la Quarantaine
Brise-Lames
Parc Alexandre
Grande Gare
Koulikovo Polé
Jardin Botan.
Jardin Litseisky
Gare aux Marchandises
Hôpital Militaire
Cimetière des Pestiférés
Société de Bienfaisance (femmes)
Stat. de Koujalnik Liman
Gravé et imprimé par Wagner & Debes, Leipzig.
Prison
Fontaine moyenne (5 km)
Grande Fontaine (8 km)

ABERDEENSHIRE, SCOTLAND

LEWIS GRASSIC GIBBON

SUNSET SONG (1932)

Modernization marauds the majestic Mearns landscape of this novel, and war annihilates the present whilst Chris Guthrie in the sanctuary of the ancient Standing Stones clings to a future.

Lewis Grassic Gibbon is the pseudonym of James Leslie Mitchell (1901–1935). He published under both names and began writing full time in 1929. He had seventeen works published before his early death in 1935.

Gibbon wrote the sequels *Cloud Howe* and *Grey Granite*, thus creating a Chris Guthrie trilogy, which his publisher, Jarrold's of London, collected and published in 1946 as *A Scots Quair*.

Sunset Song was dramatized and serialized by BBC Scotland (first broadcast in March 1971, repeated in 1975). Terence Davies directed a film version, released in 2016.

In 1932 author Lewis Grassic Gibbon burst on to the British literary scene with the harrowing, racy, and experimental novel *Sunset Song*. The novel was written partly in Doric, a North-East-Scots dialect, and set in 1911–18 in the fictional rural community of Kinraddie in the Scottish landscape of the Mearns (Kincardineshire). The Mearns is still considered as possessing outstanding natural beauty, and Grassic Gibbon was superbly adept in depicting Mearns' majesty in a non-romanticized, lyrical, yet nuanced manner.

The first edition of *Sunset Song* included end-pages with a map allowing readers to pinpoint Arbuthnott as the inspiration for the village and people of Kinraddie. The second edition excluded the map. But by the time *Sunset Song* was published in America in 1933 Grassic Gibbon's cover was blown. He was revealed to be James Leslie Mitchell, himself raised in Arbuthnott, whose family still lived in the Mearns. He was already the author of eight books of diverse genres published under his real name.

In 1911 Arbuthnott was a community of 195 people. It is perhaps unsurprising that despite Mitchell's efforts to mask identities by using fictitious names it was nevertheless a simple process for villagers to recognize themselves and others. *Sunset Song* provoked parochial paroxysms in Mitchell's home community and was banned in some libraries and bookstores in the wider district. It, and the Mitchells, soon became "the speak of the Mearns," a development the author found amusing enough to begin a new series of short stories choosing that for a title.

Sunset Song narrates Chris Guthrie's development from adolescent to married woman. A conflicted heroine, whose identity—past, present and future—is inexorably and viscerally linked to the land, Chris has intelligence, an inextinguishable spirit and possibilities that immediately have the reader rooting for her. Will she choose the old ways of servitude to the land or the freedom offered to her through education? In the end the land has a power over Chris and her tragic beau, Ewan: "nothing endured at all, nothing but the land"; "The land was forever, … you were close to it and it to you, … it held you and hurted you."

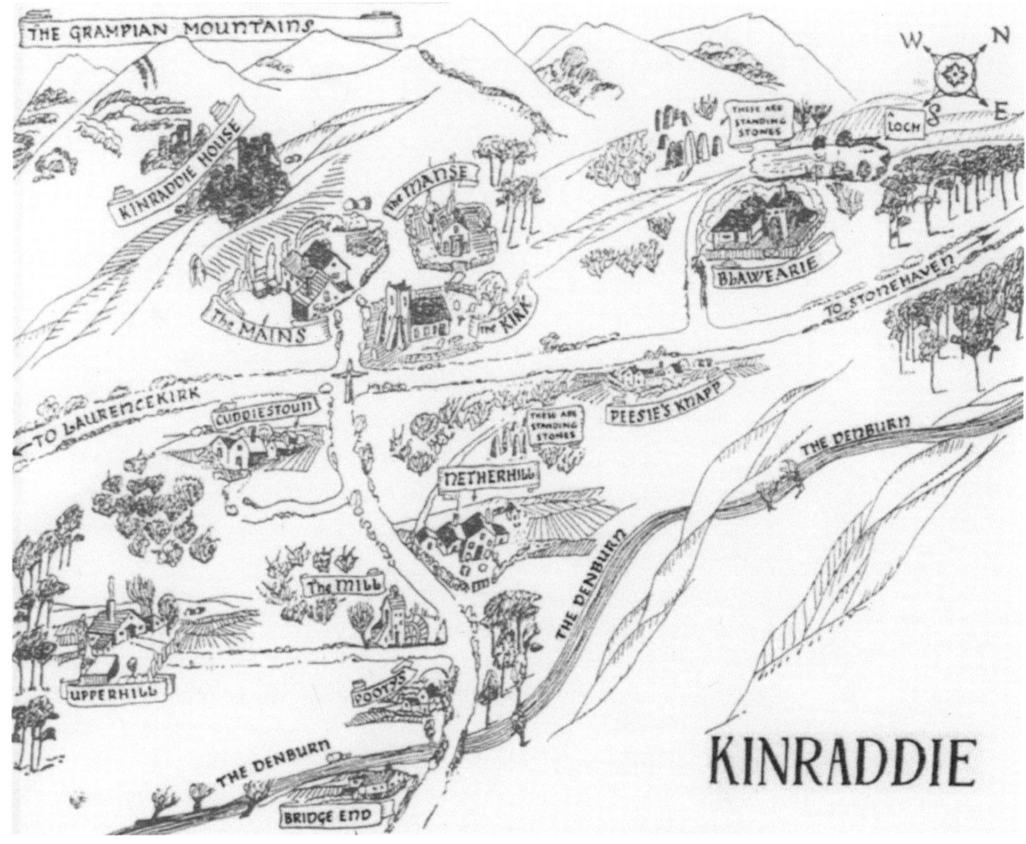

Gibbon's hometown of Arbuthnott, in Aberdeenshire, Scotland, was the inspiration for the fictional Kinraddie. Included on the endpapers of the first edition (1931), this map has deliberately distorted landmarks to hinder comparisons with the "real" town.

What was so shocking about *Sunset Song?* There are hard-hitting scenes of familial violence, suicide, infanticide, and shadowy incestuous overtures. Worse, Grassic Gibbon was unafraid to open the bedroom door after Chris and her man, Ewan, are married.

The novel's clever framing, with its Prelude and Epilude entitled the "Unfurrowed Field" and its chapters named after the phases of farming: plowing, drilling, seed time, and harvest, evidence Grassic Gibbon's modernist writing style as well as his significant knowledge of and concern with the relationship of rural communities to the land. Another notable framing device is the Standing Stones located above Kinraddie. Each chapter begins with Chris situated there, taking solace and inspiration from this landscape. The Stone Circle is simultaneously a literary framing device and a symbol of the one durable phenomenon permitting a psychological and spiritual linkage across generations. This is carved into our consciousness when the Standing Stones become Kinraddie's War memorial and Ewan's name is engraved there.

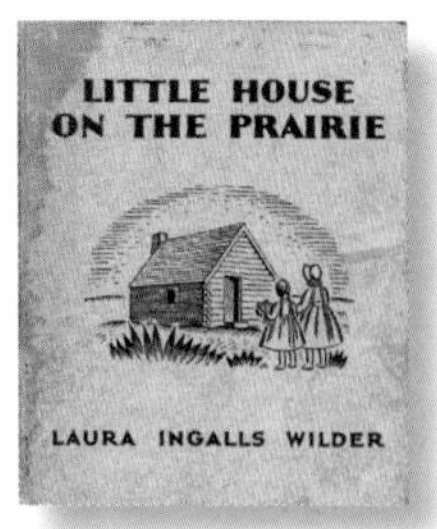

KANSAS, USA

LAURA INGALLS WILDER

LITTLE HOUSE ON THE PRAIRIE (1935)

After selling their farm in Wisconsin, the Ingalls family travels by covered wagon to make a new home on the Kansas prairie. This is the second novel in a series based on the author's own life.

In the 1930s, Wilder tried in vain to sell her memoirs before reshaping them into a sanitized version suitable for young readers. Her original autobiography, heavily annotated, was published in 2014 as *Pioneer Girl*.

The NBC-TV series *The Little House on the Prairie* (1974–1983) was set in Walnut Grove, Minnesota, where the Ingalls family lived, off and on, between 1874 and 1879.

Louise Erdrich (see *Tracks*, pp.208–209) wrote a series of books for children reversing the narrative perspective of the "*Little House*" books so that Native Americans are "us" rather than "them," beginning with *The Birchbark House* (1999).

In her sixties, aided and encouraged by her daughter, Laura Ingalls Wilder began turning her memories of childhood into a series of eight novels aimed at children and young adults. Her dramatic yet cozy depiction of a self-sufficient way of life in a vanished world was hugely influential in shaping the popular view of the westward movement in late nineteenth-century America. Published during the depths of the Great Depression, her first book (*Little House in the Big Woods)* was a great success, and the popularity of the entire series continued to grow, with *Little House on the Prairie* perhaps the most iconic, now widely recognized as a classic of American literature.

The original log cabin Charles Ingalls built almost single-handed in 1869 is long gone, but a reproduction was erected on the same site in 1977, about 14 miles southwest of Independence, Kansas. Today, visitors can see the actual well Ingalls dug with the help of his neighbor, Mr. Edwards, with the same, boundless sky above. Although there are roads and more buildings now, the area remains sparsely inhabited. But the high prairie itself is gone.

What Wilder called "high prairie" is also known as the tallgrass prairie, an ecosystem that once covered more than 170 million square miles of North America. Nearly all of the tallgrass disappeared during Wilder's own lifetime, plowed under or burned off and replaced by farms and towns. Today only a tiny remnant exists in the Tallgrass Prairie National Preserve in the Flint Hill region of Kansas and Oklahoma.

When the Ingalls arrive, the prairie appears as an unbroken sea of grass:

> Kansas was an endless flat land covered with tall grass blowing in the wind. Day after day they travelled in Kansas, and saw nothing but the rippling grass and the enormous sky. In a perfect circle the sky curved down to the level land, and the wagon was in the circle's exact middle.

Through this winds the Verdigris River, and the many creek bottoms that feed the land. Trees—chiefly cottonwood, chosen to be the State tree of Kansas—lined every creek and river, and other types of vegetation (as well as

"In the West the land was level, and there were no trees. The grass grew thick and high". Illustration by Garth Williams for the second edition in 1953.

disease-bearing mosquitos) flourished. Strangers to the midwest may describe the land as "empty," "bleak" or "barren" but the soil is rich and fertile, and, in the words of Pa Ingalls: "There's good land, timber in the bottoms, plenty of game—everything a man could want."

"Enormous" and "empty" are words frequently applied to the scene; more than once the land is described as uninhabited. Yet Charles Ingalls knew that was untrue; he knew he was encroaching on land that belonged to the Osage Nation. Like other hopeful homesteaders he expected government treaties would be broken again: "Ma said … the Indians would not be here long. Pa had word from a man in Washington that the Indian Territory would be open to settlement soon."

Wilder wrote in terms acceptable in her day, and was not entirely unsympathetic to Native Americans, but her depiction of people she called "wild Indians"—as well as the extreme right-wing libertarian politics of her daughter, Rose Wilder Lane—have since created some controversy around the book and the image it perpetuates of an American manifest destiny.

"The man in Washington" lets Pa down. Rather than wait to be evicted, he loads up the covered wagon and the family heads off to make a new start in Minnesota. In reality, the Ingalls did not settle near Walnut Grove, Minnesota, until several years later; they returned to Wisconsin out of financial necessity, when the buyer of their farm there defaulted on payments.

MISSISSIPPI AND CAMBRIDGE, MASSACHUSETTS, USA

WILLIAM FAULKNER

ABSALOM, ABSALOM! (1936)

A tragedy of rapacious ambition in the antebellum Southern US, spanning multiple generations and woven into an unorthodox detective story.

William Faulkner (1897–1962) was born and spent most of his life in northern Mississippi. Faulkner purchased the antebellum home Rowan Oak in 1930 and lived there until his death. It is now a museum dedicated to the author and maintained by the University of Mississippi.

Absalom, Absalom! offers, in Quentin Compson and his father, the continuation of characters already known to readers of Faulkner's 1929 novel *The Sound and the Fury*.

Faulkner received the 1949 Nobel Prize in Literature. He also won the Pulitzer Prize for fiction twice, first for *A Fable* (1954) and again fro his last novel *The Reivers* (1962).

Absalom, Absalom! opens in a "dim hot airless room" on a "long still hot weary dead September afternoon" in the fictional town of Jefferson, Mississippi; it concludes in "the cold air, the iron New England dark" of an unheated Harvard dormitory in December. Quentin Compson, the novel's protagonist, is present in each of these chambers, in both cases immersed in conversation yawning across the hours, and in both cases struggling with the degree to which the cruel legacy of Thomas Sutpen—Jefferson's most notorious planter—touches, implicates, or even defines Quentin himself. At the outset, the novel conjures for Quentin the spectacle of Sutpen and his slaves.

> [they] overrun suddenly the hundred square miles of tranquil and astonished earth and drag house and formal gardens violently out of the soundless Nothing and clap them down like cards upon a table beneath the up-palm immobile and pontific, creating the Sutpen's Hundred, the *Be Sutpen's Hundred* like the oldentime *Be Light*.

Between Sutpen's godlike command in 1833 and Quentin's tortured reflections in 1909 lies all that the fiat hides but also assumes, and that ultimately causes it to rebound horribly upon itself: the myriad racial and sexual depredations that ground the plantation economy and by extension that of the entire country. The novel records Quentin's fevered attempts to justify, or even to understand, his culture in the face of constant prodding by his new northern classmates: "Tell about the South. What's it like there. What do they do there. Why do they live there. Why do they live at all."

Faulkner's imagined Yoknapatawpha County, lightly superimposed on the real northern Mississippi territory where he spent almost all his life, represents one of literature's greatest and most sustained attempts to explore America's original sin. Faulkner created a sprawling, Balzacian series of over a dozen books detailing the lives and doings in the fictional Yoknapatawpha County, Mississippi. *Absalom, Absalom!*, the sixth novel, moved him to append a map of the county, appointing himself "sole owner & proprietor."

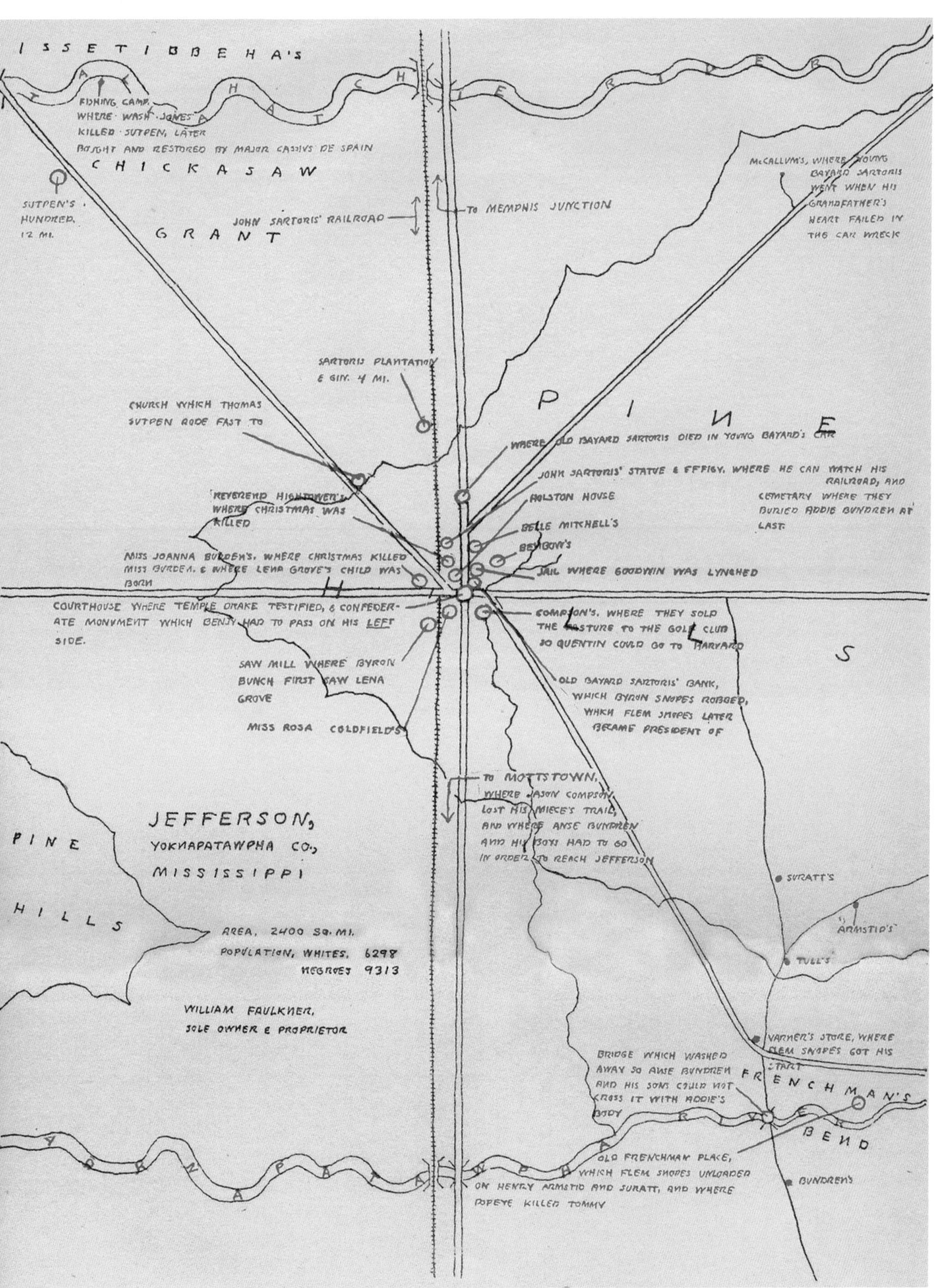
ISSETIBBEHA'S
FISHING CAMP WHERE WASH JONES KILLED SUTPEN, LATER BOUGHT AND RESTORED BY MAJOR CASSIUS DE SPAIN
CHICKASAW
GRANT
SUTPEN'S HUNDRED 12 MI.
JOHN SARTORIS' RAILROAD
TO MEMPHIS JUNCTION
McCALLUM'S, WHERE YOUNG BAYARD SARTORIS WENT WHEN HIS GRANDFATHER'S HEART FAILED IN THE CAR WRECK
SARTORIS PLANTATION & GIN. 4 MI.
CHURCH WHICH THOMAS SUTPEN RODE FAST TO
PINES
HILLS
WHERE OLD BAYARD SARTORIS DIED IN YOUNG BAYARD'S CAR
JOHN SARTORIS' STATUE & EFFIGY, WHERE HE CAN WATCH HIS RAILROAD, AND
CEMETARY WHERE THEY BURIED ADDIE BUNDREN AT LAST.
REVEREND HIGHTOWER'S, WHERE CHRISTMAS WAS KILLED
HOLSTON HOUSE
BELLE MITCHELL'S
BENBOW'S
MISS JOANNA BURDEN'S, WHERE CHRISTMAS KILLED MISS BURDEN, & WHERE LENA GROVE'S CHILD WAS BORN
JAIL WHERE GOODWIN WAS LYNCHED
COURTHOUSE WHERE TEMPLE DRAKE TESTIFIED, & CONFEDERATE MONUMENT WHICH BENJY HAD TO PASS ON HIS LEFT SIDE.
COMPSON'S, WHERE THEY SOLD THE PASTURE TO THE GOLF CLUB SO QUENTIN COULD GO TO HARVARD
SAW MILL WHERE BYRON BUNCH FIRST SAW LENA GROVE
MISS ROSA COLDFIELD'S
OLD BAYARD SARTORIS' BANK, WHICH BYRON SNOPES ROBBED, WHICH FLEM SNOPES LATER BECAME PRESIDENT OF
TO MOTTSTOWN, WHERE JASON COMPSON LOST HIS NIECE'S TRAIL, AND WHERE ANSE BUNDREN AND HIS BOYS HAD TO GO IN ORDER TO REACH JEFFERSON
JEFFERSON, YOKNAPATAWPHA CO., MISSISSIPPI
PINE HILLS
AREA, 2400 SQ. MI.
POPULATION, WHITES, 6298
NEGROES 9313
WILLIAM FAULKNER, SOLE OWNER & PROPRIETOR
SURATT'S
ARMSTID'S
TULL'S
VARNER'S STORE, WHERE FLEM SNOPES GOT HIS START
BRIDGE WHICH WASHED AWAY SO ANSE BUNDREN AND HIS SONS COULD NOT CROSS IT WITH ADDIE'S BODY
FRENCHMAN'S BEND
OLD FRENCHMAN PLACE, WHICH FLEM SNOPES UNLOADED ON HENRY ARMSTID AND SURATT, AND WHERE POPEYE KILLED TOMMY
BUNDREN'S

Sartoris
william faulkner
ULISSEIA

THE SOUND AND THE FURY
WILLIAM FAULKNER

AS I LAY DYING
WILLIAM FAULKNER

VINTAGE FAULKNER
Sanctuary

LIGHT in AUGUST
WILLIAM FAULKNER

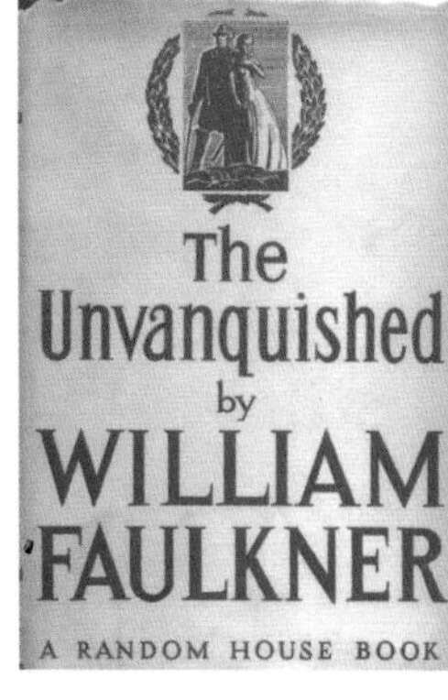
The Unvanquished
by
WILLIAM FAULKNER
A RANDOM HOUSE BOOK

95¢
William
FAULKNER
Nobel Prize for Literature, 1950
A Novel of the Snopes Family
The Hamlet
A MODERN LIBRARY PAPERBACK

INTRUDER IN THE DUST
A NOVEL BY
WILLIAM FAULKNER
RANDOM HOUSE

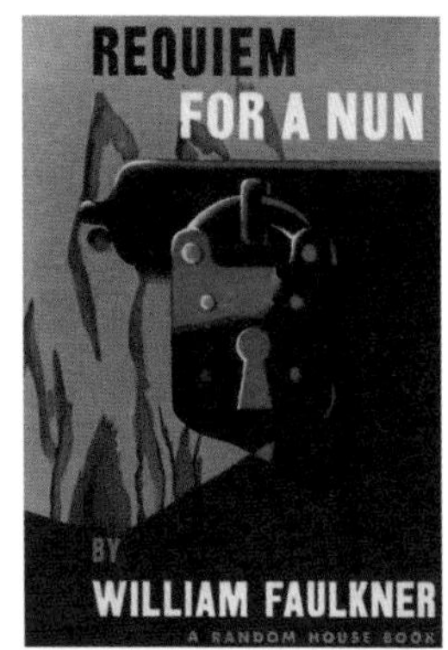
REQUIEM FOR A NUN
BY
WILLIAM FAULKNER
A RANDOM HOUSE BOOK

WILLIAM
FAULKNER
Nobel prize for literature, 1950
The Town
a novel of the Snopes family

William Faulkner
THE MANSION
A novel of the Snopes family

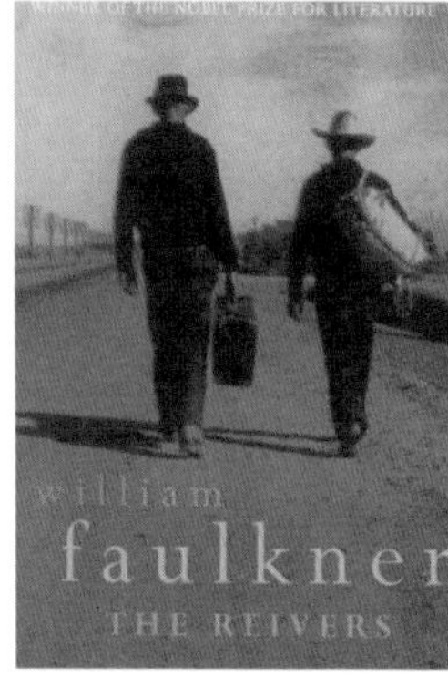
WINNER OF THE NOBEL PRIZE FOR LITERATURE
william
faulkner
THE REIVERS

It began to take shape in its same curious, light, gravity-defying attitude—the once-folded sheet out of the wistaria Mississippi summer, the cigar smell, the random blowing of the fireflies. "The South," Shreve said. "The South. Jesus. No wonder you folks all outlive yourselves by years and years and years."

For all that the most local of colors saturate the novel, seeing them accurately entails seeing as well the larger circuits of the antebellum economy and the society it produced. *Absalom* communicates Faulkner's understanding that accounting for even his "little postage stamp of native soil" requires an expansive sense of place, embracing the Appalachian hills from which Sutpen emerges, poor and uneducated; the Virginia "Tidewater" plantation where he first perceives class differences and conceives of the desire to inhabit the "big house" himself; and New Orleans, where Sutpen's ruin burgeons, seeded by his own actions along the way. Nevertheless, and pointedly, the story boils down to a series of brutal altercations at Sutpen's Hundred, and to Quentin's obsessive returns to these scenes in an effort to make sense of what, in his father's words, "just does not explain." For *Absalom*, like the Biblical episode that supplies its title, is a story of generations, and of the inheritances that constitute both places and people.

Indeed, Quentin recognizes himself as a walking repository of Southern history, "his very body ... an empty hall echoing with sonorous defeated names"—"not a being" but "a commonwealth ... a barracks filled with stubborn back-looking ghosts still recovering, even forty-three years afterward, from the fever which had cured the disease." *Absalom*'s haunted landscapes, both internal and external, play a crucial role in Faulkner's development of what has come to be called the Southern Gothic. Here, violence and grotesquerie are the province not of supernatural beings, as in the genre's European progenitor, but instead emerge from unflinching distillations of Southern society. So, too, as Quentin discovers, with the land itself: leaving Mississippi 1,000 miles behind for college does not amount to leaving it behind at all, because this, too, he carries with him. The displacement offers the anguished Quentin just enough critical distance to fabulate beyond the point at which his father reaches an impasse. Quentin and his Canadian roommate together spin out an audacious series of hypotheticals, with the implacable feel of truth, to explain what Mr Compson could not. We profoundly internalize the places we grow up with, Faulkner suggests, and then project them again wherever we go; the stories we make up are the ones we already know. Telling them is the process of recognizing—admitting—that knowledge.

Page 109: The first of a number of maps of the fictional Yoknapatawpha County drawn by Faulkner himself and used as the endpapers for the first edition of *Absalom, Absalom!*

Opposite: Faulkner set twelve of his novels and (many short stories) in Yoknapatawpha County, based on Lafayette County, Mississippi, where he lived most of his life.

FOWEY, CORNWALL, ENGLAND

DAPHNE DU MAURIER

REBECCA (1938)

This gothic drama of jealousy and suspense, narrated by Maxim de Winter's wife, traces the newly weds' return to her husband's ancestral home on the south Cornwall coast, and the narrator's growing obsession with Maxim's dead wife, Rebecca.

Rebecca was the third of nine novels set by Daphne du Maurier in Cornwall. Although she wrote a total of seventeen novels, it would remain her most successful. It has never been out of print and sold over 40,000 copies in its first month.

Ferryside was the name given by the du Mauriers to their Cornish holiday home on the River Fowey. Bought by Daphne's parents in 1926, this converted boathouse has been used by the family ever since.

Alfred Hitchcock's movie of *Rebecca* came out in 1940, two years after the book's publication.

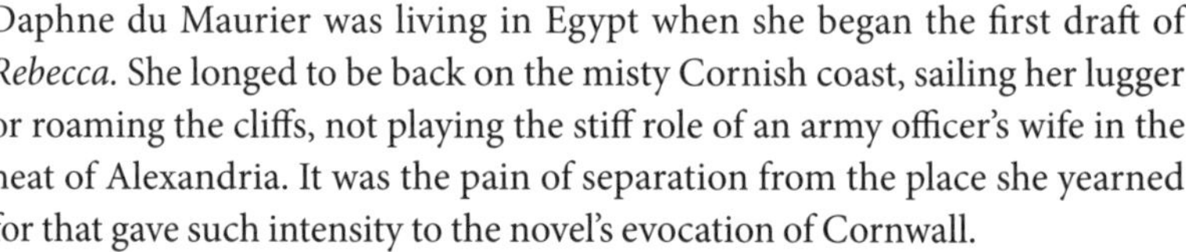
Daphne du Maurier was living in Egypt when she began the first draft of *Rebecca*. She longed to be back on the misty Cornish coast, sailing her lugger or roaming the cliffs, not playing the stiff role of an army officer's wife in the heat of Alexandria. It was the pain of separation from the place she yearned for that gave such intensity to the novel's evocation of Cornwall.

At the age of nineteen, Daphne had fallen under the spell of Fowey's handsome harbor, its busy river opening onto a wide bay edged by rugged cliffs. For a girl who had grown up in Hampstead and attended finishing school in France, Cornwall was a far cry from the life she knew. But here, she recalled, was the freedom she desired, "freedom to write, to walk, to wander, freedom to climb hills, to pull a boat, to be alone." And she quickly developed another obsession apart from the sea. Early in her exploration of the Fowey area, she had discovered the overgrown estate of Menabilly on the headland above Polridmouth Cove. Entranced, she returned repeatedly to her "House of Secrets," even on one occasion breaking into the dilapidated, ivy-covered building. The sense of trespassing in a forbidden place had only deepened her fascination, and in the heat of Alexandria she visualized Menabilly's wild gardens in almost hallucinogenic detail.

"Last night I dreamt I went to Manderley again." Although the grand mansion conjured up in the opening words of *Rebecca* is imaginary, its setting is real. Daphne re-imagined Menabilly as the far more imposing mansion of Manderley, a name suffused with exotic hints of far-off Mandalay. With the introduction of a gothic house came the palpable influence of the Brontë sisters, evident not only in the unmistakable imprint of *Jane Eyre* on the cast of *Rebecca*, but more potently in Daphne's Brontë-esque skill at merging intense feelings with haunting places—a device that would make the dramatic Cornish landscape such a gift to scores of later twentieth-century romantic novelists.

But Manderley also has its own unique topography. The monster shrubs and rampaging rhododendrons that overrun the drive to the house in *Rebecca*'s opening dream sequence have their roots in reality. The grounds of Menabilly, like those of other Cornish estates with mild valleys, were well stocked with Himalayan rhododendrons, bamboos, and a plethora of strange foreign plants brought into the country by Victorian collectors. At Manderley, these alien species seem to the dreamer to be proliferating into a menacing jungle, as uncivilized and uncontrollable as the dark desires that she unearths in her marital home.

The sensory delights of Manderley's gardens, so closely modelled on Menabilly's, resonate with the moods of the novel's susceptible narrator. Recoiling from the blood-red rhododendrons that evoke violent passion, the second Mrs. de Winter delights in the heady fragrance of delicate white azaleas as she walks in the Happy Valley with her husband. But she catches the azaleas' scent on a handkerchief belonging to Maxim's first wife, and the Happy Valley itself ends near the cove where Rebecca led her double life. She can find no lasting joy in Manderley's loveliness, for Rebecca is everywhere.

On the de Winters' return from honeymoon they take a suite in the East Wing, with its charming view of the rose garden where Maxim as a child used to play innocently with his mother; but the second wife is drawn repeatedly into the West Wing, where the demonic housekeeper Mrs. Danvers presides over the temptations of Rebecca's unchanged bedroom. Here, the changeable sea, chafing at the edge of the grounds, seems nearer and more ominous.

Daphne du Maurier with her children in front of Menabilly in 1945. Du Maurier leased the run down house from 1943 to 1969 and lovingly restored it.

Overleaf: Joseph Edward Southall, *The Botanists*, 1928, a peaceful view of Fowey harbor, where du Maurier fell in love with Cornwall. Menabilly estate, the inspiration for the novel's Manderley, is two miles west of the town.

As a sailor, Daphne understood the particular dangers of this stretch of coastline, where a daymark still stands on Gribben Head to warn navigators away from the rocks. A shipwreck, that key element of a whole genre of Cornish adventure stories, provides the turning point of her plot. When warning rockets go off in the fog, readers sense that Manderley's deepest secret is about to emerge from the black waters. The plot twists and turns, but we have known from the book's beginning that, whatever else may surface, Maxim and his new wife, like the author in Alexandria, will lose Manderley.

It proved wonderfully apt that the runaway success of *Rebecca* and its film adaptation enabled Daphne to make Menabilly her home in 1943. Though her children found the rambling house drafty and rat-ridden, she remained smitten, and she was devastated by her eventual move to a house on the other side of the headland. Like the second Mrs. de Winter, she was destined to end her life in exile. But mercifully, as a frail elderly woman, the celebrated writer of *Rebecca* could still walk the grounds of her beloved Menabilly.

GUADARRAMA MOUNTAINS, SPAIN

ERNEST HEMINGWAY

For Whom the Bell Tolls (1940)

Pitting nature against atrocity, Hemingway's classic novel of the Spanish Civil War is set among the Sierra Mountains and tells the story of an American brigadier and his experiences of love and destruction.

Ernest Hemingway (1899–1961) served as a reporter in Spain for the North American Newspaper Alliance during the Spanish Civil War and uses his firsthand experiences of this conflict for his third novel, *For Whom the Bell Tolls*.

The novel was first published in the US in 1940 by Charles Scribner's Sons, where it attracted mixed reviews from critics.

Although unanimously recommended by the Pulitzer fiction jury to receive the 1941 Pulitzer Prize, the recommendation was later reversed due to concerns over indecency.

The Guadarrama Mountains of Spain run from northeast to southwest across the central plains of Castille. They are ancient mountains, formed of pale granite and gneiss, their slopes densely wooded with pines of several species: black pines, maritime pines, sentry pines, Scots pines. To visit them is to be able to recall the scents of those days and nights, even years on: "the piney smell of … crushed needles," as Ernest Hemingway puts it in *For Whom the Bell Tolls*, "and the sharper odour of … resinous sap."

Hemingway's novel is set in the Guadarrama during the last May of the Spanish Civil War. Its hero is Robert Jordan, a young American fighting for the International Brigade. Jordan, an explosives expert with a profound disinterest in his own fate, is tasked by his Soviet commander with destroying a bridge in the Fascist-held mountains. He joins forces with Republican partisans who have gone guerrilla. Their base for the operation is a cave in the "rim-rock" at the "cup-shaped upper end" of a "little valley."

In the book's second paragraph, Jordan unfolds a photostatted map on the "pine-needle floor" of the forest. That contrast between military perception and natural presence preoccupies Hemingway throughout the novel. The landscapes of the Guadarrama are interpreted chiefly in terms of tactics: open ground is read for its lines of fire, "timber" for its cover. Those with close knowledge of the range—like Jordan's trusted guide Anselmo—are valuable because they can move discreetly through this hostile territory.

Yet these tough men remain alert to the beauty of the mountains. When a two-day blizzard blows in, Jordan relishes its wildness, though he knows it will betray their position. Pilar, a fellow partisan, agrees: "What rotten stuff is the snow and how beautiful it looks." The hurry-up-and-wait aspects of war mean there is time to appreciate the "afternoon clouds … moving slowly in the high Spanish sky". Maria, Jordan's lover, speaks of her passion for the pine forest: "the feel of the needles under foot … the wind in the high trees and the creaking they make against each other." Even their target is assessed both aesthetically and militarily—it is a "steel bridge of a single span", possessing a "solid-flung metal grace," standing "dark against the steep emptiness of the gorge."

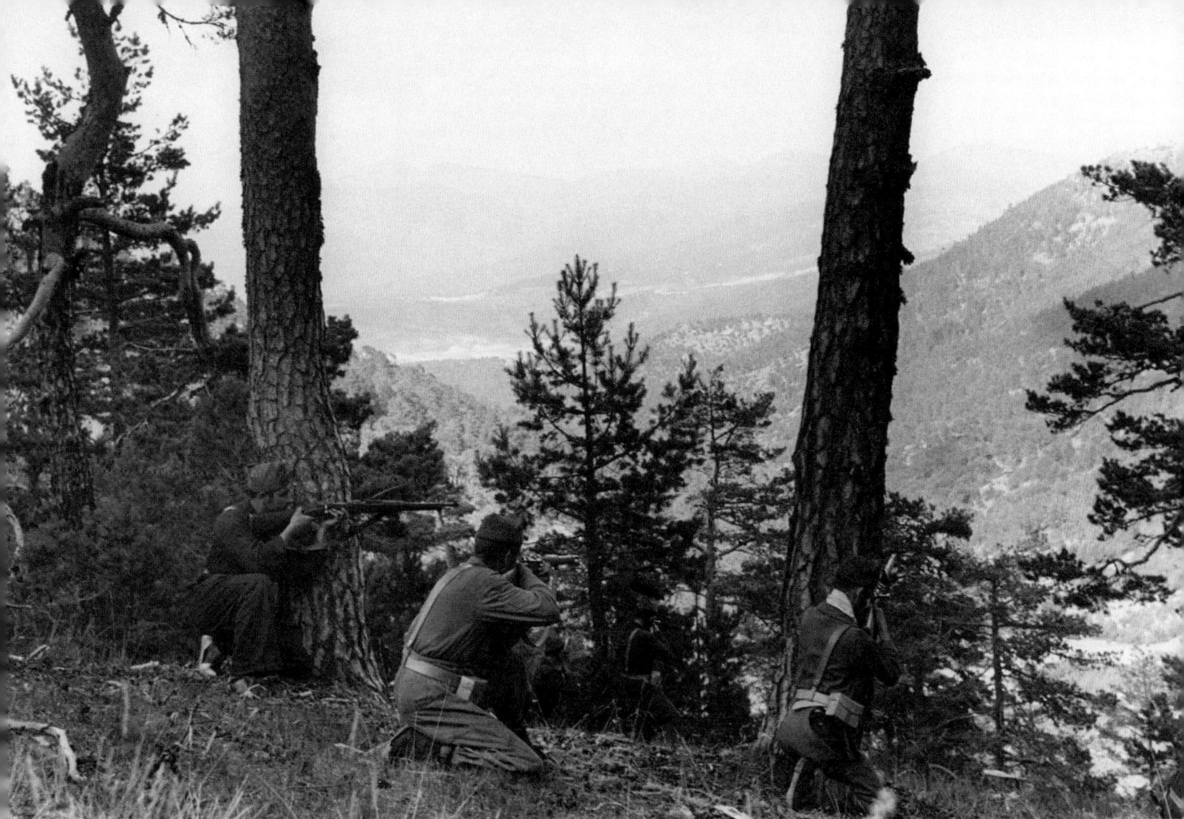

This uncredited photograph taken during the height of the Spanish Civil War (1936–1939) depicts Franco's Nationalist snipers attacking Republican rebels, 7,000 feet up in the pine forests of the Guadarrama Mountains.

The upper pine forests aren't the only landscape of the novel, though. Hemingway splices in atrocious scenes from earlier in the war: a dusty village square in which supposed Fascists are flailed, cudgelled and then hurled over a cliff, or an attack on a *guardia civil* barracks, after which the wounded are dispatched with pistol shots to the skull. The sky is a scape, too, through which pass Franco's glittering aeroplanes: Heinkel bombers of the Condor Legion, moving "like no thing there has ever been … like mechanised doom," or Messerschmitts turning among the vultures.

The novel's first and last sentences describe almost the same situation: Jordan, flat on the forest floor, watching the ground below. In the first, he is planning his assault on the bridge; in the last, waiting for his death. The attack has gone wrong, and a shell blast has broken his leg appallingly. Fascist troops are approaching. Despite the circumstances, these closing paragraphs are oddly uplifting. Jordan touches "the palm of his hand against the pine needles where he lay," and "the bark of the pine trunk that he lay behind." Such gestures are a means of reassuring himself of the existence of matter, in advance of its annihilation. Dying, he has begun to meld with the forest in which he has fought. The landscape shimmers into a mindscape: "he was," writes Hemingway, "completely integrated now." Jordan has fulfilled the novel's title: he has become a piece of the continent, a part of the main.

BAHIA STATE, BRAZIL

JORGE AMADO
THE VIOLENT LAND (1943)

An epic novel about the conquest of the Atlantic Forest in Northeastern Brazil and the bloody conflicts among cacao farmers in the beginning of the twentieth century

As a child, Jorge Amado (1912–2001) experienced the power struggles in Bahia, the Brazilian state in which *The Violent Land* is set. His own father was a cacao farmer who survived ambushes by rivals in Bahia.

Amado's fiction—almost thirty novels—has been translated into nearly fifty languages. They may be divided by two location-related themes: the rural novels, set in southern Bahia during the cacao economic cycle in the early twentieth century, and the urban novels, which take place in Salvador, Bahia's capital.

The Violent Land was adapted for film, theatre, television and radio in 1965.

Places are sirens in Jorge Amado's novels. Their melodies evoke both appeal and threat to a sailor's ears. The migrants and adventurers who embark on a ship to the port of Ilheus, Bahia, in the beginning of Amado's *The Violent Land* cannot resist the siren's song that promises gold.

Gold, in this case, is a golden fruit, cacao, the seeds of which are the source of chocolate. Its trees, originally grown in the Amazon area, found more fertile soil when they were transplanted to the Atlantic Forest zone in southern Bahia, a Brazilian state in Northeast Brazil. The ensuing economic boom saw many migrate from all over the country in search of quick riches.

Ilheus, the port town turned into city, would become larger and richer than Salvador, the capital of Bahia and Brazil's first capital. It was the gateway into the feud of powerful cacao plantation farmers—a no man's land, or rather an only-man's land, where testosterone-laden bravery, front and backstabbing, realpolitik, and proper networking guaranteed another day to lives. As the ship from the first chapters of *The Violent Land* arrives in Ilheus, its passengers quickly get involved in the main plot of the novel, an all-engrossing land-grabbing conflict: the dispute between the most powerful cacao plantation farmers in the area, the Badarós and Horácio da Silveira, for Sequeiro Grande, a vast and promising swath of virgin forest. It's a given that they will destroy whatever or whoever stands in their way, including themselves.

There is much to destroy here: Horácio's wife, Ester, a transplant from the city who falls in love with his lawyer, Virgilio; Damiao, the illiterate gunman who faces a sudden burst of conscientiousness; Antonio, the migrant worker who realizes he will never return to his homeland; Don'Ana Badaró, who wants to prove herself to her father and uncle; the local prostitutes and everyone else between Tabocas, a frontier town, and Ilheus.

Even though the novel presents a cast of dozens, with their own individual stories and backstories, they coalesce into a mosaic that eventually forms the history of this place and time. One of its sections, "The Forest," starts with a rapturous description of the Bahian Atlantic Forest, its centuries-old ecosystem and the myths that men attached to it. Then, Amado

A cacao plantation in Bahia, Brazil, 1933. In the 1990s an invasive fungus epidemic decimated most of the Bahian cacao trees. Today, all that is left in Ilheus are touristic cacao farms that double as chocolate boutiques.

introduces Man, one of the Badaró brothers who forces his men to venture into the jungle and chop it down to give way to his seedlings. This event sends ripples across the entire area. The whole section charts its consequences from the perspective of major and minor characters revealing a human ecosystem set against a natural one. The section ends with a hermit witch-doctor cursing all those who are invading this sacred green ground with his final words: may they harvest their cacao on blood-soaked land. In *The Violent Land*, Man is himself the Miltonian fallen angel with Paradise Lost reconfigured as Paradise Crushed.

Amado's writing mimics the luscious Bahian settings with operatic aplomb. He stretches time by way of interior monologues and alternating scenes to create a suspenseful crescendo. If the sounds of the forest carry their own drama, sentence repetition recaps key plot points, but it also functions as a chorus to an aria that marches breathlessly to its apocalyptic ending. It is typical of Amado's social realist style at the time. Being a member of the Communist Party in the 1940s, he used literature to raise social awareness. Thus, *The Violent Land* ("Endless Land" in the more poetic original) aims at denouncing a savage capitalist system that is a redressing of an old exploitative colonial one with warts, castes, and all: cacao, indentured servitude, and forests replace sugar, slavery, and forests. The author's ability to juggle crowds and landscapes in an adventurous rhythm overcomes the hints of condescension

MONTEREY, CALIFORNIA, USA

JOHN STEINBECK
CANNERY ROW (1945)

Set on Monterey's Cannery Row, where sardines were canned from the early twentieth century until 1973, when Hovden Cannery closed, Steinbeck's novella is about an interconnected community of bums, prostitutes, a marine biologist, and a Chinese grocer.

John Steinbeck (1902–68) published over twenty books during his lifetime and set the majority of his fiction in his home state, California.

Published in January 1945 by Viking Press, *Cannery Row* sold for $2.00 in hardcover; a pocket-sized Armed Service edition, T-5, was issued the same year to be read by soldiers in the Second World War, one of several such pocket editions; the novel has been translated into over thirty languages.

A sequel to *Cannery Row* called *Sweet Thursday* was published in 1954.

Immediately after completing *The Grapes of Wrath* in 1938, John Steinbeck started writing a little novel about Cannery Row on the Monterey Peninsula, 118 miles south of San Francisco, a place he had known and loved since he was a boy. Although born in 1902 in the agricultural town of Salinas, 17 miles inland, he went often to the peninsula, where his family had a summer cottage in the sleepy town of Pacific Grove, two blocks from Monterey Bay and a mile from Cannery Row, which stretched along the bay in Monterey. Steinbeck loved the ocean, admitting he was a "water fiend", and he lived much of his life near water. In the 1930s, when he and his wife Carol moved into the Steinbeck family cottage to write and work, another important bond to Cannery Row was his closest friend, marine biologist Edward F. Ricketts. During the 1930s, Steinbeck would compose stories during the day and often visit Ricketts in late afternoons to talk about ecology, religion, music, and philosophy. In many ways, the novel *Cannery Row* is dedicated to Ed Ricketts and captures the complexity of Ricketts's kaleidoscopic vision of the world and of place. The dominant metaphor of the book is the intertidal, noted at the end of the opening chapter, and Steinbeck's *Cannery Row* describes a human intertidal zone, with each specimen/character interconnected.

The opening sentence of the novel maps the geographical location—"Cannery Row in Monterey in California…"—and then captures the street's physical vitality:

> [Cannery Row] is a poem, a stink, a grating noise, a quality of light, a tone, a habit, a nostalgia, a dream. Cannery Row is the gathered and scattered, tin and iron and rush and splintered wood, chipped pavement and weedy lots and junk heaps, sardine canneries of corrugated iron, honky tonks, restaurants and whore houses, and little crowded groceries, and laboratories and flophouses. Its inhabitants are, as the man once said, "whores, pimps, gamblers, and sons of bitches," by which he meant Everybody. Had the man looked through another peephole he might have said, "Saints and angels and martyrs and holy men," and he would have meant the same thing.

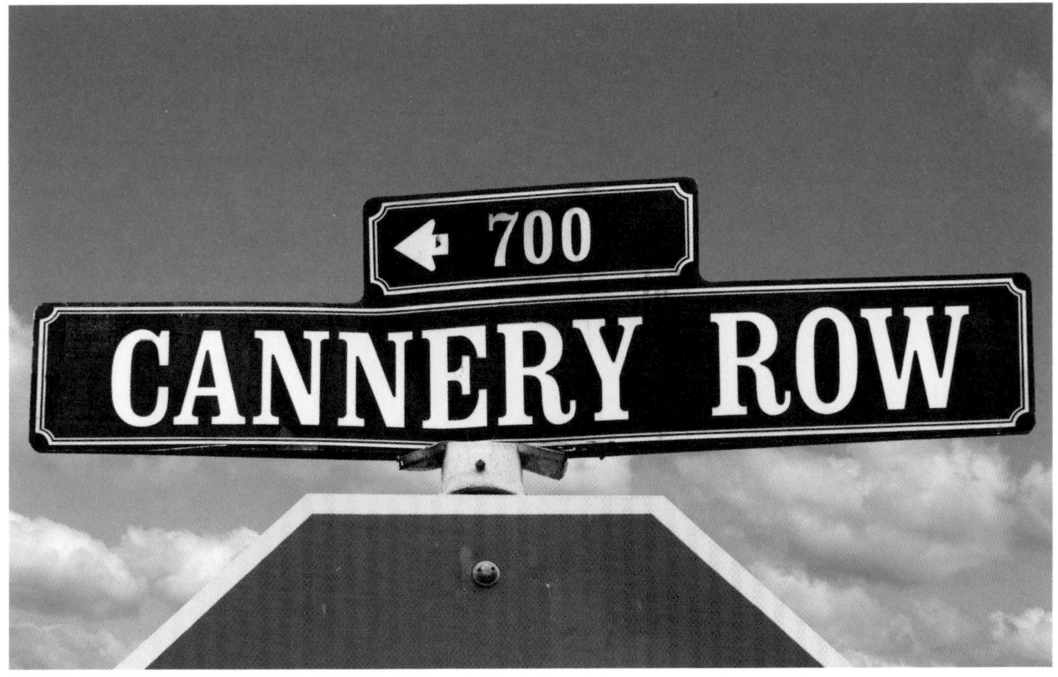

Formerly called Ocean View Avenue, this half-a-mile stretch along the Monterey seafront was officially renamed Cannery Row in 1958 in honor of Steinbeck's novel.

The sentence moves from the particular to the general, from factual to abstract, as does the book itself. In the 1930s, Cannery Row was an industrial enclave of some 20 sardine canneries lined up along Monterey Bay, a place characterized by smell and noise. When the sardine canneries were in operation, from August through February, the lucrative reduction process created a "stink"—two-thirds of the sardine catch was reduced to fish oil and fish meal used for fertilizers and chicken feed.

Steinbeck's Cannery Row, however, was not the busy industrial zone of the 1930s and '40s—he dispenses with that history in a paragraph. His Cannery Row is an enclave where the marginalized live; a place envisioned in half light, a "time of magic", the "hour of pearl—the interval between day and night when time stops and examines itself."

Steinbeck noted the book's complexity when he declared that *Cannery Row* was written on four levels. That statement is a reminder that this novel is about real people and places; that it is about ecological connections among people and their environment; that it's about loneliness and laughter, maybe peace and war (Steinbeck was overseas as a war journalist in 1943, immediately before writing this novel), individuals and communities; and that it suggests a dreamlike reality that was, for scientist/philosopher Ed Ricketts (Doc in the novel), a vital quality of the human mind—"breaking through" to spiritual, holistic understanding, Ricketts called it (the puzzling interludes in the novel about a Chinaman's eyes, an artist's dream, a woman in the intertidal).

The fictional occupants of Steinbeck's Cannery Row were, in fact, real-life denizens, and Steinbeck describes each *in situ*: the grocer Lee Chong; the bums, Mack and the boys; the madam who operates a Cannery Row brothel, Dora Flood; and the marine biologist "Doc." Steinbeck maps the location where each of these characters lives: "To the right of the vacant lot" is Lee Chong's grocery, "a miracle of supply," which was, in fact, a store opened in 1918 by Won Yee, a Chinese grocer whose establishment included a gambling room at the back. The Wing Chong building—still standing—was one of several Chinese establishments in the area. Beginning in the 1850s, Chinese came to the Monterey Peninsula to fish—largely squid—and to dry squid to send back to China. Won Yee was involved in this business as well. The old Chinaman who "flap flaps across the street" was probably a familiar figure collecting sea urchins, abalones, or snails at low tide.

Early morning is a kind of magic in Cannery Row. In the gray time after the light has come and before the sun has risen, the Row seems to hang suspended out of time in a silvery light.

Steinbeck's Mack and the boys were, in real life, bums who often slept in abandoned boilers from the canneries—boilers used to steam the sardines after the fish were packed in cans. The "Chicken Walk" leading to the Palace Flop House, where Mack and the boys live, wound through a vacant lot (now a park) between the grocery and the fictional Bear Flag Restaurant, site of a real brothel owned by Flora Wood (the site now occupied by a concrete block building that hawks souvenirs). Steinbeck's fictional madam, Dora Flood, is every bit as salty and good-hearted as the real Flora, a well-known figure in the community in the 1930s who also, like Steinbeck's Dora, had "trouble with her income tax." When a fire burned the Row in 1936, a front-page story in the *Monterey Herald* announced that firemen managed to save Flora Wood's establishment.

"Western Biological," where Doc lives, is "across the street and facing the vacant lot." In life it was Ed Ricketts's Pacific Biological Laboratories, his workplace and, from the mid-1930s on, his residence as well. Steinbeck describes the lab's interior in exact detail, as it was when Ed lived there.

In short, art is a "fantastic pattern" woven from life itself. "The Word is a symbol and a delight," Steinbeck writes in chapter 2, "which sucks up men and scenes ... Then the Thing becomes the Word and back to the Thing again, but warped and woven into a fantastic pattern."

The novella's form is open and meandering, like life itself. Traced in alternating chapters, the plot, as it is, tells of Mack and the boys' efforts to throw a party for Doc. Other chapters, all thematically linked, describe Monterey denizens who are lonely, isolated, yearning for beauty and meaning. The book's form traces the delicate bonds that unify all life.

Today's tourists are drawn to Cannery Row to retrace Steinbeck's map of the street. They yearn to find Steinbeck's Cannery Row intact, decades later. They want to meld fiction and fact, past and present, dream and reality. And

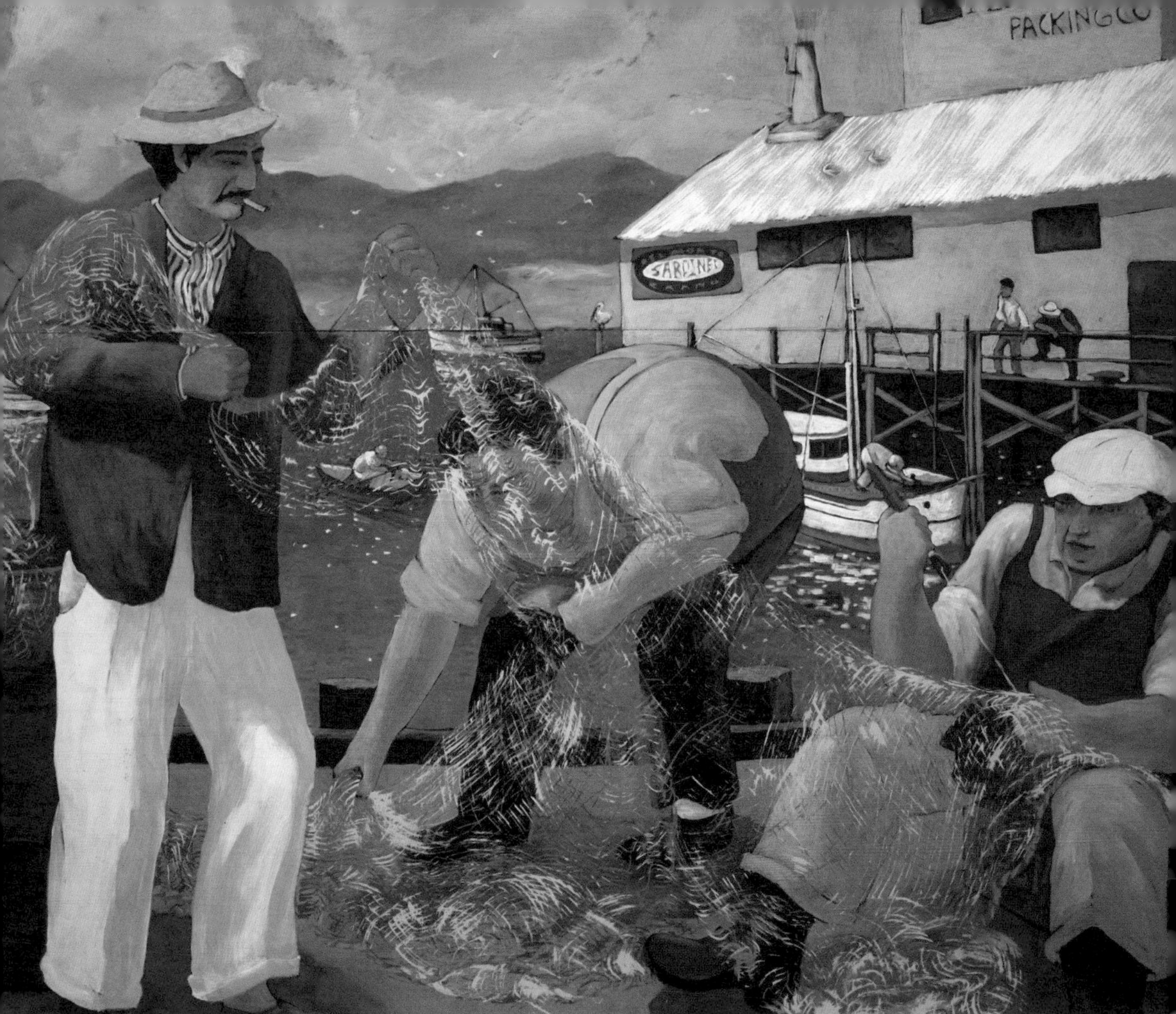

this may, in fact, be close to what Steinbeck intended—immersion in reality as a first principle. *Cannery Row* is a novel about seeing, a novel full of eyes. It moves from concrete and delightful reality to abstract and sometimes puzzling reflection. Fact and fiction blend seamlessly in Steinbeck's novel as well as in the place that is today's Cannery Row, Steinbeck's imprint intact.

Mural of sardine fishermen repairing their nets along Cannery Row, California. Photograph by Carol Highsmith, 2011.

1946–1974

3 Postwar Panoramas

As the world was rebuilt after the Second World War violently redrew the contours of the map, hopeful new horizons were reflected in narratives that tracked the increasing popularity of the holiday, the spread of suburbia, and the politics of postcolonial space.

AMSTERDAM, NETHERLANDS

GERARD REVE

THE EVENINGS: A WINTER'S TALE (DE AVONDEN: EEN WINTERVERHAAL) (1947)

In the gloomy fogs and frosts of post-war Amsterdam a disaffected young man struggles to get through the last ten days of 1946.

Gerard Kornelis van het Reve was twenty-three when he wrote this masterpiece, his first novel, which was to become a classic of modern Dutch literature.

The Evenings has never been out of print since its first publication in 1947.

It was first translated from Dutch to German in 1987 and has since been translated into French (1989), Hungarian (1999), Slovak (2008), Swedish (2008), Spanish (2011), and English (2016).

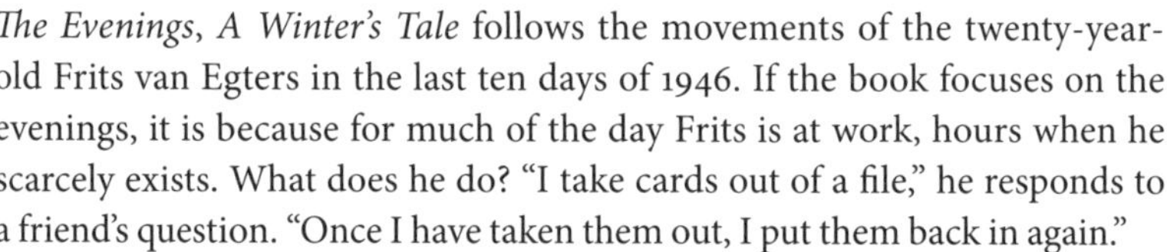

The Evenings, A Winter's Tale follows the movements of the twenty-year-old Frits van Egters in the last ten days of 1946. If the book focuses on the evenings, it is because for much of the day Frits is at work, hours when he scarcely exists. What does he do? "I take cards out of a file," he responds to a friend's question. "Once I have taken them out, I put them back in again."

But Frits never complains about his job, nor expresses any desire to change it. Those hours are at least taken care of. His problem is his evenings and his days off—Christmas in particular—and his one ambition is to get through them without losing his mind. For both hero and author, this novel is a tour de force of filling space. Never has the business of arriving at bedtime been more urgently and richly dramatized.

Everything takes place in a few suburban streets in Amsterdam, which in their icy winter gloom and post-war seediness rapidly present themselves as an extension of Frits's unhappy, obsessive mind and invariably threatening dreams. Condemned to sharing a small apartment with a half-deaf father and well-meaning but clumsy mother, he describes the couple's eating and grooming habits with a mixture of savage fury and grudging affection. They argue endlessly and repetitively to the point that Frits can predict exactly what platitude is coming next, often taking masochistic pleasure in prompting what he doesn't want to hear. Meantime, his only ally, between stoking the stove, feeding guilders into the electricity meter, and criticizing Mother's cooking or Father's table manners, is the radio, whose scattered fragments of news and music offer themselves to the shipwrecked Frits as life-saving flotsam in an ocean of wasted time. "All is lost," he thought, "everything is ruined. It's ten past three."

One thing that astonished and infuriated first critics of this precocious debut was that amid so much despairing realism nothing was said about the war. It had been barely two years since the Nazi occupation of the Netherlands, only three since the "Hunger Winter" of 1944 when 18,000 people died of starvation. The extent of Dutch collaborationism was at the center of heated debate. But Frits simply isn't interested, recalling the conflict in passing merely as an inconvenience that prevented him from retaking failed school exams.

All the same Reve's novel is drenched in an intensely phobic atmosphere that must surely be the legacy of war. Again the urban setting, the wintry streets, frozen canals, dark stairways of decaying tenements, and cold rooms where friends warm themselves around dying fires, all reinforce a profound sense of fragility. You feel the story simply had to happen here, would be unthinkable anywhere else. "The frozen street glittered. 'It's as though the paving stones are filled with tiny pieces of glass,' he thought."

Utterly frustrated, having no girlfriend, nor making any attempt to find one, Frits moves like a ball in a bagatelle between his lonely bedroom, where he is terrified by the materiality of his body, the sitting room where he confronts the horror of his parents' aimlessly hostile lives, and fitful forays to the houses of friends and relatives where he allays his own fears by playing on everyone else's. At this he is a past master. Barely has he greeted someone before he is wryly commenting on their sickly complexions, imminent baldness, early ageing and likely demise, always with a frightening wealth of detail and an imagination as reckless as it is jaundiced. Other characters differentiate themselves by their reaction, humoring him, growing anxious, assuming he's joking, or even joining in, often trading truly gruesome anecdotes of accident, illness, and violence in a mood that fuses hilarity and horror.

Frits picked his way down the front steps. The street lights were mirrored in the icy canal. He stamped his feet, closed his collar tightly and walked on with his head bowed. The hands of the clock on the front of a bank read eighteen minutes past nine.

If this seems dire, Reve's sparkling collage of acute observation, droll internal monologue, and pitch-perfect dialogue keep the reader breathless right through to the grand finale, which sees Fritz tying himself in knots to survive an interminable New Year's Eve with his all-too-human but actually rather wonderful parents and a bottle his mother is convinced is wine and Frits knows, alas, is berry-apple cordial. "Eternal, only, almighty, our God," he begs in one of many appeals for divine mercy, "fix Your gaze upon my parents. See them in their need. Do not turn Your eyes from them."

The achievement of this book is to establish an entirely convincing fusion between realism and existential comedy, and again between a place and psychology, individual and collective. You feel that to rediscover these icy canals in a threatening winter gloom would be inevitably to move into this dangerous state of mind.

Overleaf: Artwork by Bill Bragg from the cover of the first English-language edition of the book, published in 2016.

CAIRO, EGYPT

NAGUIB MAHFOUZ

MIDAQ ALLEY

(ZUQĀQ AL-MIDAQ) (1947)

Capturing the various stories of the inhabitants of a small but lively secluded alleyway in 1940s Cairo, Mahfouz's novel brings vividly to life a portrait of Egypt confronting the changes of modernity.

Naguib Mahfouz (1911–2006) wrote a total of 33 novels, 13 collections of short stories, numerous film scripts, and five plays in a career that lasted over five decades. He became the first Arab writer to win the Nobel Prize for Literature in 1988.

Considered his best novel, *Midaq Alley* made little impression when it was first published in Egypt in 1947. On republication in 1970, however, translations into French and fourteen other languages followed, and now it is recognized as one of the twentieth century's leading depictions of life in the Middle East.

In a small, faintly sleazy backstreet in Cairo's teeming Gamaliya district, where he was brought up, Naguib Mahfouz finds a microcosm of the whole of Egypt. Midaq Alley, the setting for Mahfouz's novel of the same name, is a tiny backwater. It is largely isolated from the rest of the city, with no more than a couple of shops, a bakery, an office, and two three-storey houses, but it is inseparably connected with Egypt's ancient civilizations—the worlds of the Fatamids, the Mamelukes, and the Sultans.

Ancient stone paving joins it to the historic Sanadiqiya Street, and Mahfouz refers to its own vanished and unspecified "ancient glory" in Cairo. Now, it is home for a disparate cast of characters, all of whom are trying in their various ways to deal with the conflicting pressures of poverty, wartime, British rule, and personal ambition. When first described by Mahfouz, the street is associated with a gloomy sense of entrapment:

> The sun began to set and Midaq Alley was veiled in the brown hues of the glow. The darkness was all the greater because it was enclosed like a trap between three walls. It rose unevenly from Sanadiqiya Street. One of its sides consisted of a shop, a café and a bakery, the other of another shop and an office. It ends abruptly, just as its ancient glory did, with two adjoining houses, each of three storeys.

Yet Mahfouz makes the alley much more than a setting for his characters. From the first page of the book it is presented as a character in its own right, depicted through not just its physical appearance but the textures of its crumbling walls, the smells of spices and folk cures, the deep colors of a city sunset, and the intimate evening whispers as the daytime noises die down.

It has the reassurance of home for those who live there and frequent Kirsha's café, but it has a dark and sinister underside. The three walls that enclose it mean that the sun appears only late in the day, and night comes early; poverty and destitution are only a step away for most of its inhabitants. The sinister Zaita cripples beggars so they can beg more successfully; it

Many things combine to show that Midaq Alley is one of the gems of times gone by and that it once shone forth like a flashing star in the history of Cairo. Which Cairo do I mean? That of the Fatimads, the Mamlukes, or the Sultans? Only God and the archaeologists know the answer to that, but in any case, the alley is certainly an ancient relic and a precious one.

is revealed that Dr. Booshy, the popular but unqualified dentist, manages to supply cheap false teeth only by stealing them from freshly buried corpses.

The Second World War and the British military presence hang over the landscape of the novel like a dark cloud. The British Army provides a relatively quick and easy route to prosperity for several of the inhabitants of the alley, and the young Hussein Kirsha and Abbas, the young barber, both find well-paid work at the Army base. Hamida—who Mahfouz later accepted had been subconsciously presented, like Midaq Alley itself, as a symbol of Egypt under occupation—eventually works as a prostitute for British soldiers. But the prosperity is illusory: Kirsha ends up back in Midaq Alley when the Army lays off local labor at the end of the war.

When Abbas finds Hamida, his former fiancée, flirting with British soldiers in a bar, he attacks them and they beat him to death. This is the climax of the novel, but although people in the alley are initially shocked, indifference quickly returns. The alley is ageless, and the characters in the book are only a very few of those who will pass through its long history and be forgotten.

Previous page: This vintage 1920s print by Mortimer Menpes depicts an archetypal "Cairo Street," as immortalized by Mahfouz's novel.

MADRID, SPAIN

CAMILO JOSÉ CELA

THE HIVE (LA COLMENA) (1951)

The canonical novel of the Spanish postwar era, this sophisticated "colony" of interlocking vignettes follows in the path of those modernist "choral" city novels, chronicling the myriad lives of citizens under Franco's regime.

The protagonists of *The Hive* are the inhabitants of Madrid, whose lives are fully invested in attending to their most basic needs: food, work, sex. The one character who appears in all chapters is Martín Marco, a homeless writer who travels through the city and acts as connection and partial representation of the author. It is narrated in the third person by a sarcastic and patronizing narrator, who embodies another side of Cela. This narrator shows Cela's profound knowledge of Madrid. He lived there during his formative years.

The Hive (New York, 1953), narrates three days in Madrid in 1943, a mere four years after the Spanish Civil War (1936–39). The 1940s are known in Spanish history as the "years of hunger," and as a period of brutal reprisals. This demoralized Madrid stands in radical contrast to the heroic city portrayed in pro-Spanish Republic documentaries, films, plays, novels, and poems of the 1930s, such as Langston Hughes's and Pablo Neruda's, and to the jazzy Madrid of Almodovar's *Movida* in the 1980s.

The geography of Madrid in *The Hive* is classified here in five groups: accurate, cognitive-emotional, aesthetic, phantasmagoric, and ideological. First, the novel is highly "mappable." The routes followed by Martín Marco closely correspond with the map of the city in 1945 (Carbajo Lago). He travels by foot and metro, from the old center of the city, through the more modern and expensive areas to the east, to the outskirts where shantytowns and the cemetery are located. Marco almost closes a circle back to the old town; we do not know if he will be allowed to do it.

Madrid's urban geography (streets, monuments, districts, gathering places, subway stops) is also Marco's emotional and cognitive one. To use the terms of urban studies scholar Kevin Lynch, it is full of "paths," "edges," "districts," "nodes" and "landmarks" of deep significance to him. Imaginary cafes are gathering or unwelcoming places; homes of family and friends and brothels are shelters; the outskirts are liminal areas that announce transformations.

Madrid has aesthetic relevance in this novel, which Cela describes as "a bunch of pages through which flows with disorder the life of a disorderly city."

Camilo José Cela Trulock (1916–2002) was the first Spanish novelist to be awarded the Nobel Prize for Literature in 1989. During his lifetime, he was a complex and conflicted writer: a "provocateur" of Francoism who was made canonical by it. He was ideologically rejected by the left and mistrusted by the most conservative right.

Cela was a soldier in Franco's army and worked as a censor during the dictatorship. *The Hive* (*La colmena*) was itself censored and had to be published in Argentina in 1951.

CÍRCULO DE LECTORES

CAMILO JOSÉ CELA

LA COLMENA

Con ilustraciones de Lorenzo Goñi

In order to depict Madrid as a suffocating space of isolation, lack of solidarity, randomness, and lack of values, this novel breaks traditional linear narrative and chronology. It narrates simultaneous events and utilizes montage, collage, and fragmentation into more than 217 vignettes or "cells," which at least as many characters randomly enter and exit like bees.

Cell-like fragmentation is not the only explanation for the title. Spanish anarchists, inspired by Belgian writer Maurice Maeterlink (*The Life of the Bee*), equated beehives with perfect cities. Cela's Madrid is as far from being an egalitarian anarchist city as its inhabitants are from being able to imagine it. Death is a central theme in *The Hive*—one of the last scenes occurs in a cemetery, the marble tables of the Café La Delicias are recycled gravestones, and Madrid is called "sepulcher, greasy pole and beehive." Death in *The Hive* not only represents the more than one million killed in the war and the postwar, but also the annihilation of the ebullient egalitarian ideals of the Spanish Republic.

A phantom geography is superimposed on to the material, cognitive-emotional and aesthetic ones. Everywhere, the city evokes what is not present. New street names created by Franco to commemorate Fascist heroes (the avenues "de Jose Antonio," "del Generalisimo," "de Calvo Sotelo") remind "Madrileños" of the traditional names ("Paseo de la Castellana," "Gran Via" or "Paseo de Recoletos"—incidentally and happily, the same names they now have). The dreary Cafe Delicias recalls prewar ebullient intellectual, artistic, and political *tertulias* (artistic gatherings) in iconic cafes like Pombo, Universal, Gijón, significantly not mentioned in the novel. Stylistically, Cela alludes to and pays homage to earlier Spanish writers closely connected to Madrid who were active members of prewar *tertulias*: Gómez de la Serna, Baroja, Valle-Inclán.

A final type of geography is ideological. The novel is frequently criticized for its conservatism in that it does not openly criticize the dictatorship. In the 1940s, Cela was involved in writing *The Hive* and had already been broadly recognized for an earlier novel. Regardless, *The Hive*, was to be censored due to sexual scenes and lack of patriotic ardor. Martín Marco and the narrator of *The Hive* help us chart the fears, concerns, and characteristics of the young Cela that help explain his ambiguous political attitude. He stands at a crossroads of vulnerability and arrogance, of involvement and distance. A moment of tenuous hope described at the end of the novel provides a third relevant pinpoint. As characters unite under the common goal to save Martín Marco from an unspecified ominous fate at the hands of the Fascist state, a precarious sense of community, even hope, begins to emerge. Cela in *The Hive* stands at a confluence of emotional and vocational streets that will mark his work in general: paternalistic sarcasm and tenderness, fear for his own vulnerability; ideological ambiguity; wish for recognition; a tremendous sense of loss; and a vague, wishful-yet-skeptical belief (or disbelief) in his fellow citizens. In this sense, Madrid, geographic center and capital of Spain, represents the whole country.

Opposite: 1989 anniversary edition cover illustrated by Lorenzo Goñi, showing Café La Delicia, a local haunt for the main characters in the novel.

LOS ANGELES, USA

RAYMOND CHANDLER

The Long Goodbye (1953)

In postwar Los Angeles, private detective Phillip Marlowe's search for justice sets him against crooked cops, brutal racketeers, and the entire might of a corrupt city government.

Raymond Chandler (1888–1959) did not take up writing professionally until his mid-forties, after losing his job as an oil executive in the Great Depression. He reportedly never intended to be a genre writer, bur rather wished to be a poet.

Chandler lived most of his adult life in Los Angeles, moving frequently with an estimated twenty-four different residences.

The Long Goodbye is the sixth novel featuring Phillip Marlowe, adapted by Robert Altman into a 1973 film of the same name.

Like the city in which it takes place, *The Long Goodbye* is a peculiar, rambling novel, filled with unexpected digressions and strange interludes. It is the story of Phillip Marlowe, a two-bit private detective with a dingy office in downtown Los Angeles, a few hundred in the bank, and an unbreakable code of ethics, one which stands in unforgiving contrast to the loose morals of post-war America. Incorruptible, antisocial, caring nothing for money and little more for sex, Marlowe's sole vice—albeit one which proves as ruinous as liquor or dope—is for lost causes, the weak and the foolish and the misbegotten. His quest to clear the name of a dead friend sees him exploring a Los Angeles reflecting the dark side of the American dream, in which love is a commodity like any other, and money can buy everything but happiness.

As Los Angeles is the anti-city, a hundred diverse communities stuck against one another into a sprawling metropolis, so is *The Long Goodbye* the anti-crime novel. Peculiarly for an author who all but defined the genre, Chandler had few of the skills generally associated with writers of pulp fiction, and readers used to the cheap, violent thrills of Chandler's imitators will likely come away bored. For that matter, the through-line at the heart of the classic mystery—a stolen necklace, a butler murdered in the study—is nowhere to be found. In its place is a work full of odd asides, of side plots that go nowhere, of characters that appear and then disappear, of loose ends that a competent editor would almost certainly have strangled. While the final sting remains as sharp as anything in fiction, it is precluded by 50 pages that could be cut without affecting the work in any significant way.

And yet, in the half-century since it was written, *The Long Goodbye* has become widely recognized as the defining example of what is the only truly American literary form. Chandler's great and abiding genius resides in two areas; first, a talent for language that is shared by few twentieth-century writers, irrespective of genre; and second, a profound sense of place, a vision of Los Angeles that has defined the city in the minds of millions of readers. It is, on the surface at least, an unkindly depiction. Chandler's Los Angeles is a city of gamblers and dope addicts, of decent men rendered amoral by time and misfortune, of woman lost to drink and lust and sadness, of unjust police officers and titans of industry unconcerned with the brutal effects of their wealth. Its great natural beauty is ever at contrast with the sins and vices of its inhabitants, and the sunny optimism that was the hallmark of the 1950s America seems a sick joke.

Visitors to Los Angeles often find themselves agreeing with Chandler's estimation. For those used to the uniform charms of cities to the east, where the only direction one needs to know is uptown or down, it can come across as confusing, too vast, and tacky. It lacks any of the consistency of architecture by which cities are generally judged beautiful, with Spanish haciendas sharing space with Art Deco skyscrapers, as if each structure had been designed and built without any reference to those beside it. The city's development boom came during what was surely the least attractive architectural epoch in recent history, and one can, quite literally, drive 100 miles in LA and never lose sight of some or other concrete monstrosity.

And yet, beneath the scuzz and commercial squalor is a place of unique and magnificent charm. Los Angeles is, in some sense, the least believable city on the planet, a maddening hodgepodge, impossible to neatly categorize.

Much of the Los Angeles that Chandler describes has long since disappeared. His largely monochromatic metropolis has been replaced by a city, in practice, more diverse than almost anywhere else on the planet, 1,000 ethnic enclaves merging together, where you can drive from Yerevan to Bangkok in less time than it takes to change the radio station. The unincorporated cities of Santa Monica and Malibu, in Chandler's time distinct entities, have amalgamated to the general Los Angles sprawl, and the Southern California scenery, some of which, in his day, remained relatively pristine, has long since been plowed over. But scratch the surface and you can still see the city he all but created, its sun-baked grandeur, its endless corruption, the occasional occluded decency of its citizens. The riddle hidden in *The Long Goodbye* is that Marlowe, whose patter is so hard-boiled you might roll it across the White House lawn, who portrays himself as a man so jaded by life as to be immune to its charms, is in fact every bit as much the knight-errant as Don Quixote, willing to sacrifice everything and anything for a moral principle. Likewise, scattered amid the author's seeming contempt for his home is an abiding affection for a dreamlike city nestled between the desert and the sea, in which the full range of human behavior is on exhibit, and, for better or worse, anything is possible.

A city no worse than others, a city rich and vigorous and full of pride, a city lost and beaten and full of emptiness. It all depends on where you sit and what your own private score is.

Overleaf: 1932 map of LA drawn by Karl Moritz Leuschner and edited by Loren Latker in 2014 to highlight key locations in *The Long Goodbye* (see key).

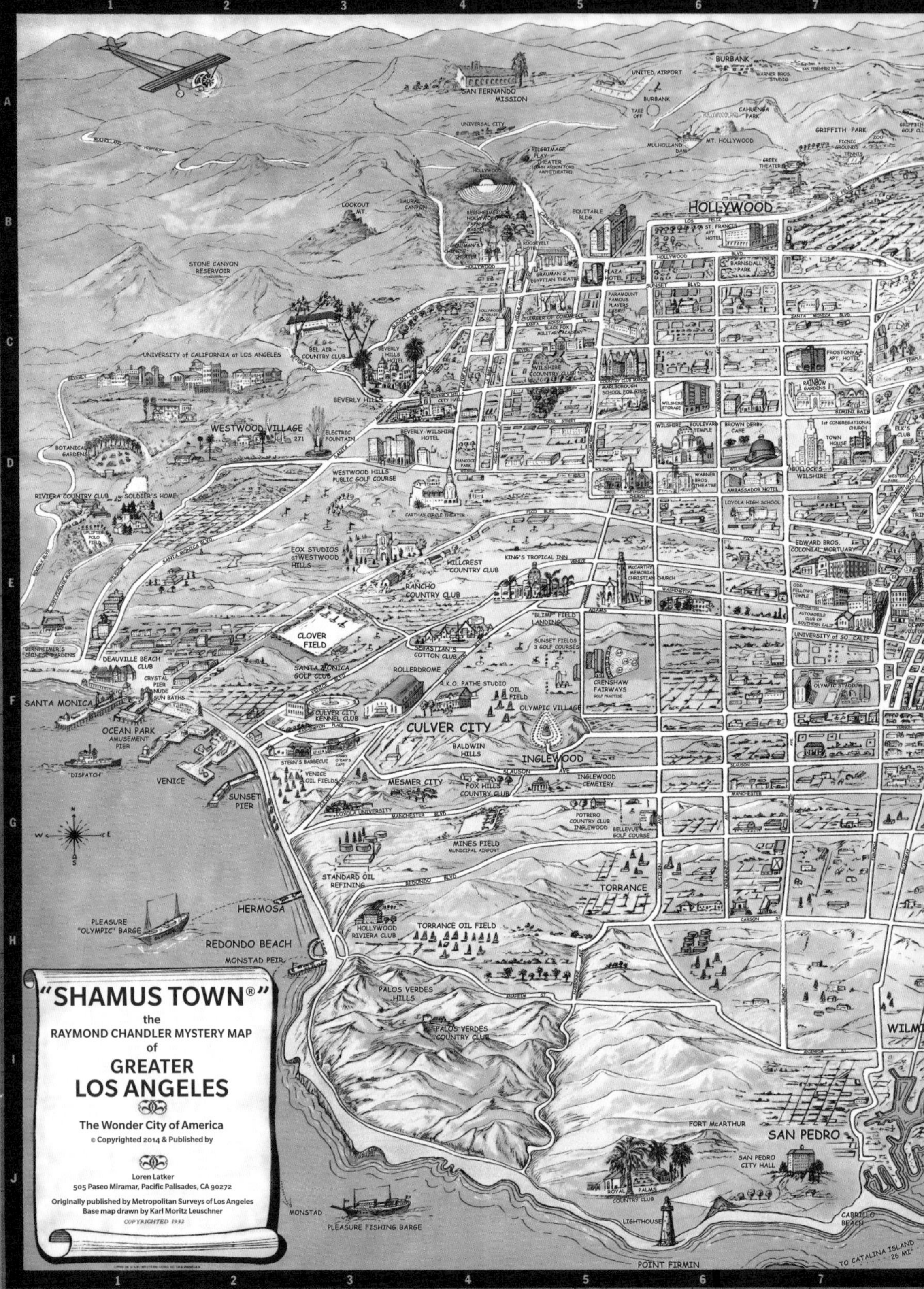

"SHAMUS TOWN®"
the
RAYMOND CHANDLER MYSTERY MAP
of
GREATER
LOS ANGELES
The Wonder City of America
© Copyrighted 2014 & Published by
Loren Latker
505 Paseo Miramar, Pacific Palisades, CA 90272
Originally published by Metropolitan Surveys of Los Angeles
Base map drawn by Karl Moritz Leuschner
COPYRIGHTED 1932
SAN FERNANDO MISSION
UNITED AIRPORT
BURBANK
WARNER BROS. STUDIO
TAKE OFF
CAHUENGA PARK
UNIVERSAL CITY
GRIFFITH PARK
MULHOLLAND DAM
MT. HOLLYWOOD
PILGRIMAGE PLAY THEATER
GREEK THEATER
LOOKOUT MT.
LAUREL CANYON
EQUITABLE BLDG.
HOLLYWOOD
ST. FRANCIS APT. HOTEL
ROOSEVELT HOTEL
STONE CANYON RESERVOIR
PLAZA HOTEL
BARNSDALL PARK
GRAUMAN'S EGYPTIAN THEATRE
PARAMOUNT FAMOUS PLAYERS LASKY
BEL AIR COUNTRY CLUB
BEVERLY HILLS HOTEL
UNIVERSITY of CALIFORNIA at LOS ANGELES
BEVERLY HILLS
WILSHIRE COUNTRY CLUB
FROSTONYA APT. HOTEL
RAINBOW GARDENS
MARLBOROUGH SCHOOL FOR GIRLS
WESTWOOD VILLAGE
ELECTRIC FOUNTAIN
BEVERLY-WILSHIRE HOTEL
BOULEVARD TEMPLE
BROWN DERBY CAFE
1st CONGREGATIONAL CHURCH
TOWN HOUSE
BOTANICAL GARDENS
WESTWOOD HILLS PUBLIC GOLF COURSE
WARNER BROS THEATRE
AMBASSADOR HOTEL
BULLOCK'S WILSHIRE
RIVIERA COUNTRY CLUB
SOLDIER'S HOME
CARTHAY CIRCLE THEATER
LOYOLA HIGH SCHOOL
SANTA MONICA BLVD
FOX STUDIOS at WESTWOOD HILLS
KING'S TROPICAL INN
EDWARD BROS. COLONIAL MORTUARY
HILLCREST COUNTRY CLUB
McCARTHY MEMORIAL CHRISTIAN CHURCH
RANCHO COUNTRY CLUB
ODD FELLOWS TEMPLE
"BLIMP" FIELD LANDING
AUTOMOBILE CLUB OF SOUTHERN CALIF
CLOVER FIELD
SUNSET FIELDS 3 GOLF COURSES
UNIVERSITY of SO. CALIF
BERNHEIMER'S CHINESE GARDENS
DEAUVILLE BEACH CLUB
SEBASTIAN'S COTTON CLUB
SANTA MONICA GOLF CLUB
ROLLERDROME
CRYSTAL PIER
NUDE SUN BATHS
R.K.O. PATHE STUDIO
OIL FIELD
CRENSHAW FAIRWAYS
SANTA MONICA
OLYMPIC VILLAGE
OLYMPIC STADIUM
CULVER CITY KENNEL CLUB
OCEAN PARK AMUSEMENT PIER
CULVER CITY
BALDWIN HILLS
INGLEWOOD
STERN'S BARBECUE
"DISPATCH"
VENICE OIL FIELDS
MESMER CITY
INGLEWOOD CEMETERY
VENICE
FOX HILLS COUNTRY CLUB
SUNSET PIER
LOYOLA UNIVERSITY
POTHERO COUNTRY CLUB INGLEWOOD
BELLEVUE GOLF COURSE
MINES FIELD MUNICIPAL AIRPORT
STANDARD OIL REFINING
TORRANCE
PLEASURE "OLYMPIC" BARGE
HERMOSA
HOLLYWOOD RIVIERA CLUB
TORRANCE OIL FIELD
REDONDO BEACH
MONSTAD PEIR
PALOS VERDES HILLS
PALOS VERDES COUNTRY CLUB
WILMI
FORT McARTHUR
SAN PEDRO
SAN PEDRO CITY HALL
ROYAL PALMS COUNTRY CLUB
MONSTAD
PLEASURE FISHING BARGE
LIGHTHOUSE
CABRILLO BEACH
POINT FIRMIN
TO CATALINA ISLAND 26 MI.

MT. LOWE
JOHN BROWN PARK
ECHO MT
MT. WILSON OBSERVATORY
FOREST LAWN
EAGLE ROCK
ROSE BOWL
ANNANDALE GOLF CLUB
OCCIDENTAL COLLEGE
BROOKSIDE PARK
A MILE OF CHRISTMAS TREES
ALTADENA
SIERRA MADRE
HOTEL VISTA DEL ARROYO
SILVER LAKE
EDENDALE
ELYSIAN PARK
TUNNEL THROUGH PARK
YAGODA SATSANGA HINDU-AMERICAN TEMPLE
SOUTHWEST MUSEUM
COLORADO ST. BRIDGE
PASADENA CITY HALL
HOTEL RAYMOND
PASADENA COMMUNITY PLAYHOUSE
HOTEL HUNTINGTON
PASADENA JR. COLLEGE
CAL. TECH. UNIVERSITY
HUNTINGTON LIBRARY
CAWSTON OSTRICH FARM
SYCAMORE PARK
LINCOLN PARK TOURIST CAMP
SAN GABRIEL MISSION
OLD MILL PASADENA
ASCOT SPEEDWAY
LINCOLN PARK
COUNTY HOSPITAL
CHINA TOWN
TO COUNTY FAIR GROUNDS
GAY'S LION FARM
TO KELLOGG FARM
MIDWICK COUNTRY CLUB
SANTA FE DEPOT
WESTERN LITHOGRAPH CO.
REPETTO PARK
MONTEBELLO GOLF CLUB
BELVEDERE GARDENS
MONTEBELLO
OVERLAND TERMINAL WAREHOUSE
PECK-HILLS FURNITURE CO.
SEARS-ROEBUCK & CO.
BALL PARK
GOODYEAR RUBBER CO.
CENTRAL MANUFACTURING DISTRICT
FIRESTONE RUBBER CO
HUNTINGTON PARK
WILLYS-OVERLAND PLANT
GOODRICH RUBBER CO.
U.S. RUBBER CO.
CHRYSLER PLANT
ANGELES ABBEY MAUSOLEUM
SANTA FE SPRINGS OIL FIELD
ATLANTIC BLVD.
DOMINGUEZ OIL FIELD
RICHFIELD OIL FIELDS
GOODYEAR
SIGNAL HILL
LONG BEACH CITY HALL
LONG BEACH
BREAKERS HOTEL
HOTEL VIRGINIA
VILLA RIVIERA
BIXBY PARK
BELMONT SHORES
ALAMITOS BAY
"JOHANNA SMITH" PLEASURE (Gambling) SHIP
9
10
11
12
13
14
15
16
A
B
C
D
E
F
G
H
I
J
KEY
Numbers Correspond to Numbers in Downtown Area
6- BILTMORE HOTEL D-9
17- CALIFORNIA HOSPITAL E-8
3- CALIFORNIA STATE BLDG C-10
16- CHAMBER OF COMMERCE E-9
1- CITY HALL, LOS ANGELES C-11
10- EDISON BUILDING D-9
GOODYEAR BLIMP, INF PHONE LA 2151 ..... H-12
2- HALL OF JUSTICE: 211 W. Temple C-10
13- HOTEL CECIL E-10
12- HUNTINGTON BUILDING E-10
20- JONATHAN CLUB C-9
JOHANNA SMITH PLEASURE SHIP J-10
21- L.A. ATHLETIC CLUB D-9
5- L.A. LIBRARY D-9
15- MAY CO D-9
11- MILLION DOLLAR THEATRE C-9
MT. HOLLYWOOD A-6
MT. LOWE A-14
MT. WILSON OBSERVATORY A-16
MULHOLLAND DAM A-6
24- ORPHEUM BLDG D-9
23- OLYMPIC AUDITORIUM E-8
OLYMPIC FISHING BARGE, CPT ANDERSEN H-2
22- PATRIOTIC HALL E-8
7- PERSHING SQUARE PARK D-9
8- PHILHARMONIC AUDITORIUM D-9
PLAZA SQUARE C-11
4- POST OFFICE C-11
POINT VICENTE LIGHTHOUSE J-6
26- OUEEN OF ANGELS CHURCH C-11
14- RICHFIELD BLDG D-8
ROLLERDROME F-4
SANTA MONICA PIER F-1
SOUTHWEST MUSEUM B-12
SO PACIFIC & UNION PACIFIC DEPOT E-11
STANDARD OIL REFINERY G-3
9- TITLE GUARANTEE BLDG D-9
25- TRINITY BUILDING D-8
VENICE PIER G-2
VENICE OIL FIELD G-3
WESTERN THEATRE D-6
WRIGLEY BALL PARK F-9
RAYMOND CHANDLER MYSTERY MAP KEY
Italics = Fictionalized Locations
SOME COMMON LOCATIONS
HOLLYWD-CAHUENGA: *Marlowe's office* B-5
YUCCA OFF LAUREL: *Marlowe's home* B-4
ON OR NEAR FRANKLIN: *Marlowe's home, i.e., Bristol Apts on "Bristol"* B-5
FRANKLIN-KENMORE: *Marlowe's home (Hobart Arms)* B-7
7000 BLOCK FRANKLIN AVE: *Sternwood Mansion, 3765 Alta Brea Crescent* B-4
THE LONG GOODBYE (1954)
WESTWOOD: *Terry Lennox's Apt* D-2
6409 HOLLYWOOD: American Bus Lines B-5
1735 N. CAHUENGA: Santa Fe Trailways B-5
1625 N. CAHUENGA: Interurban Buse B-5
369 N. BEDFORD, BEVERLY HILLS, VICTOR HUGO'S RESTAURANT: *Victor's* D-4
211 W. TEMPLE: LA County DA's office C-10
401 N. AVE 19: Los Angeles City Jail B-12
9500 WILSHIRE, BEVERLY WILSHIRE HOTEL: *Beverly-Ritz Hotel* D-3
55 LA CIENEGA BLVD: Lawry's D-4
BEVERLY HILLS: *Carne Organization* C-4
SEPULVEDA CANYON: *Verringer's Clinic* ..... QR
STERN'S B-B-Q, 12664 W. WASHINGTON: *Rudy's BBQ on La Cienega Blvd* D-4
8240 SUNSET BLVD, THE MARQUIS: *Mendy Menendez's Club, El Tapato* C-4
6667 HOLLYWOOD BLVD: Musso & Frank B-5
TIJUANA, MEXICO: Tijuana Airport ..... QR
MAZATLAN, MEXICO: Mazatlan ..... QR
TOREON, MEXICO: Toreon ..... QR
NOTES: Chandler put El Pueblo de Nuestra Señora la Reina de los Ángeles de Porciúncula on the literary map by using disguised and actual locales for his canvas. From his first short stories, readers have been trying to figure out what and where the *disguised* places are. Some are obvious. Some have been accepted for years, and many are open to interpretation and debate.
I have checked the short stories and novels to verify, add, delete, or alter the locations on this map. Some are gone. Some existed only in Chandler's imagination. Others have changed, and despite the herculean efforts of fans, the locations of some defy discovery.
For example, this from *Farewell My Lovely*: "The place was one of the many canyons off the foothill boulevard that turns into town from the coast highway north of Bay City. ... It seemed to be at the end of a street called Camino de la Costa."
Bay City was Chandler's name for Santa Monica, taken from the actual 1930s *Bay Cities Directories* that included Santa Monica.
But note the street name: "... at the end of a street called Camino de la Costa."
In 1946 the Chandlers moved to La Jolla on *Camino de la Costa*! Eight years earlier, in *Farewell My Lovely*, Chandler plunked his future La Jolla street down in Pacific Palisades.
He continues: "Those lights off to the right are the Belvedere Beach Club. The next canyon is Las Pulgas and the next after that Purissima..." This puts the action along Sunset. There actually is a Las Pulgas (Flea) Canyon, and today Bienveneda runs North from Sunset through it, but not in the 1930s. The Canyon after Las Pulgas? Temescal Canyon, and it has a road running North from Sunset. So Purissima is Temescal, but where Marlowe gets sapped and his client murdered was probably off of Paseo Miramar.
In the above examples, Chandler plays with both places and names, disguising them and confusing readers.
The end result is that in 2014 readers are still trying to figure out what and where his actual places are, and readers will probably still be trying in 2114.
Maybe this map will help. Enjoy!
Loren Latker, ©November 2014.
Designed by K.M. Leuschner, M.R.A.

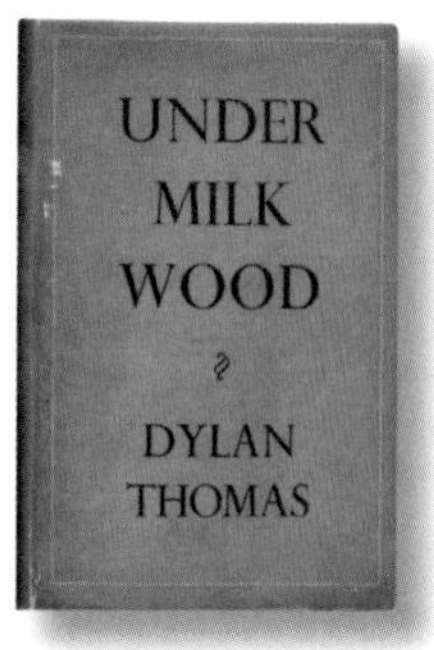

LAUGHARNE, WALES

DYLAN THOMAS

UNDER MILK WOOD, A PLAY FOR VOICES (1954)

Regaling the audience with the antics of an eclectic ensemble of eccentrics, who never existed except in the author's imagination, this classic radio play provides a fecund vision of Wales.

Born in 1914 in Swansea, Wales, Dylan Thomas published his first book of poetry when he was nineteen years old.

Under Milk Wood was first performed on 14 May 1953 before a live audience at The Poetry Center in New York City. One of the readers was Thomas himself.

Conceived as "a play for voices," it gained prominence after being broadcast on radio by the BBC on 25 January 1954.

It was written of Dylan Thomas that he "liked small towns by the sea best, and small Welsh towns by the sea best of all." Here, then, can be found the roots of what was to become *Under Milk Wood*, a work ten years in the writing with the final pages unrevised at the time of the poet's death on 9 November 1953.

It is no coincidence that *Under Milk Wood, a Play for Voices* was written whilst Thomas was living in New Quay and, later, with wife Caitlin and their children, in a sea-shaken house in a breakneck of rocks in the rough and tumbling harbour village of Laugharne. And it is no further coincidence that the seaside town of Llareggub (read it backwards), populated by characters that are romantic, earthy, mad, sane, parochial, universal, and wildly comic, reflects the good folk of Laugharne ... or at least Thomas's fantastical version of them. In a radio broadcast for the BBC he described Laugharne as "a legendary lazy little black-magical bedlam by the sea."

After Thomas's early death, the actor Richard Burton—his friend, contemporary, and rollicking co-roisterer, who had given voice to his final and most enduring work—said that *Under Milk Wood* was about "religion, sex and death." And indeed it is deeply suffused equally with whimsy, nostalgia, and "hiraeth," that sense of melancholic yearning for home that the Welsh claim as their own, and the south Welsh most of all.

Taking place over the course of a spring night and day, Thomas's surreal tapestry is a dreamscape of life and death, illustrated via the collective imagination of the town's multitudinous inhabitants: the 69 characters of Thomas's play. They include Captain Cat, a retired blind sea captain who dreams of his shipmates, lost to the Davy dark, and weeps for his long-dead sweetheart, the harlot Rose Probert: "Lie down, lie easy./Let me shipwreck in your thighs."

Prim dressmaker Myfanwy Price, lavender fragrant, proffers her heart to draper Mog Edwards, and together they glory in their love. Twice-widowed Mrs. Ogmore-Pritchard organizes her ghostly husbands' daily chores in acid fashion: "And before you let the sun in, mind it wipes its shoes."

The Rev. Eli Jenkins greets each new beauteous morn with a prayer/poem and resolves to "never, never leave the town."

Dylan Thomas's writing shed where he wrote parts of *Under Milk Wood*, in his birth town of Laugharne, on which he loosely based elements of Llareggub. He described the shed as "my word-splashed hut" and it is here he worked for the last four years of his life.

Willy Nilly the postman opens every letter before it is delivered. Pretty Polly Garter hangs out the washing with a babe in her mothering arms, and sees in the child the image of its father. Was it Tom, Dick, or Harry, or Little Willy Wee, now six feet deep? Martyred nightly by the men of the town, she hums and sings eulogies of the loved and lost: "O Tom Dick and Harry were three fine men/And I'll never have such loving again."

Proud schoolmarm Gossamer Beynon is the object of publican Sinbad Sailor's affections. Organ Morgan is the Bach-obsessed organist. Mae Rose Cottage, aged 17, has never been sweet in the grass. ("You just wait. I'll sin till I blow up!")

Thomas grew up in Swansea during and immediately after the Great War. His middle-class, comfortable childhood was founded on a landscape of dreams: of shipped-pictured bars, zinc-roofed chapels, splashed churches, salt-white houses, pink-washed pubs, and yellow seashores. In that fantasy of sleep and of dreams grew Milk Wood, and with it the lulled and dumbfound town of Llareggub.

In Laugharne Thomas, who, Caitlin said, had no urge to travel (though he liked to fantasize about traveling to exotic, faraway places) found and embraced an inborn insularity. It was there he found Llareggub and Milk Wood: a silent, sleep-world sea-town, starless and bible-black, that would become and forever represent his dream memory of Wales.

UTA-JIMA, ISE BAY, JAPAN

YUKIO MISHIMA

THE SOUND OF WAVES

(SHIOSAI) (1954)

The Sound of Waves is the story of two star-crossed lovers on a remote Japanese island in the years after World War II. Fisherman Shinji competes with the richer and more powerful Yasuo for the affections of Hatsue, a pearl diver, leading to a dramatic conclusion.

Yukio Mishima is the pen name of Hiraoka Kimitake (1925–1970). Mishima is regarded as one of the most important Japanese writers of the twentieth century.

The Sound of Waves has been adapted for film five times, including one animated film.

Mishima said the story is a reworking of *Daphnis and Chloe*, a romance from second-century Greece.

The Japanese archipelago, with its steep alpine and forested interior, narrow strip of livable space around the rim, three fertile rice-growing plains, and 6,852 islands has long played a key role in the country's literature—for example, in the terrifying isolation of Kobo Abe's *The Woman in the Dunes*; the unspoiled purity of Yasunari Kawabata's *Snow Country*; Shusaku Endo's dark coasts and dangerous roads in *Silence*; Hideo Furukawa's post-meltdown Fukushima in *Horses, Horses, in the End the Light Remains Pure*. But perhaps more than any other Japanese author, Yukio Mishima was in tune with the shades and meaning of the landscape.

His 1954 novel *The Sound of Waves* is a strident example. It's a classic of the "love-triangle" genre and a book that has held such romantic sway over Japanese culture that it has been adapted for the screen no fewer than five times. It is set on the fictional island of Uta-jima, which so closely resembles Kamishima in Ise Bay that the island markets itself to fans looking to touch the book's swelling romanticism. It is a book where the protagonists seem to have been molded from the ground, their plasma and sinews made of the same stuff as their surroundings. The plot, with its dramatic peaks and treacherous cliffs, sheltered coves and bare, open spaces, seems to have been drawn out of the island.

Our hero, Shinji, is a fisherman, his routine controlled by the tides and the weather. He is a survivor, poverty stricken, living hand-to-mouth, just managing to keep his head above water. He falls for Hatsue, a pearl diver sent to another island for her apprenticeship. She emobodies beauty, tradition, a bridge to the world beyond the island both as a traveler and in her economic role bringing money to the community through the sale of pearls. She in turn attracts Yasuo, son of the big fish in this small pond. Trees that grow too tall on islands tend to get blown down by the first storm to come along. On Japanese islands, a storm is always just over the horizon.

Novelists love an island. Enclosed, easily mappable, small enough to hold conceptually in the mind, varied enough to allow plot developments and contrasting locations to echo emotions and moods. Mishima

冨士三十六景
伊勢二見ヶ浦
廣重畫

Photograph of the MeotoIwa; the sacred rocks represent the husband and wife, the union Shinji wishes between himself and Hatsue. They are connected by a *shimenawa* rope acting as the division between the spiritual and earthly realms.

Previous page: Hiroshige print of Meoto Iwa (the "wedded rocks") off the shore of Futamigaura in the Ise province, with Mount Fuji in the background.

uses the cone-shaped Uta-jima as a funnel down which his characters can't help but spiral. Each step, each twist, each scene is closely wedded to a specific point on the island—the encounter at the lighthouse, the attempted rape by the pure water spring, the climax offshore amongst the turbulent waves of a typhoon. It's a cliché to describe place as a character within a work of fiction. In this case it's not only a cliché but an inadequate description. All of Mishima's novels depend heavily on location for a literal and figurative grounding, before his powerful philosophy and fierce emotions can be unleashed. But *The Sound of Waves* is the book where, more than any other, place is everything. Uta-jima is creator, catalyst, explanation, the beginning and end, the structure and the tone. From the very start a sense of impending threat and isolation is cast as Mishima introduces us to Uta-jima:

> At the foot of the cliff the current of the Irako Channel sets up an unceasing roar. On windy days these narrow straits connecting the Gulf of Ise and the Pacific are filled with whirlpools. The tip of the Atsumi Peninsula juts out from across the channel, and on its rocky and desolate shore stands the tiny, unmanned beacon of Cape Irako.

Mishima knew exactly what he wanted when he chose Kamishima to model for him. The characters, the story, and the reader have landed on the island and we're there to stay. Relocate the story and you'd tear the heart out of it. On an island, the sound of waves is everywhere, inescapable.

CÔTE D'AZUR, FRANCE

FRANÇOISE SAGAN

BONJOUR TRISTESSE (1954)

Set under the baking sun and amid the beautiful resorts of the fashionable Côte d'Azur, this cool, dispassionate novel observes the amorous lives and deep unhappiness of the wealthy bourgeois.

"Cet été-là, j'avais dix-sept ans et j'étais parfaitement heureuse"—"That summer I was seventeen and perfectly happy." A simple, direct line from the first page opens this short, intense, unforgettable novel first published in 1954, set under the blazing sun of the Côte d'Azur on the southeastern most tip of France: the favored playground of the wealthy, with its gorgeous beach resorts, rocky coves, and dramatic cliff tops, promising hedonism and intrigue in abundance.

The appearance of *Bonjour Tristesse* provoked acclaim and opprobrium in equal measure. Its author, who went by the pen name of Françoise Sagan, after the Princesse de Sagan (a character invented by her literary hero Marcel Proust), was herself a mere eighteen, and needed parental approval for the contract she signed with her publishers. The novel had been written during the previous summer in which the young Françoise had been forced to miss the annual family holiday in the south of France and stay in Paris, attending a crammer in order to retake her failed baccalaureate. After passing the exam that autumn, Françoise enrolled at the Sorbonne, like her heroine Cécile in the novel. Yet, instead of studying she spent most days writing in a cafe in St-Germain-des-Prés, invoking an indelible picture of the indolent days and nights of a supposedly carefree summer on the Riviera around Saint-Raphael and Juan-les-Pins: public mornings on the beach and private afternoons in the pine woods; chaotic nights at the casino; danger under the sun and along the hairpin bends of the roads. A tranquil Mediterranean surface with turbulence underneath.

The novel, which takes its title from the first lines of a melancholic 1932 poem by Paul Eluard, was a sensation, focusing on an unusual ménage à trois: a playboy widower, his teenage daughter, and the woman who, at least from the daughter's point of view, comes between them, with tragic consequences. Raymond, a businessman, and his daughter, Cécile, who has been sequestered at boarding school since the early death of her mother, take a summer holiday on the fashionable Côte d'Azur, near the resort town of Saint-Raphael. Joining them are Raymond's lover Elsa, a young woman in

Françoise Sagan (1935–2004) was the *enfant terrible* of French letters. *Bonjour Tristesse* was her first novel, published to a scandalous reception in 1954. It was written when she was seventeen and a student at the Sorbonne.

It was first published in France in 1954. By 1958 it had been translated into twenty languages.

Early celebrity led to excess, much of it public: despite her literary success, by the time of her death Sagan had debts of $1.3 million.

her twenties, attractive but unsophisticated, who is nowhere near either Raymond or Cécile's intellectual level. Her pale skin and red hair lead her to burn in the merciless sun of the Riviera.

> We spent hours on the beach, overwhelmed by the heat, and gradually acquiring a healthy golden tan, except for Elsa, who was having a terrible time, going red and peeling ... I was in the water from dawn. It was cool, clear water and I would get thoroughly immersed in it and tire myself out with uncoordinated exertions in an attempt to wash away all the murk and dust of Paris.

Shortly after the holiday begins, Cécile meets the handsome Cyril; he has a sailboat, and their flirtation quickly becomes ardent—real on his side, more experimental on hers. First passion, against the backdrop of the Mediterranean, is reflected in ongoing impressions of sensuality, such as Cécile's morning ritual at breakfast: "I bit into the orange and its sweet juice burst into my mouth. That was swallowed straight away by a gulp of scalding black coffee and then again came the coolness of the fruit." Cécile and Cyril's trysts, their lovemaking away from the beach amid the dry heat and aromatic scents of the pine forest, are forever associated with a summer in this time, this place.

The sun was becoming detached from the sky. It was bursting open and fallen on me..Where was I? It was as if I were at the bottom of the ocean, I was lost in time, I was in extremes of pleasure ... Then came the coolness of the salt water. We were laughing together, dazzled, languid, grateful. We had sun and sea, laughter and love..

The semi-idyll is interrupted by the abrupt appearance of Anne, a cool, intelligent and elegant woman of Raymond's age. Anne had been a friend of Cécile's mother and it swiftly becomes clear that her romantic target is Raymond. Despite her youth, Elsa is no match for the older woman and is treated abominably, while Anne and Raymond soon announce their intention to marry. Anne's treatment of Cécile is ambiguous—is she a rival, or a maternal figure? Anne orders Cécile to study, to eat more, to break off with Cyril; Raymond, her father, is passive. Cécile rebels and becomes Cyril's lover, while hatching a disastrous plan to rid herself and Raymond of Anne forever.

Bonjour Tristesse remains shocking today: written in detached, exquisite prose, it has been misunderstood as an amoral book, largely perhaps because the world was not ready for such a forensic skewering of relationships, the paradoxical allure and repellence of the characters. Sagan wrote formidably about the "jet-set" of the Riviera, who decamped from their sweltering cities for weeks at a time to drink, eat, flirt, and frolic in boats, on beaches, in villas. *Bonjour Tristesse* is an achingly stylish, eternally poignant work of youth and innocence compromised in one scorching Mediterranean summer.

Opposite: Bathers absorb the summer heat on crescent beach, Cannes, part of the French Riviera where Sagan's novel is set. Photograph by Howell Walker, c.1960.

LONDON, ENGLAND

SAMUEL SELVON

THE LONELY LONDONERS (1956)

In this crucial story of race and survival, a crew of Windrush immigrants try to carve out a life for themselves in 1950s London. Written using elements of the Trinidadian vernacular, Selvon's brilliant portrait gives voice to this community with both wit and pathos.

Samuel Selvon (1923–1994) emigrated to London in April 1950, on the same boat as Barbadian writer George Lamming (whose novel *The Emigrants* (1954) has a similar focus to *The Lonely Londoners*).

It was one of the first novels to record the experience of black immigrants in England, and can be seen as a precursor to such novels as *The Buddha of Suburbia* by Hanif Kureishi and *White Teeth* by Zadie Smith.

Selvon first tried to write the novel in "standard English," but found it "just would not work." Once he decided to write in dialect, though, the book "just shot along" and he completed it in six months.

London as myth and London as lived experience meet in this novel by Trinidadian writer Sam Selvon, which opens with the lines:

> One grim winter evening, when it had a kind of unrealness about London, with a fog sleeping restlessly over the city and the lights showing in the blur as it is not London at all but some strange place on another planet, Moses Aloetta hop on a number 46 bus at the corner of Chepstow Road and Westbourne Grove to go to Waterloo to meet a fellar who was coming from Trinidad on the boat-train.

Within this first, single sentence, London appears at once as a place of legend, basking in the glow of its literary heritage—the "unreal city" of T. S. Eliot, bathed in a Dickensian fog—and as somewhere one might casually "hop" onto a specific bus, from the corner of two specific roads. The day-to-day mechanics of life in this city, the reality of its geography, coexist with the grandeur of its status as a place imagined and dreamed of—and this tension is one of the themes at the very heart of this wonderful, witty, meandering book.

First published in 1956, *The Lonely Londoners* follows a set of (mainly) West Indian men (and a couple of women), more or less recently arrived in London as part of the wave of post-war immigration that came to be known as the Windrush. It is a loosely structured book that, rather than following a plot, "coasts" along with one or another of its characters before drifting off to the next—an (apparent) aimlessness that echoes the bewildered roaming of Selvon's "boys" through this foreign, alienating city.

In a loose, playful prose that blends "standard English" with Trinidadian vernacular, Selvon gives us brief insights into the lives of these men—how Captain, a crafty Nigerian, sponges off the many women who inexplicably find him irresistible (with frequently disastrous consequences), how Galahad, the cocksure recent arrival Moses meets at the beginning of the book, ends up catching pigeons for food, how they all hustle for work, hustle for

The Lonely Londoners

Samuel Selvon

So, cool as a lord, the old Galahad walking out to the road, with plastic raincoat hanging on the arm, and the eyes not missing one sharp craft that pass, bowing his head in a polite "Good evening" and not giving a blast if they answer or not. This is London, this is life oh lord, to walk like a king with money in your pocket, not a worry in the world.

girls—creating an assemblage of anecdotes that, together, form a novel and a portrait of a city.

Selvon's use of a dialect-inflected English was a major landmark in the development of the Caribbean literature that was having something of a renaissance at this period—his contemporaries included V. S. Naipaul and Derek Walcott, as well as the writers associated with the London-based Caribbean Artists Movement—but it is also one of the things that make this novel such a fitting portrait of London itself. Walk down the streets of the city today, and it is not rare to hear a dozen different languages being spoken within a 50-yard stretch: London, the cosmopolitan megalopolis, is nothing if not a huge, sprawling amalgamation of wildly different communities, all speaking their own languages, following their own customs, and making the city their own by getting on its underground trains, roaming its streets.

Like countless immigrants before and after them, Selvon's "boys" incorporate London into their language by naming the territory that is theirs, such as when Moses explains to Galahad that he lives "in the Water. Bayswater to you until you living in the city for at least two years." It is through language that we lay claim to places, that we gain a hold over the brick and mortar that may or may not have made room for us (and Selvon's characters, frequently faced with "Keep the Water White" signs in boarding room windows, are only too keenly aware that room has not always been made).

But it is also these names that make places themselves have a mysterious hold over us, as Selvon points out toward the end of the novel:

> Oh what it is and where it is and why it is, no one knows, but to have said: "I walked on Waterloo Bridge," "I rendezvoused at Charing Cross," "Piccadilly Circus is my playground," to say these things, to have lived these things, to have lived in the great city of London, center of the world...

Previous page: The original cover artwork produced for the Allan Wingate edition of ***The Lonely Londoners*** (1956)—a small but influential press run by André Deutsch.

"Piccadilly Circus—that circus have a magnet for him, that circus represent life, that circus is the beginning and the ending of the world." A group of Jamaican immigrants scrutinize a map of the Underground, c.1948.

> What it is that a city have, that any place in the world have, that you get so much to like it you wouldn't leave it for anywhere else? What it is that would keep men, although by and large, in truth and in fact, they catching their royal to make a living, staying in a cramp-up room where you have to do everything—sleep, eat, dress, wash, cook, live.

London as an exhausting, beguiling beast, so expensive you have to break your back working just to survive, alienating its inhabitants by confining them miles away from each other in the only tiny rooms they can afford—it's an impression of the city that will be just as familiar to many a modern-day Londoner as to Selvon's characters. And yet, then as now, the city's myth, the poetry of its names, continue to enchant people—and on they hustle, lonely Londoners all....

NEW HAMPSHIRE, USA

GRACE METALIOUS
PEYTON PLACE (1956)

The woods of New England frame Grace Metalious's blistering, pioneering exposé of what was really happening behind the lace curtains and pretty white shutters of the postcard towns along the Connecticut River.

Grace Metalious (1924–1964) finished the first draft of her manuscript of *Peyton Place* within six months.

When it was published in 1956, it sold 60,000 copies in ten days. It went on to become the bestselling book of the century, deposing classics like *Gone with the Wind*.

The novel became the first ABC primetime soap opera, running from 1964 to 1969, and launching the careers of Mia Farrow and Ryan O'Neal.

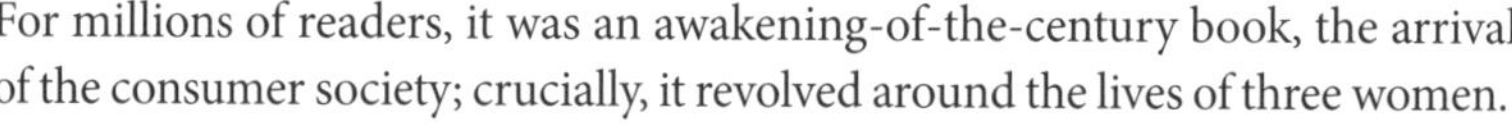

For millions of readers, it was an awakening-of-the-century book, the arrival of the consumer society; crucially, it revolved around the lives of three women.

Peyton was a mash-up of places Metalious lived, including Gilmanton where she was born and would return to, up to Plymouth where the book was finished. The original book and portrait of New England are rather different from usual perceptions, which have been whitewashed and sanitized in two Hollywood movies and the world's first TV soap opera after her death. As Professor Ardis Cameron details in her preface to Virago's 2002 edition, the novel was deemed scandalous and offensive to the down-home and much-loved image of small-town America.

The prose, though, had already found its mark, a fanfare for a new age, a new emancipation, for female sexuality. It was the flag for the pent-up outpourings of a repressed generation. The more it was banned—as it was in US libraries and also in Canada—the more copies sold and the more Metalious herself became a celebrity. Arguably, it was the first feminist blockbuster.

From the opening pages the pathos of the glorious countryside is apparent. Schoolgirl Alison MacKenzie strolls through the town bookmarked by two churches at either end, basking in the warmth of a capricious Indian summer. The New England trees provide an iconic commentary of their own: "The conifers stood like disapproving old men on all the hills around." Cut down they provide the weatherboard fascias to the houses so familiar from tourist guides. But these same trees are the woodsman's insurance, a natural resource to return to when other work dries up—"when one was given a shove by life." For young Alison they are her secret hideaway. Prophetically they are her first love: "She paused and put her nose against the wood's bare, green-whiteness, sniffing its fresh wet small, running her fingertips over its unprotected surface until she felt the dampness of the sap on her hands."

As the characters come into view we start to feel the fury and passions lurking underneath, a whole chocolate box of frustrations, desires, and warped passions: "Constance felt a vague restlessness within herself, she told herself sharply this was not sex, but perhaps a touch of indigestion."

The famous view when Allison MacKenzie, played by Mia Farrow, and Norman Page, played by Russ Tamblyn, stand on the hill overlooking Peyton Place. It is actually Mount Battie in Camden, Maine.

Not least among these characters is the drunken, dissolute, and terrifying Lucas Cross, who locks himself up with his mates in Kenny Stearns's cellar with barrels of cider. In one of the epic X-rated binges that might have been paid for by the Temperance society, with instructions to show all the evils that drink can bring in one scene, they drink themselves to oblivion until the money runs out—men turned feral, beasts collapsing under their perceived burdens.

Sadly Metalious did not heed her own warnings. She died of cirrhosis of the liver eight years after the book was published. She blew her fortune away faster than the royalties came in. By the time of her death—which was before the film or TV series had launched—she was broke and owed the Internal Revenue Service three times more than she had in the bank. Known for her extravagances in New York, behind the scenes she had used the money to buy her dream house in Gilmanton. She stayed faithful to the town whose secrets she had washed and hung out on the line, and went back to live and die among the many people she had so offended.

OUTBACK, AUSTRALIA

PATRICK WHITE

VOSS (1957)

An acclaimed retelling of the fate of Australia's archetypal explorer, Ludwig Leichhardt (here called Voss), and his battle with the country's unforgiving landscape.

Born in London to Australian parents, Patrick White (1912–1990), was a novelist, playright and poet. His family emigrated to Australia when he was six months old and he lived in Sydney for most of his life. In 1973 he became the only Australian to be awarded the Nobel Prize for Literature.

First published by Eyre & Spottiswoode in London in 1957, *Voss* has since been translated into twenty-three foreign languages.

Although regarded as a classic text today, on first publication *Voss* attracted polarized opinions.

The Australian landscape is known colloquially as the Outback, the Bush, or the Never-Never. To Australians, these highly evocative terms are such a towering presence in their imaginations that they are rendered with capitals. And beyond the mere civilized fringe of this island continent, the overwhelming spread of landscape is as arid and hostile to settlement as these metaphors might suggest. Even so, to the first white settlers this alien landscape exerted a magnetic allure, both fearful and fascinating. It challenged them to conquer its vast spaces and to name its furthest reaches as if this act alone could confer authority and dominion.

Patrick White enshrined this dichotomy in his novel *Voss*, which first appeared in 1957. As the fifth of his twelve novels published between 1939 and 1986, it received wide international acclaim. British and American critics even invoked comparisons with Tolstoy and Melville and the book claimed two inaugural literary prizes: Australia's Miles Franklin Award and Britain's W. H. Smith Award. Thereafter, *Voss* was widely translated. Then, when White was awarded the Nobel Prize for Literature in 1973, the citation specifically celebrated his depiction of the unique Australian landscape by an "epic and psychological narrative art which … introduced a new continent into literature."

In its home country, however, White's dislocated syntax (which one critic called "over-literary arabesque"), alienated many readers. Yet White was forging a new style in an attempt to convey the metaphysical; in his own words striving "to create completely fresh forms out of the rocks and sticks of words." The writer himself therefore became an explorer, wrestling with new stylistic territory as, seemingly, out of the very landscape itself, he struggled to give it a voice. Others found the book's unapologetic German mysticism, which depicts a central character consumed by Nietzschean pretensions and Hitlerian megalomania, impenetrable. And thus, with distinct echoes also of Melville's Captain Ahab, Voss sets off with heaven-storming arrogance to conquer the landscape by sheer will. His retort, when asked if had studied a map, is that he will "first make it." In his godlike stance Voss bestows animus upon this landscape, considering it his only worthy opponent.

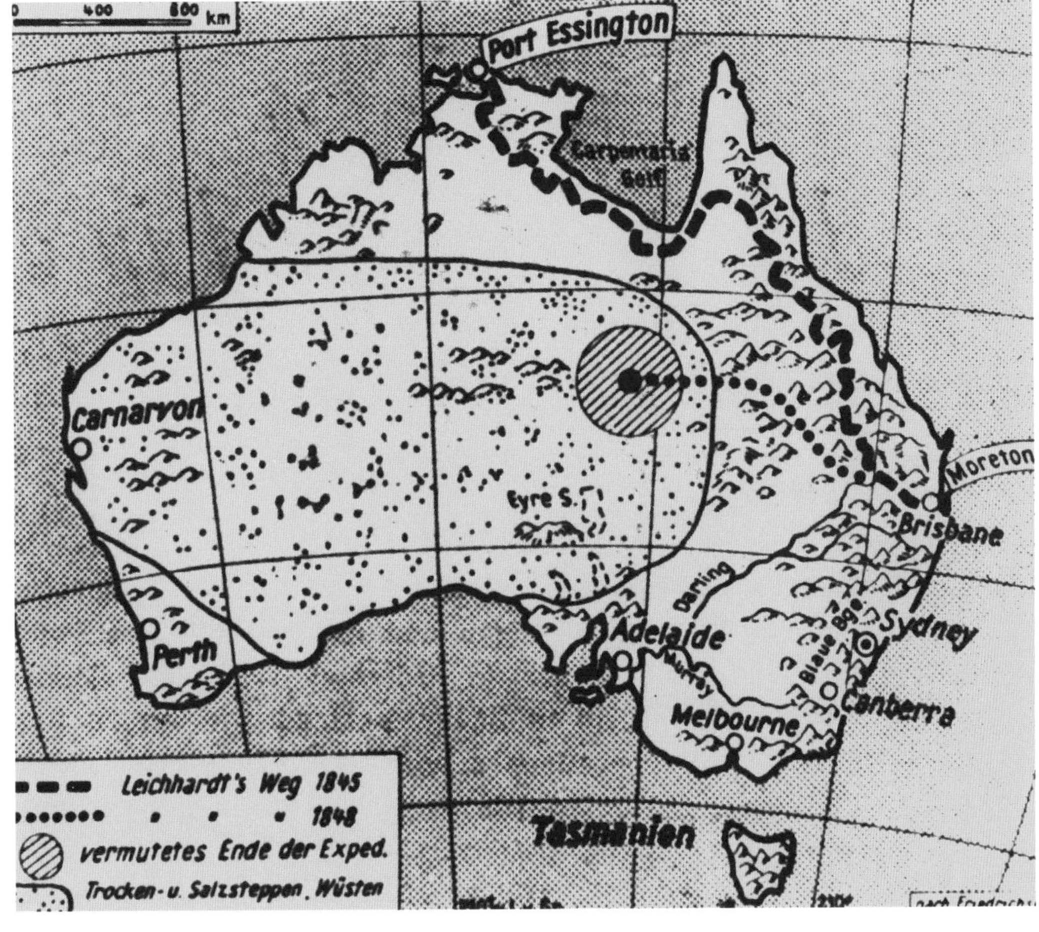

German explorer Ludwig Leichhardt's route for his expeditions through Australia, which White used as a basis for *Voss*.

By White's own admission the novel was conceived during the London Blitz and anchored in his wartime experiences in the Western Desert. Its specific inspiration was as much the Australian landscape as the Prussian explorer Ludwig Leichhardt (1813–1848) who perished while attempting to cross the continent from east to west. In White's retelling, the inner landscape of Voss becomes manifest in the outer landscape he traverses: alien, prickly, unforgiving and inexplicable. By "winding deeper into himself, into blacker thickets of thorns" Voss internalizes the landscape that assumes mythic, even gothic dimensions. The Outback becomes a protagonist itself as Voss travels to the very horizon of his known self and into an equally "disturbing country."

While White's desert metaphors have biblical overtones they also resonate with the archetypal myth of Odysseus's wanderings. Ultimately, however, the land becomes a place of dispossession rather than one that man can possess. Voss's arrogance cannot conquer the landscape. If only he had been content with a mortal's earthbound destiny. Laura Trevelyan, his

Sydney Nolan illustrated several covers for Patrick White, beginning with *Voss* and ending with *A Fringe of Leaves* in 1958.

Opposite: "I am compelled into this country." McFarlane and Erskine print from *The History of Australasia* by David Blair, McGrady, Thomson and Niven, 1879.

psychic companion in the country of his mind, recognized this when she declared: "*You* are *my* desert!"

When the expedition sets out, Leichhardt's men begin an apotheosis into mythical status. They become akin to the figures depicted in the austere art of the Australian artist, Sidney Nolan. Initially, the explorers set out from a fertile coastal landscape, which devolves into "the approaches to hell" where they are "writing their own legend." The first setting epitomizes the superficial and the finite, the other, the mystical, and the infinite and critics responded to this vision of landscape. Some discerned it as Wordsworthian or as individual in character as Thomas Hardy's Wessex.

Ultimately, any wisdom wrung from Voss's wrestling with landscape is vouchsafed to Laura: "Knowledge was never a matter of geography … it overflows all maps that exist [and] … only comes of death by torture in the country of the mind." The explorer thus becomes a metaphor for all men whose lives are an unexplored desert and where suffering and humility are the preconditions of his spiritual quest.

PROCIDA, BAY OF NAPLES, ITALY

ELSA MORANTE

ARTURO'S ISLAND

(L'ISOLA DI ARTURO) (1957)

Perfectly poised between myth and reality, this Italian classic evokes a blissful Mediterranean boyhood inexorably transformed into an adolescent's existential nightmare.

Elsa Morante (1912–1985) was married for twenty years to the novelist Alberto Moravia, making Italy's most celebrated literary couple.

Published in 1957 just as Italian neo-realism was at its most doctrinal and dour, *Arturo's Island* ran entirely contrary to contemporary fashion in fiction.

"Arturo, c'est moi," Morante told an interviewer; having always wanted to be a boy herself, she poured the creativity of middle age into evoking boyishness on the page.

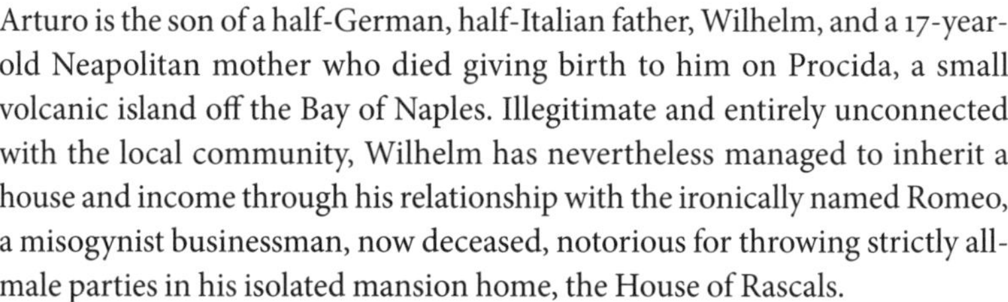

Arturo is the son of a half-German, half-Italian father, Wilhelm, and a 17-year-old Neapolitan mother who died giving birth to him on Procida, a small volcanic island off the Bay of Naples. Illegitimate and entirely unconnected with the local community, Wilhelm has nevertheless managed to inherit a house and income through his relationship with the ironically named Romeo, a misogynist businessman, now deceased, notorious for throwing strictly all-male parties in his isolated mansion home, the House of Rascals.

It is here, in what is actually an ex-monastery, that our narrator and hero Arturo grows up. His father is almost always absent. After an early infancy with a male nanny, the boy is left entirely to his own devices with just a dog—Immacolatella—for company. Unkissed by any woman, roaming his tiny island kingdom (Procida measures just 1.5 square miles), reading the books available in the House of Rascals, all written by men for men about male heroism, he dreams of the day when he will be able to leave the island together with his father, whom he supposes to be a great traveler and explorer, perhaps a military hero. Instead, as Arturo approaches 15, Wilhelm brings home a second 17-year-old bride, photocopy of the long-dead mother, whom he promptly gets pregnant, before returning to his mysterious wanderings. Arturo's first kiss will thus be with the one woman forbidden to him, Nunziatella, his stepmother.

Along with its intense evocation of the Mediterranean coastal landscape and a wild, seaside boyhood, Morante's novel is steeped in the vocabulary of sovereignty, enchantment, and imprisonment. The three are related. Apparently a paradise, the island houses at its rugged center a high-security prison. Arturo feels that the island, like his boyhood, is a kind of prison, precisely because it is so enchanting. Every time he tries to row away from it and escape to mainland Naples in his little rowboat, he is overtaken by a terrible nostalgia that inevitably draws him back. Positive and negative understandings of the same experience are constantly intertwining. The boy's father, Wilhelm, exercises complete, sometimes cruel sovereignty over him, but this is strangely beautiful, because Arturo is enchanted by his father.

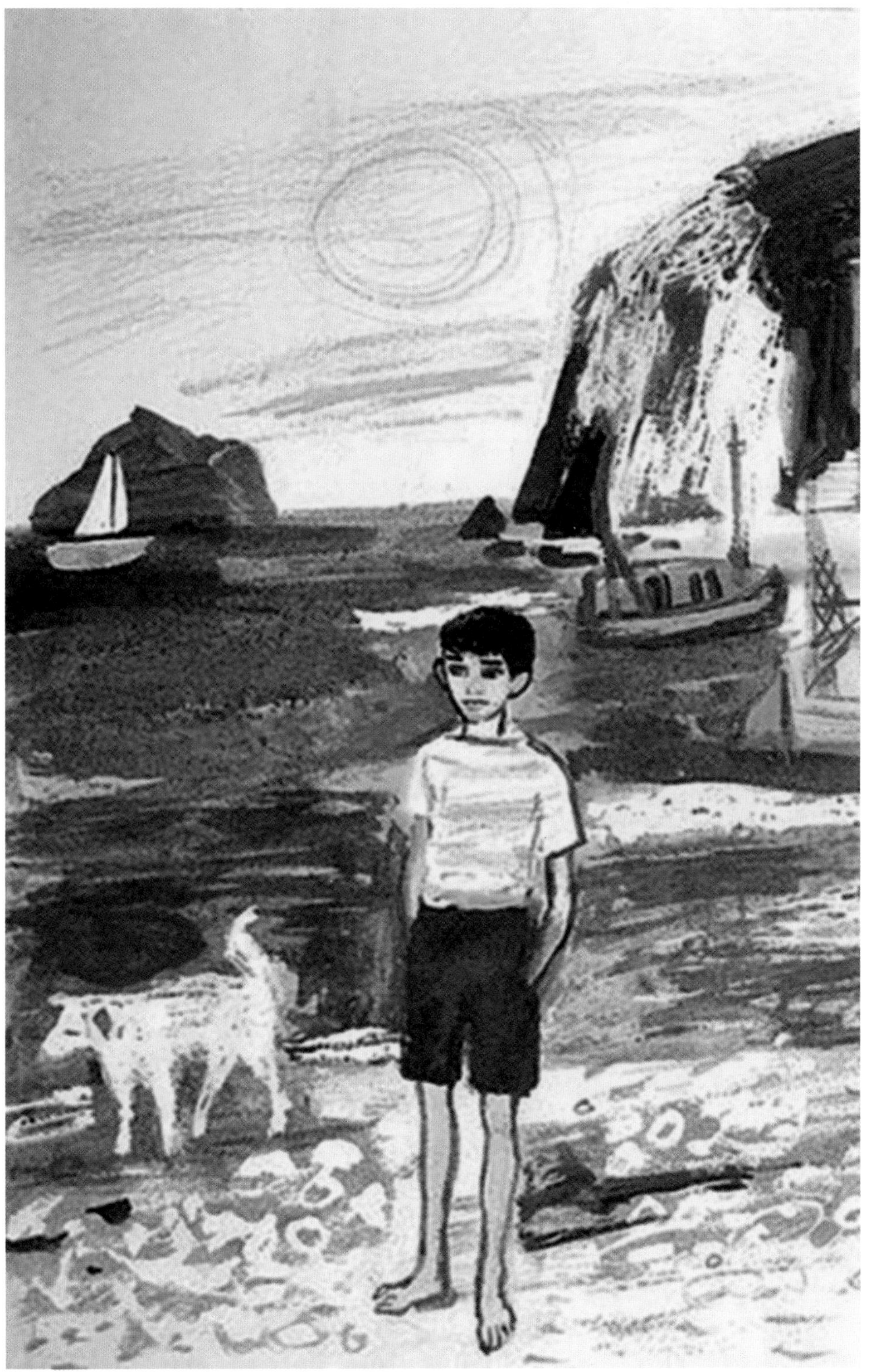

It seemed to me that everyone on earth was busy kissing: boats, tied one close to the other along the shore, were kissing! The movement of the sea was a kiss, running towards the island; sheep were kissing the soil while grazing, and air flowing among the leaves and the grass was a kissing lament.

Wilhelm, on the contrary, rejects any authority. Raving against the reproach of his wife as he sets off on another trip he announces: "Obligations and duties don't exist for me, I AM A SCANDAL." A woman, he says, "always wants to hold you prisoner, like the time she was pregnant with you."

In complete opposition to her husband's modern ideas of freedom and individuality, the child-wife Nunziatella has an entirely traditional sense of duties and relationships. Subjected to a tirade of appalling, drunken misogyny from her husband, she nevertheless lays a blanket over him when he falls asleep. The gesture drives Arturo quite mad for its beauty and blind self-sacrifice, especially because, despite being in love with Arturo, Nunziatella will never go beyond that first kiss, because "Wilhelm is my husband." The last violent scenes of the novel where a desperate Arturo tries to get his unwilling stepmother to understand that Wilhelm is in fact "IN LOVE WITH A MAN," imprisoned by his passion for a young convict incarcerated in the island's penitentiary, are among the strongest that readers are likely to encounter anywhere.

The achievement of Morante's novel is its investigation of the relationship between beauty and power in the reality of enchantment and the relation between the sexes. Her own prose is very much part of the equation. The whole novel presents itself as a magnificent spell that seizes the reader's mind from page one. Only at the end are we released at last into the plain world of history; leaving Procida for the first time, immediately after his seventeenth birthday, Arturo discovers that war, the Second World War, is imminent. He will volunteer. It is the first time the reader is given an inkling of a date.

Considered by many as one of the finest Italian novels of the twentieth century, *Arturo's Island* captures all the themes of modern Italy, above all the intense desire to belong and the equally intense fear of being possessed or demeaned by those we love. But Morante's supreme stroke of genius is the setting; fabulous as it is constricting, Procida becomes emblematic of a whole society's dilemma.

Previous page: Ronald Glendenning's illustration from a 1959 US edition of *Arturo's Island*. Arturo stands at the forefront with his dog and only friend, and the evocative Mediterranean coast behind.

ONITSHA, EAST BANK NIGER RIVER, NIGERIA

CHINUA ACHEBE

THINGS FALL APART (1958)

Wrestling hero Okonkwo has ambitions to become a great clan leader but he is sent away from his tribe after a lethal accident. This is the story of his return to his village after a seven-year exile, during which time Christian missionaries have brought about drastic changes to the indigenous culture.

In his first and best-known novel, Nigerian writer Chinua Achebe uses the folk tales of the Igbo people to explore culture, myth, religion, and gender in a fictional village called Umuofia in pre-colonial Nigeria at the turn of the nineteenth century. Achebe uses the language of the colonizers, English, but incorporates Igbo speech patterns and syntax to create a narrative that had not been read before in mainstream literary fiction. Achebe's English is written with a Nigerian aesthetic—a flavor local to the region he writes of, and the poetics of the Igbo. *Things Fall Apart* is a book that portrays Nigeria (and is to many readers representative of West Africa) as a country that is more than just anarchic violence. Here is a book that is finally—simply put—not racist or viewed through a Western lens. Here is a book that tells the complex story of colonialism from the perspective of the colonized, that challenges Eurocentric perspectives on Imperialism.

Achebe is often referred to as the father of modern African writing, with *Things Fall Apart* considered his most successful book—a book, he has said, that "seized me, and almost wrote me."

It is the story of Okonkwo, who must straddle both pre- and postcolonial life in his village, which is at a historic threshold, unbeknownst to Okonkwo or his clan. He is determined to become a powerful leader in Umuofia, but when he accidentally causes the death of another, he is exiled by the tribal leaders. It is then also the story of Umuofia, a village that functions on Igbo culture and myth, and a clan that is forced to rescind to the Christian missionaries who arrive with Bibles to convert the natives and set up their own system of governance. Okonkwo, who has been in exile for seven years, returns to find that the way of life he knew and regarded as sacrosanct no longer exists. Change for the Umuofia is inevitable, and Achebe's narrative is concerned with how resistance to or acceptance of change (whether it be change for the better or worse) can destroy a man. As Okonkwo's friend Obierika explains, the white man "has put a knife on the things that held us together and we have fallen apart."

Chinua Achebe (1930–2013) won the Man Booker International Prize in 2007. Born in Ogidi, Nigeria, he has suffered periods of semi-exile from his homeland due to threats following publication of his books.

The title of the novel comes from a line in W. B. Yeats's poem "The Second Coming."

The novel was initially rejected by several publishers, before being bought by Heinemann. The initial print run was 2,000 copies but the novel has sold over ten million copies worldwide and has been translated into fifty languages.

THINGS FALL APART
ARTISAN RELEASING CORPORATION presents
THINGS FALL APART
Produced in Nigeria, A Calpenny Nigeria Films/Nigram Production
Starring JOHNNY SEKKA and PRINCESS ELIZABETH OF TORO
Executive Producers FERN MOSK and EDWARD MOSK
Produced by FRANCIS OLADELE and WOLF SCHMIDT
Screenplay by FERN MOSK based on the novels
"Things Fall Apart" and "No Longer At Ease" by CHINUA ACHEBE
Directed by JASON POHLAND Music by MILT HOLLAND Color by TECHNICOLOR®
Distributed by ARTISAN RELEASING CORPORATION 9200 SUNSET BOULEVARD, SUITE 616, LOS ANGELES, CALIF. 90069

A man who calls his kinsmen to a feast does not do so to save them from starving. They all have food in their own homes. When we gather together in the moonlit village ground it is not because of the moon. Every man can see it in his own compound. We come together because it is good for kinsmen to do so.

Achebe also explores Umuofia through the village's dependence on the very land it stands on. By weaving Igbo beliefs deftly into the narrative, Achebe is able to explore the physical landscape of the village as well, for the Umuofia are entirely dependent on their land for survival and so their religious systems are rooted in their natural environment—so much so that an annual Feast of the New Yam is held to herald the new year. The "Evil Forest" is a god—feared, respected, revered—as is Ani, the goddess of the earth and fertility. We are reminded of the very physicality of the everyday lives of the clan in many ways—Okonkwo is a wrestler, grappling with bodies so that he may earn a title; the tribe's drums, powerful and always in unison as their one combined heartbeat; the fire that Okonkwo is associated with, that reminds us not just of the climate but also of Okonkwo's fatal flaw—that of uncontrollable anger.

"There is such a thing as absolute power over narrative," wrote Achebe. "Those who secure this privilege for themselves can arrange stories about others pretty much where, and as, they like." With *Things Fall Apart,* Achebe took back the narrative of Nigeria, of the Igbo, and of the landscape that formed their belief system and society from the empire, from Western writers who had previously secured the privilege to tell stories about parts of Africa. Achebe took back the power of his people and their stories, and retained the privilege for the writers who belong.

Opposite: The 1971 poster for the movie adaption, produced by Hollywood lawyer Edward Mosk and screenplay by his wife, Fern.

MONROEVILLE, ALABAMA, USA

HARPER LEE

TO KILL A MOCKINGBIRD (1960)

Seen through the eyes of young Scout Finch, the attitudes of the Depression South are tested as she encounters various people of different social and economic classes and watches her father defend in court an African-American falsely accused of raping a white woman.

Nelle Harper Lee (1926–2016) was born in Monroeville, Alabama, which was her inspiration for Scout's hometown of Maycomb. The novel has never been out of print since its initial publication.

Truman Capote was a lifelong friend of Lee's and was the inspiration for Scout's best friend Dill.

Gregory Peck and Harper Lee became fast friends after the film was made in 1962, and Peck's grandson was named Harper.

Saying that "landscape creates separation" when looking at the spectrum of landscapes across North America seems both overly obvious and enormously varied. This view of the physical environment might suggest the Rockies separating states and meteorological environments, or the Mississippi dividing the entire continent of North America. The use of space, how people survive in that space, and how we conceptualize it politically are practically visible from an airplane window when flying over Colorado or Louisiana. Physical separation, however, is only a visible manifestation; legal, emotional, and social separation can also be products of landscape that only become evident as people are seen working in the landscape (or not, which is equally telling), and are separated (either voluntarily or not) within a landscape.

The sole location of the characters we meet in *To Kill a Mockingbird* is southern rural Alabama, in the fictional town and county of Maycomb. Approximately 70 miles north of Mobile, Maycomb looks like many rural southern towns. Southern Alabama is flat, pine forested, and not generally the home of the large plantations associated with the Deep South; those locations tend to be in northern Alabama, a wealthier area mentally distant and somewhat questionable to those living nearer the Gulf. Maycomb County residents farm smaller plots or depend on the Tombigbee or Alabama Rivers for their livelihood in fishing or transport. The main physical feature of this environment is the weather, and that factor affects its inhabitants deeply. Corporeal ennui caused by climate is a constant in life in the southeastern American states: engulfing heat, brain-fogging humidity, the slow drone of cicadas, and the overwhelming nature of semi-tropical vegetation that grows so quickly and profusely that battling it eventually becomes pointless. Maycomb is described as "tired," the dirt streets turning to "red slop" in the rain, even the shade of the oaks is "sweltering." Over time people can become immobilized in body, unlikely to move briskly and with energy without becoming fatigued and enervated. Clothing and people wilt by midday and movement is slow: people "ambled across the square, shuffled in and out of stores around it, took their time about everything."

Wall mural depicting Scout, Jem, and Dill spying on the road. The mural is located in historic downtown Monroeville, Alabama, Harper Lee's hometown and theinspiration for Scout's hometown of Maycomb. It is also where the first stage adaptation of *To Kill a Mockingbird* was performed in 1991.

But lethargy in body is not the only result of an environment that tangibly oppresses its inhabitants. The Depression has taken most sources of income away from the area, and inhabitants on all economic levels are affected; the poverty-wracked Cunninghams pay Atticus in stovewood and bags of nuts instead of money, and Mr. Cunningham refuses any assistance: "Mr. Cunningham could get a WPA job, but his land would go to ruin if he left it, and he was willing to go hungry to keep his land and vote as he pleased." Sticking to the land as one's forefathers did is a political and moral obligation that trumps economic security. With little to do, time seems to take longer, but productivity is not a part of life in Maycomb: "There was no hurry, for there was nowhere to go, nothing to buy and no money to buy it with, nothing to see outside the boundaries of Maycomb."

Attitudes as stagnant and fruitless as the slow-moving rivers and overworked land are presented, not with narrative commentary, but to be viewed by the reader for what they are. When Scout's cousin Francis calls Atticus a "nigger-lover," when the children's maid Calpurnia takes them to her church and is told that she has no business bringing white children there, or when Scout describes the North Alabama home of her first-grade teacher as "full of Liquor Interests, Big Mules, steel companies, Republicans, professors, and other persons of no background," we hear echoes of generations of separation based on where and how one lives.

Her class's apprehension of their "foreign" teacher is not the only geographic marker of personhood in the novel. Family genealogy attaches a person to a particular area and sometimes even a piece of property in perpetuity, and locating one's specific territory is crucial to understand the

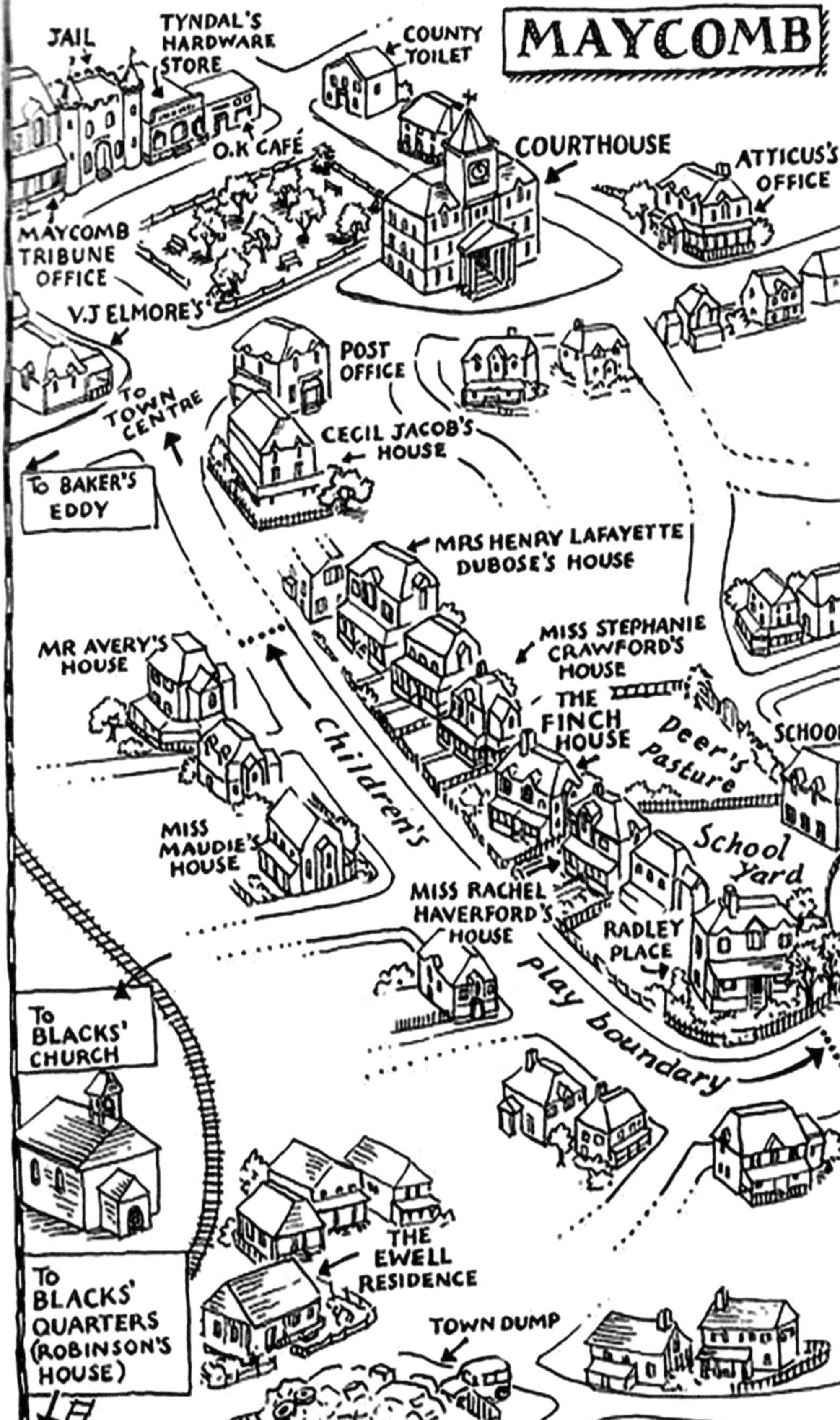
MAYCOMB
JAIL
TYNDAL'S HARDWARE STORE
COUNTY TOILET
O.K CAFÉ
COURTHOUSE
ATTICUS'S OFFICE
MAYCOMB TRIBUNE OFFICE
V.J ELMORE'S
POST OFFICE
TO TOWN CENTRE
CECIL JACOB'S HOUSE
To BAKER'S EDDY
MRS HENRY LAFAYETTE DUBOSE'S HOUSE
MR AVERY'S HOUSE
MISS STEPHANIE CRAWFORD'S HOUSE
THE FINCH HOUSE
Deer's pasture
SCHOOL
Children's
MISS MAUDIE'S HOUSE
School Yard
MISS RACHEL HAVERFORD'S HOUSE
RADLEY PLACE
play boundary
To BLACKS' CHURCH
THE EWELL RESIDENCE
To BLACKS' QUARTERS (ROBINSON'S HOUSE)
TOWN DUMP

Maycomb was spared the grubbiness that distinguished most Alabama towns its size. In the beginning its building were solid, its court-house proud, its streets graciously wide.

very nature of a human being. The very first thing Scout says about her family laments their lack of family connections with mild derision: "Being Southerners, it was a source of shame to some members of the family that we had no recorded ancestors on either side of the Battle of Hastings." Still slightly suspect because of the absence of notable ancestors, the Finch family had been based "on the banks of the Alabama River some forty miles above Saint Stephens" on a homestead called Finch's Landing, and Maycomb, where Atticus Finch settled to practice law, is twenty miles east of there. Atticus is specifically situated in this county:

> he was Maycomb born and bred; he knew his people, they knew him, and because of Simon Finch's industry, Atticus was related by blood or marriage to nearly every family in the town.

Scout attempts to explain to her teacher the poverty of Walter Cunningham by simply saying, "he's a Cunningham." This word conveys a wealth of information about the Cunningham "tribe—one branch, that is." Both Scout's and Walter's ways in the world will be unchangeably determined by where their families live and how that separates them in social and economic class from others.

The Ewell family is another local, low-class tribe who is at the heart of the second half of the novel; its most famous plot thread is Tom Robinson's tragic trial after Mayella Ewell lies about Tom raping her. The dismal nature of 1935 race relations in southern Alabama is a palpable example of every kind of separation among human beings. This book was published only five years after teenager Emmett Till was lynched in Mississippi after being falsely accused of whistling at a white woman; no circumstance would raise strong, irrational emotions more in this time and place than the mere suggestion of sexual assault by a black man toward a white woman. The crux of the case depends on the fact that Mayella was beaten by someone left-handed; it is casually mentioned that Tom's left arm is a foot shorter than his right as the result of a nearly fatal cotton gin accident "when he was a boy." King Cotton, child labor, the lack of medical care for a poor black child, a poor white woman who must not show any affection toward a black male, and Tom's eventual conviction and death in a trumped-up "jailbreak"—all of these are products of the control that the landscape has had for generations on its inhabitants and their codes of belief and behavior.

Opposite: An illustrated map of Maycomb, showing the novel's key locations. The map also visualizes the segregation that divides the town's populace.

TELEMARK, NORWAY

TARJEI VESAAS

THE ICE PALACE (IS-SLOTTET) (1963)

Set in a remote village at the height of winter, this slim novel by one of Norway's most beloved writers explores themes of friendship, childhood, community, and loss.

Tarjei Vesaas (1897–1870) was born to a farming family in Vinje, Telemark, in southern Norway, in 1897, and died there in 1970.

He was awarded the Nordic Council Literature Prize for *The Ice Palace* in 1964.

Norway has two official languages, Nynorsk and Bokmål. Vesaas wrote all of his books, plays, and poems in Nynorsk, which is rooted in rural Norwegian dialects (Bokmål—"Book language"—is more closely affiliated with written Danish).

Ice and darkness play a central part in Tarjei Vesaas's *The Ice Palace*, which opens in midwinter in a rural community in Norway. From the outset, the ice is portrayed to be a threat: "It thundered like a gunshot, blasting long fissures, narrow as a knife-blade." The sound startles Siss, a young girl navigating her way after school to visit a newcomer to the village, Unn, who has recently arrived to live with an aunt after the death of her mother. The sinister descriptions at the start of the novel prove to be portentous; the girls' fate is forever impacted by the callous, frozen environment they inhabit.

An awkward moment occurs between the pair, and the next day, embarrassed, Unn plays truant from school. She decides to explore the so-called ice palace: a sculpted, many-chambered structure nearby, the husk of a frozen waterfall. Symbols recur in Vesaas's work—here, the ice palace represents something beyond the control of human society, accessible only to children.

Unn finds a fracture in the ice and enters the palace, moving, in doing so, from the realism of Siss and the adults toward a stranger realm, the beguiling world of fairytale and folklore. She discovers a room containing "a petrified forest," a "room of tears," which "seemed to trickle and weep," and a room full of "jagged walls with many angles". Finally, unable to make her way out, scrutinized by what she perceives to be "a tremendous eye … in the middle of the ice," she succumbs to the cold: "She wanted to sleep; she was languid and limp and ready."

A blizzard descends and a thick layer of snow prevents the villagers from recovering Unn. The blanketing snowfall reflects the growing numbness Siss feels as she yields to a deep depression. Weeks pass, and she finds herself caught between the forward-looking perspective of her parents and school-friends and her loyalty to the memory of Unn. Meanwhile, tension mounts between the ordered world of the humans and the wild winter landscape around them. Vesaas realizes this tension structurally, weaving plot-driven passages with lyrical fragments describing nature scenes.

As winter passes into spring, and the ice palace thaws and eventually collapses, Siss comes to terms with her grief. The darkness of which she was so

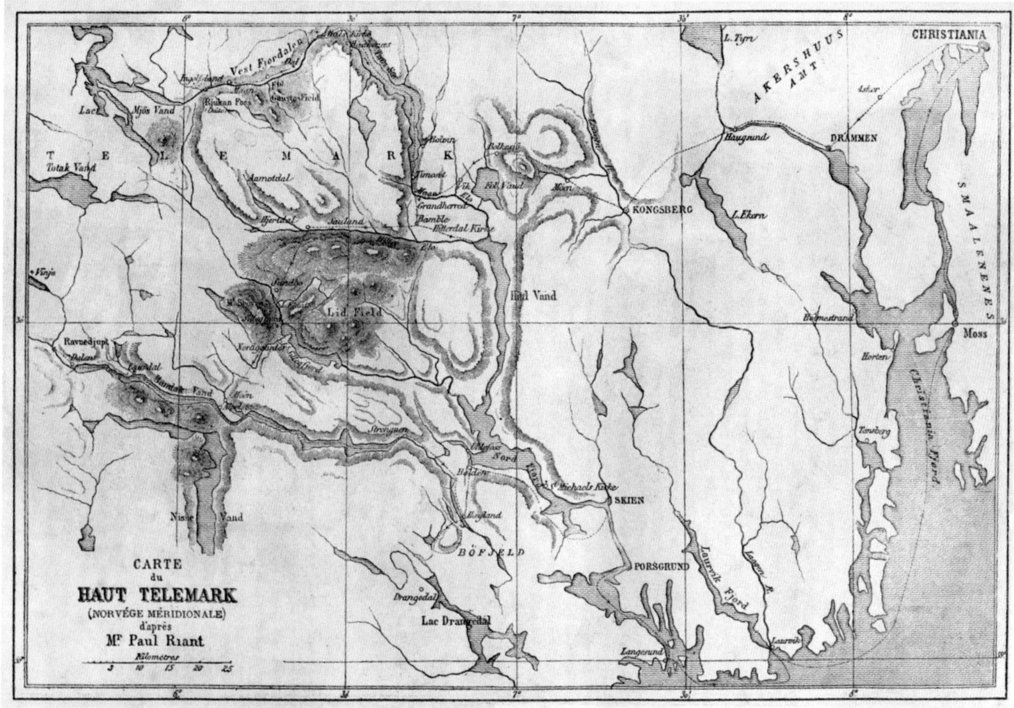

frightened at the start of the novel has become something she is comfortable with. "Afraid of the dark?" Vesaas writes. "No. Bright woodwind players had appeared and were walking along the sides of the road."

Map of Telemark, Norway, created by Riant and Erhad, 1860. Telemark is an isolated mountainous district in southern Norway, where Vessas was born and spent most of his life.

Vesaas has been praised for his realistic depiction of the rural Norwegian landscape, yet he also invests this setting with supernatural elements, drawing on Nordic folklore to give his seemingly straightforward story of friendship and loss an extra dimension. Common to Scandinavian mythology is the representation of nature as wild and unbiddable, with people frequently submitting to its whims; see, for example, the trope of *bergtagning* (taken to the mountain), in which humans vanish into nature, stolen by supernatural forces. The disappearance of Unn, who is erased forever by ice and snow, has been linked to this folkloric motif.

The remarkable blending of the real and the figurative in *The Ice Palace*, and the extraordinarily evocative portrait it paints of a remote, ice-covered region in Norway, cement this novel's reputation as Vesaas's masterpiece.

Unn looked down into an enchanted world of small pinnacles, gables, frosted domes, soft curves and confused tracery. All of it was ice, and the water spurted between, building it up continually. Branches of the waterfall had been diverted and rushed into new channels, creating new forms. Everything shone.

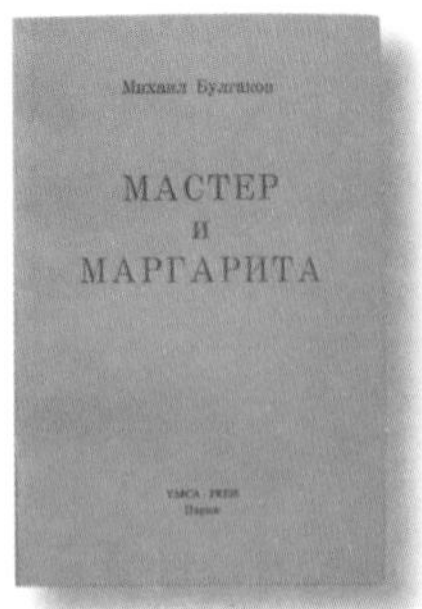

MOSCOW, RUSSIA

MIKHAIL BULGAKOV

THE MASTER AND MARGARITA (MÁSTER I MARGARÍTA) (1966)

In this classic of twentieth-century fiction, the Devil and his retinue (including a talking cat), visit atheist Moscow during the era of Stalin's Terror. The Master's secret lover Margarita enters into a pact with the Devil.

Mikhail Bulgakov (1891–1940) originally trained as a doctor before abandoning medicine to pursue journalism.

"Manuscripts don't burn," the most famous phrase from *The Master and Margarita*, is a courageous affirmation of the enduring power of art to survive political oppression.

After Bulgakov's death in 1940, his widow Elena preserved his subversive novel in secret for over a quarter of a century, until a more liberal atmosphere made publication thinkable in Soviet Russia.

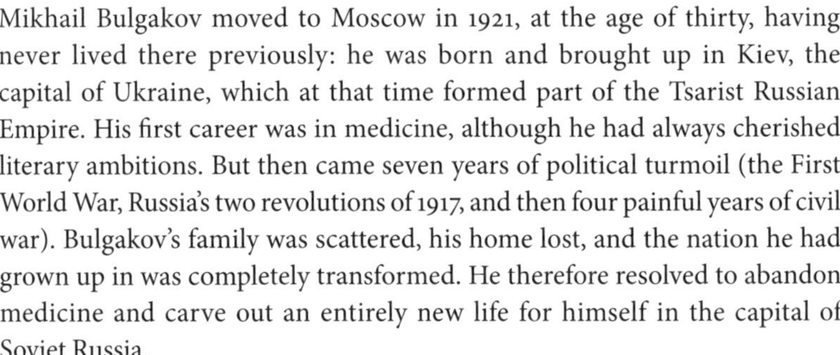

Mikhail Bulgakov moved to Moscow in 1921, at the age of thirty, having never lived there previously: he was born and brought up in Kiev, the capital of Ukraine, which at that time formed part of the Tsarist Russian Empire. His first career was in medicine, although he had always cherished literary ambitions. But then came seven years of political turmoil (the First World War, Russia's two revolutions of 1917, and then four painful years of civil war). Bulgakov's family was scattered, his home lost, and the nation he had grown up in was completely transformed. He therefore resolved to abandon medicine and carve out an entirely new life for himself in the capital of Soviet Russia.

Bulgakov soon became entirely identified with his adopted city. In the early 1920s he wrote humorous sketches of Moscow life, as the Bolsheviks rebuilt the ruined economy and infrastructure of the capital. His first marital home in Moscow was a room in a communal apartment, crammed full of residents squabbling over shared bathroom and kitchen facilities. He detested this apartment (no. 50) at 10 Bol'shaya Sadovaya Street, Moscow's inner-city ring road, which makes it particularly ironic that it has now become the principal Bulgakov museum in the city. Many visitors come especially to see the stairwell, covered in doodles and phrases scrawled there by Bulgakov fans.

In the late 1920s he embarked on the writing of *The Master and Margarita*, a novel unlike any other, in which the Devil Woland investigates the moral standing of Moscow's inhabitants under Communism and metes out retributive justice, along with hilarious mischief. There is a moving love story between Margarita and her lover, the Master, who is persecuted for the novel he has written about Pontius Pilate, a kind of fifth Gospel. After the bravura description of Satan's Spring Ball (closely modelled on a ball at the American Embassy held in April 1935), the narrative takes Woland, the Master, and Margarita to an encounter with Pilate in the afterlife.

There is a discreet level of political satire concerning life in a police state that runs through the text; and the very fact of presenting Christ, Pilate, and Satan as real people offered a defiant challenge to militant Soviet atheism. This explains why it was unthinkable for Bulgakov to offer the novel for publication in his lifetime, particularly as the Terror intensified in the 1930s, and why its existence remained a closely guarded secret for decades thereafter.

The chapters set in the ancient world provide a vivid sense of Pilate in Herod's Palace in Jerusalem, the bustling, volatile city, its cool balconies, narrow, winding lanes near the bazaar, and the oppressive heat on Golgotha during the crucifixion. The modern settings, by contrast, are paradoxically less sensual in their specific detail, but they delineate Bulgakov's Moscow. Foremost amongst these is the small park called Patriarchs' Ponds near Sadovaya Street, essentially a square pond surrounded by shaded alleyways. It is here, as they are sitting on a bench, that the Devil Woland first appears to a couple of Soviet writers, an encounter with a tragic ending involving a recently installed tram.

Bulgakov's former "accursed" apartment on Sadovaya figures as the home to protagonists who will rue their acquaintance with Woland once he and his retinue move in. By contrast, Satan's Spring Ball takes place in a building recognizable as the lavish residence of the American Ambassador, Spaso House. Other locations important to the plot include the Moskva River; the Alexander Gardens along the Kremlin walls; the foreign currency grocery store Torgsin, filled with desirable produce; and the restaurant at Griboedov House, modeled on the real Moscow Writers' Club on Tverskoy Boulevard, and satirized in the novel as a temple of material pleasures rather than true art. And when Woland finally decides to leave the city, he gazes over it at sunset from the parapet of a grand old merchants' residence, Pashkov House, which commands a magnificent view over the entire ensemble of the Kremlin with its red walls and golden-domed churches.

Illustration by Tatyana Alyoshina from the 1976 edition of the book. The Master stands atop the Griboedov House and Margarita over the Pashkov House with its imposing white pillars.

Bulgakov was fascinated by the founding cities of Christendom: ancient Jerusalem; Kiev, the cradle of Christianity in Russia since the tenth century; and Moscow, present-day home of Russian Orthodoxy. In Moscow, the tensions between spiritual values and materialism became especially acute in the Soviet era. Bulgakov's Moscow in *The Master and Margarita* maps that conflict on to the topography of the city.

Map of Bulgakov's Russia by Jamie Whyte showing where the main action in *Master and Margarita* takes place. Koroviev, Behemoth, and Azazello (left to right) from Satan's retinue frame the novel's key locations, such as the burning apartment and the Alexander Gardens.

Bulgakov's

[...]skva

[...]ster and Margarita

The Spectacles Commission

'A certain Moscow Institution'

Hotel Metropol

Margarita meets Azazello

Sadovaya Kol'tso

Sadovaya-Spasskaya Ulitsa

Petrovsky Bul'var

Kreml'

LYME REGIS, DORSET, ENGLAND

JOHN FOWLES

THE FRENCH LIEUTENANT'S WOMAN (1969)

At once a postmodern period romance and a study in the hypocrisy of the Victorian era, this ambitious novel also captures the intricacies of the cozy seaside town that hosts the tale.

John Fowles (1926–2005) retired with his wife and her daughter to Lyme Regis in Dorset in 1965. Here he experienced recurring visions of a woman in black Victorian clothing staring out at sea, which inspired him to write *The French Lieutenant's Woman.*

The metatextual nature of *The French Lieutenant's Woman* made it a challenge to adapt to film, but Harold Pinter was up for it. His screenplay earned one of the film's five Academy Award nominations, as did Meryl Streep's performance as Sarah Woodruff.

By the time the film adaptation came out, the book had sold four million copies.

The French Lieutenant's Woman is a book about contrasts—with the romance between gentleman Charles Smithson and the outcast Sarah Woodruff foremost amongst them. The novel also juxtaposes the primness of Victorian society and its burgeoning sex trade; the glorification of progress and the stasis of the class system; the dependence on trade and the genteel abhorrence of the business. John Fowles's period romance gleefully tilts at the many hypocrisies of the Victorian era.

The peaceful seaside village of Lyme Regis seems like an unlikely host for this turmoil. A half-forgotten town, its defining moment is a fictional stumble—Louisa Musgrove's fall in *Persuasion.* But Lyme, hidden on the beautiful Dorset coast, provides Fowles with a perfect metaphor for the Victorian era, as despite the town's innocuous appearance, it is home to its own conflicts.

At first appearance, the streets of Lyme Regis may seem clean and cheerful, but they serve as a shadowy panopticon. Sarah, frustrated, comments that "I live among people the world tells me are kind, pious, Christian people. And they seem to me crueller than the cruellest heathens, stupider than the stupidest animals." Reigning from their parlors and their pulpits, the town's ruling elite are petty and judgmental tyrants.

Immediately to the west of Lyme Regis lurks the Undercliff, "a dark cascade of trees and undergrowth." The landscape has gone spectacularly awry due to an unlikely landslip; as uncultivated and uncontrollable as the town itself is neatly groomed. The Undercliff is a place of secrets and of rebellion. To even be seen walking there, as Sarah often does, is deemed an improper act. But Fowles notes that the Undercliff is possessed of its own natural beauty. "Flat places are as rare as visitors in it. But this steepness in effect tilts it ... towards the sun." While the good people of Lyme Regis portray it as a dark and shadowy place, the Undercliff is, in actuality, naturally and brilliantly lit.

Fowles is careful to point out that Lyme Regis has remained largely unchanged since Charles's time but there are a few notable exceptions. By the time of writing, he notes, the beautiful Assembly Rooms, the intellectual

Above: Still from the 1981 film adapted by Harold Pinter and directed by Karel Reisz, starring Meryl Streep as Sarah Woodruff and Anna. Streep promised John Fowles that she would not try to explain Sarah, leaving it to viewers to decide her nature.

Previous page: View of the Cobb at dawn, Lyme Regis's iconic stone jetty. Fowles describes the Cobb as "primitive yet complex, elephantine but delicate, as full of subtle curves and volumes as a Henry Moore or a Michaelangelo."

and aesthetic heart of Lyme, have been "sacrificed to the Great British God, Convenience" and become, he adds, "the worst-sited and ugliest public lavatory in the British Isles." This aside isn't solely therapeutic—it reinforces the book's themes of inevitable change, for the better and for the worse. It is also a gentle, if back-handed, compliment: there is something romantic, if not entirely noble, about the passions of Charles and his Victorian ilk.

One of Lyme Regis's many attractions is its location on England's Jurassic Coast—a geological treasure trove for fossil hunters. As an amateur natural historian, Charles finds a rebellious passion in "Darwinism," enjoying the sense of *frisson* that comes from being part of this punk-progressive scientific movement. But in yet another of the book's hypocrisies, Charles is also an elitist, as quietly opposed to social advancement as he is loudly in favor of biological evolution. Lyme is both surrounded by fossils and inhabited by them.

Lyme Regis, with its pocket-sized community and well-defined social strata, encapsulates the tranquility—and the underlying tension—of the Victorian era. Surrounded by its deceptively immutable routine, Charles is blind to the larger picture, that this provincial pocket, and everything it represents, is doomed to extinction. "He was a Victorian. We could not expect him to see what we are only just beginning … to realize ourselves: that the desire to hold and the desire to enjoy are mutually destructive." Those twin impulses underpin the town, the era and, of course, the book's legendary central romance.

LORAIN, OHIO, USA

TONI MORRISON

THE BLUEST EYE (1970)

A story of poverty, human depravity, and cultural measurement, which has come to be regarded as one of the most important novels in the articulation of the black female experience in America in the twentieth century.

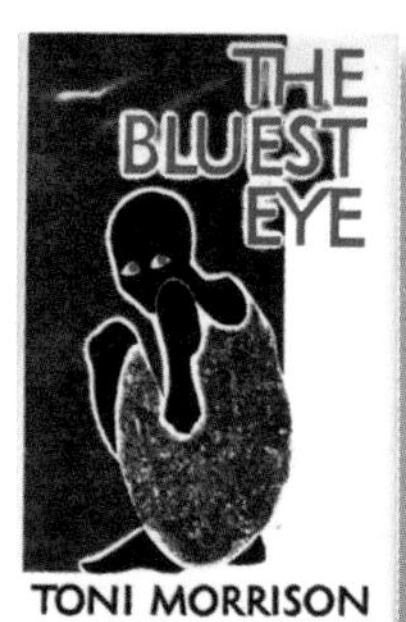

The Bluest Eye is set among the working-class African-American community just after the Great Depression, in the author's home town of Lorain, Ohio, during the early 1940s. The then small, industrialized town, now a small city, is situated at the mouth of Lake Erie and later became part of what is now known as America's Rust Belt.

The main theme of this short, melancholic book is of the self-hatred engendered by racism, with whiteness, and blond hair and blue eyes in particular, setting the standard for accepted beauty. Eleven-year-old Pecola Breedlove believes—and is encouraged to believe—that because she is black she is ugly, and therefore cannot be beautiful, or loved—and indeed, her life is one of violence and disaster, with even the most hopeful, ravishing elements of the natural world around her being used systematically as objects as punishment: "the spring is shot through with the remembered ache of switchings and forsythia holds no cheer. Sunk in the grass of an empty lot on a spring Saturday I split the stems of milkweed and thought about … death and where the world went when I closed my eyes."

Toni Morrison was born in Lorain at 2245 Elyria Avenue, a two-storey frame house with a backyard full of weeds, very close to Lake Erie. Morrison used this house as a setting in *The Bluest Eye*, as well as a rundown store downtown, which became, in the novel, the home of the Breedlove family. "There is an abandoned store on the southeast corner of Broadway and Thirty-fifth Street in Lorain, Ohio," she wrote. "It does not recede into its background of leaden sky, nor harmonize with the gray frame houses and black telephone poles around it. Rather, it foists itself on the eye of the passerby in a manner that is both irritating and melancholy."

The Bluest Eye is a novel about seeing and being seen, about invisibility and privilege, still as relevant in America today as it was in 1970 or 1941. The language of the urban dispossessed in poor neighborhoods, of lack of space, of the freedom of the outdoors, and being perpetually stuck in a cycle of privation is urgent, yet reflective:

Toni Morrison was born into a working-class African-American family in Lorain, Ohio, in 1931. She studied at Howard and Cornell universities, became the first black senior woman editor in book publishing, and published the first of her powerful novels on race and the African-American experience from 1970 onward.

Morrison was awarded the Nobel Prize in Literature in 1993, the first African-American writer to be given the accolade.

Since its publication, the book has been controversial in the US for its graphic depiction of sexual assault.

Toni Morrison, born Chloe Wofford (second row, third from left), was the only African-American girl in her class of 1949 at Lorain High School. Photograph from the Lorain Historical Society.

> Knowing that there was such a thing as outdoors bred in us a hunger for property, for ownership. … Propertied black people spent all their energies, all their love, on their nests. Like frenzied, desperate birds, they overdecorated everything; fussed and fidgeted over their hard-won homes … And these houses loomed like hothouse sunflowers among the rows of weeds that were the rented houses.

Morrison has a way of taking beauty into every line, calling up the attention she remembered having been paid in her own family to African-American heritage and language through folk tales, stories, and singing; an extraordinary recollection of a place and a time, the Midwest of America in the middle of the twentieth century, where joy and oppression coexist. The most autobiographical of her works, *The Bluest Eye* subtly addresses the impact of racial segregation in the US. The former Confederate States (the thirteen secessionist slave-holding states) of the South, segregated US citizens in public spaces by means of dehumanizing race legislation, known as the Jim Crow Laws, from 1861 until as late as 1965. For this reason many African-Americans—including Morrison's own family, the Woffords, like Pecola's parents Pauline and Cholly Breedlove in the novel—migrated from Alabama and Georgia, respectively. Yet as "transplanted Southerners" they were to quickly discover that there was, as Morrison later put it, a pernicious "de facto segregation" at work in the supposedly more liberal states—and also among the black community itself. This is the controversial seed from which *The Bluest Eye* grows.

PELLINKI ARCHIPELAGO, FINLAND

TOVE JANSSON

THE SUMMER BOOK

(SOMMARBOKEN) (1972)

A vivid, simple yet surprisingly profound novel about the summer experiences of an old woman and her six-year-old granddaughter on a tiny island in the Gulf of Finland.

For Tove Jansson, life on an island represented freedom. She loved the sea, and wrote to a friend, "You become different and think new thoughts when you live a long time alone with the sea and yourself." In an essay on "The Island" in 1961 she wrote, "An astonishing number of people go about dreaming of an island."

Tove Jansson (1914–2001), author and artist, was the daughter of two professional artists who belonged to the Swedish-speaking population of Finland.

She is internationally famous as the writer and illustrator of a series of books for children about the Moomins, which have been translated into 35 languages.

In 1947, Tove fulfilled her dream when she signed a 50-year lease to Bredskär, a tiny island in the Pellinki archipelago. She spent the summer living in a tent and working on a new Moomin book while she built a one-room wooden cabin. She called the house *Vindrosen* or "Windrose" (the name for a diagram showing the relative frequency of wind directions). It measured just four yards by five and had windows on three sides. (Later it was expanded just enough to include a "guest room" and veranda.)

Her mother, father, and brother Lars joined her when the house was finished; another brother, Per Olov, had his own summer place on a nearby island. Bredskär could get very crowded with relatives and visiting friends. In 1963, she finally managed to get permission to build on another tiny island, the barren rock of Klovharu, where she built a house to share with her long-term companion Tuulikki Pietila. Neither Bredskär nor Klovharu was the island of Tove's dreams. She always dreamed of living and tending the lights on Kummelskär, which had two beacons and was the largest and most beautiful island in the chain.

The island in *The Summer Book* is not named, but it is obviously Bredskär, and the three main characters were based on the author's mother, her brother Lars, and his daughter, Sophia.

Visitors to Bredskär may be surprised by its size: it is possible to walk all the way around the island in five minutes. In the novel we are permitted to share a child's view, in which everything seems larger and more mysterious. As she walks with her grandmother across "the ravine" of bare granite boulders, Sophia exclaims, "I've never been this far before."

Most of the island has been turned into "an orderly, beautiful park," with paths that spare the beautiful, delicate carpet of moss, and a tidy, sand beach,

Jansson wrote the book in this cottage, which she built just below the cliff top on Klovharu, a small rocky island in the Gulf of Finland. She spent many summers at the cottage and also based her more well-known Moomin series on the island.

but wilderness remains in "the magic forest," a thicket of spruce trees forced into strange, distorted shapes by the winds, and in the hidden bogs.

The surrounding sea and neighboring islands where the family goes adventuring, are equally important, as is the weather. When bored, Sophia prays for something to happen, and gets a storm. She is thrilled, enjoying witnessing and surviving the destructive power of the wind. An island may be tidied up and built upon, but nature is never conquered.

The Summer Book is a celebration of the wild beauty of the Gulf of Finland with its multitude of rocky skerries and tiny islands. It depicts a way of life familiar to Scandinavians, and was an immediate success in Sweden and Finland, where it was embraced as a celebration of summer, the time of year when Scandinavians feel they come back to life after the long, dark nights of winter. Yet Tove Jansson should not have been surprised when it also proved popular abroad. Its appeal is universal. It is a beautifully judged story of relationships between generations, about growing up and growing old, and the conflict between our desire for comfort and need for freedom.

Sophia and Grandmother sat down by the shore to discuss the matter further. It was a pretty day, and the sea was running a long, windless swell. It was on days just like this—dog days—that boats went sailing off all by themselves. Large, alien objects made their way in from sea, certain things sank and others rose, milk soured, and dragonflies danced in desperation.

SOLOVETSKY ISLANDS, WHITE SEA, RUSSIA

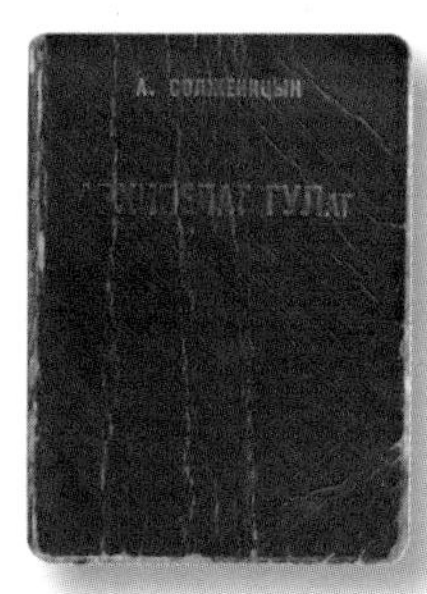

ALEKSANDR SOLZHENITSYN

THE GULAG ARCHIPELAGO (ARKHIPELÁG GULÁG) (1973)

Far exceeding personal narrative in scale and scope, Solzhenitsyn's monumental chronicle of the Soviet prison camp system demands not just reading as a book but understanding as an event in world literature and political culture.

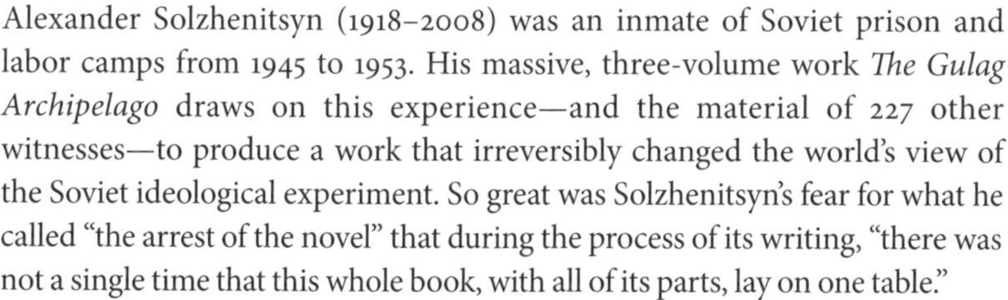

Alexander Solzhenitsyn (1918–2008) was an inmate of Soviet prison and labor camps from 1945 to 1953. His massive, three-volume work *The Gulag Archipelago* draws on this experience—and the material of 227 other witnesses—to produce a work that irreversibly changed the world's view of the Soviet ideological experiment. So great was Solzhenitsyn's fear for what he called "the arrest of the novel" that during the process of its writing, "there was not a single time that this whole book, with all of its parts, lay on one table."

Written between 1958 and 1968, *The Gulag Archipelago* was smuggled out of the Soviet Union to the West on microfilm in June 1968.

The Gulag Archipelago was first published in Paris, in English, by the YMCA Press—an event that led to its author's deportation from the Soviet Union on 13 February 1974. Its first official publication in Russian came in late 1989.

In September 2009, *The Gulag Archipelago* was included in Russia's high school literature curriculum.

The metaphor of the title describes a vast landscape, an archipelago of islands that form the "amazing country of Gulag," the network of forced labour camps that extended across Soviet territory. Solzhenitsyn's work added a new word to the international lexicon; *GULag* had been a little-known Soviet acronym referring to the management of the prison camp system (Main Administration of Corrective Labor Camps and Colonies) but now came to designate the individual camps themselves.

Far from being confined to the remote, blank expanses of Siberia or Central Asia, "this Archipelago crisscrossed and patterned that other country within which it was located, like a gigantic patchwork cutting into its cities, hovering over its streets." Indeed, most of Solzhenitsyn's first year of imprisonment was spent in Moscow, in proximity to the city's main parks and boulevards.

If there is one emblematic setting of *The Gulag Archipelago*, it is the Solovetsky Islands (also known as Solovki), lying just south of the Arctic Circle in the White Sea. Solovki was, in Solzhenitsyn's words, the "mother of the Gulag," the site of a "Special Purpose Camp" that operated from 1923 to 1933. But Solovki's carceral history extends far back: the Solovetsky monastery was founded there in the fifteenth century, soon growing into a wealthy monastic center of spiritual and military-strategic importance, including the imprisonment of religious and political heretics.

The monastery was dissolved in the early years of Soviet rule (and re-established in 1990). As monastic center, Solovki's solitude and marvellous natural setting inspired prayerful contemplation; as prison camp, the harshness of nature was unleashed by a darker imagination to add to the

Photograph of the Russian entrance to the forced labor camp of the Moscow-Volga Canal (1935–1943), guarded by the GPU.

torture of those imprisoned here. It was on Solovki that many aspects of prison camp administration solidified, including the principle that the labor of the camp system could be economically profitable. Solovki was the original archipelago—the archipelago that "metastasized" and spread insidiously through the Soviet Union.

Solovki is described in a chapter called "The Archipelago Rises from the Sea" which situates the landscape outside of the usual diurnal rhythms of human life and within the geological time of its glacial formation:

> On the White Sea, where the nights are white for half a year at a time, Bolshoi Solovetsky Island lifts its white churches from the water within the ring of its bouldered kremlin wall, rusty-red with the lichens which have struck root there—and the grayish-white Solovetsky seagulls hover continually over the kremlin and screech... Without us these isles rose from the sea; without us they acquired a couple of hundred lakes replete with fish... The glaciers came and went, the granite boulders littered the shores of the lakes.

There is no singular setting of *The Gulag Archipelago*. A non-fiction work of documentary, memoir, and history it may be, but its landscape is an

Painting of a Gulag 'zombie' by Igor Obrosov (1930–2010), whose work was shaped by his experiences of the Stalinist purges during the 1930s and 1940s. One of many paintings that were forbidden in the USSR and only came to light after the fall, it depicts the horrors of life in the Gulag.

imagined geography. Solzhenitsyn's "experiment in literary investigation" challenged its original readers to piece together "an almost invisible, almost imperceptible country" and still challenges its readers today as tangible, material traces of the Gulag have receded, decayed, or been wiped away.

Today, Solovki is a popular destination for Russians and odd handfuls of adventurous foreigners. The layers of the past are uneasily accumulated here, the frames through which one looks uneasily aligned. Pilgrims, sightseers, whale watchers all arrive on boats accompanied by the circling gulls, eager for the first glimpse of the monastery, with its clusters of delicate onion domes surrounded by the mighty walls. Just as Solzhenitsyn describes, built environment and landscape merge: the fortifications are constructed from Solovki granite, the material offered up by the glacial islands, material that is still living, with its covering of orange-red lichen. But the lichens are being removed from the kremlin walls in ongoing "restoration" work, a violence that disregards and wipes away an ecologically fragile life form and wipes clean a historical landscape.

1975–PRESENT

4 Contemporary Geographies

From sinister sprawling metropolises to diverse emergent neighborhoods, the city, in all its color and confusion, is often the site of these contemporary grapplings with the meaning of place. But beyond the urban, secluded islets and indomitable ice fields raise the same questions: to what extent do we shape our environment, and to what extent does our environment condition us?

SAN FRANCISCO, USA

ARMISTEAD MAUPIN

TALES OF THE CITY (1978)

A rambunctious chronicle of life in 1970s San Francisco, Maupin's bestselling medley of tales became a cultural touchstone for the LGBT movement, as well as an iconic and much-loved portrait of the Californian city.

Armistead Maupin (born 1944) grew up in North Carolina, moving to San Francisco in 1971 to take up a position as a reporter at the Associated Press bureau there. The author of nine novels, including the six-volume *Tales of the City* series, he still lives in San Francisco, his adopted city.

Prior to its novelization, *Tales of the City* was published as installments in the *Pacific Sun* and the *San Francisco Chronicle* in 1976.

Tales of the City was first published as a novel in 1978, and has since sold over six million copies worldwide.

Heaven, an angel informs a character in Tony Kushner's dramatic epic *Angels in America,* is "a city much like San Francisco." If that's true, the version of San Francisco most likely to be reproduced in paradise is Armistead Maupin's. For four decades, Maupin's *Tales of the City,* nine novels that began as a serialized column in the *San Francisco Chronicle,* spun an image of the city that has charmed, comforted, and enchanted readers around the globe. The *Tales* are a twisty soap opera, filled with disguises, long-lost relatives, deep dark secrets, and such preposterous narrative devices as amnesia, but they were also grounded in the real world of everyday San Franciscan life. A journalist when he began them, Maupin ventured to a disco called Dance Your Ass Off and a supermarket renowned as a pick-up spot to research the first of the *Tales* in 1976. He wrapped things up in 2014 by camping out at Burning Man, a trippy, sybaritic festival staged every year in the Black Rock Desert of Nevada.

The original goal of the *Tales,* Maupin has said, was "an elaborate inside joke on the way life worked in San Francisco." In the late 1970s, that meant a peculiar combination of stuffy, old-school Pacific Heights socialites (San Francisco has long regarded itself as the sophisticated superior to the vulgar megalopolis to the south) and the giddy explosion of gay liberation happening in the Castro, with a dash of leftover hippiedom for good measure. Maupin himself moved easily among all these milieus. Raised in the South as an "uptight, archconservative, racist brat," he worked briefly for the notoriously bigoted senator Jesse Helms. Not long after arriving in San Francisco at the age of 27, Maupin came out of the closet and into his own. His characters, like their author, are reborn in the city; it's the place people head to when they're finally ready to be themselves, where a thousand freak flags fly to general applause.

Previously, the fictions most closely identified with the city were Dashiell Hammett's Sam Spade novels, chiaroscuro depictions of a city where the grittiness of a gold-rush boomtown still lingered, and the melancholy nostalgic trance of Alfred Hitchcock's *Vertigo.* Despite the lovelorn nights and frustrated dreams that sometimes afflict Maupin's pilgrims, the joy of the freedom and

"She rose and went to the window, confronting a panorama of almost ludicrous exoticism: the sylvan slope of Telegraph Hill, the creed grandeur of a Norwegian freighter, the bold blue sweep of the bay." The view of Telegraph Hill, c.1975, that Maupin's characters experience in the *Tales*.

fellowship they find with each other suffuses the *Tales*. The city may be wrapped in fog, but for Maupin, its heart remains fundamentally sunny.

For the first several novels, the *Tales* centered around 28 Barbary Lane, a boarding house on one of San Francisco's 670 pedestrian and stairway streets. (Maupin modeled Barbary Lane on Russian Hill's Macondray Lane.) The landlady, Anna Madrigal, discreetly cultivates a fine strain of sinsemilla and plays mother hen to her young tenants, adroitly intervening now and then to nudge them back on the right track. Four of them—Mary Ann, Michael (nicknamed Mouse and modeled on Maupin himself), Brian, and Mona—became mainstays of the series, but the *Tales* have no traditional protagonist. Maupin's short chapters ping from character to character, storyline to storyline, a half-dozen pots perpetually on the boil. There are bad guys—a closeted bisexual heartbreaker, a sleazy society-magazine editor, a man so normal he can't be up to anything good—but the series' most fearsome antagonist, the AIDS virus, lay a few years in the unforeseeable future. When the crisis hit, Maupin was one of the first popular novelists to face it head-on.

The house was on Barbary Lane, a narrow, wooded walkway off Leavenworth between Union and Filbert. It was a well-weathered, three-story structure made of brown shingles. It made Mary Ann think of an old bear with bits of foliage caught in its fur. She liked it instantly.

Michael loses his lover to the disease. AIDS makes the idyll of the first three volumes of the *Tales* seem even rosier in retrospect.

For non-San Franciscans, the city of Maupin's *Tales* is a little like the Emerald City of Oz, a kind of fantasy. For anyone who has ever lived there, and especially those who lived there during the heyday of the *Tales,* the books are Proustian madeleines in printed form. From the Irish coffees Mary Ann downs in the Buena Vista Cafe (where the cocktail was invented) while working up the courage to move to the city on the very first page, to the Wonder Bread plant on Bryant Street that once perfumed its industrial neighborhood with the chemical aroma of Twinkies snack cakes, to the ferris wheel spinning atop the (now defunct) Emporium department store at Christmas time, to the Swiss orange chip served at Swensen's Ice Cream Parlor—the *Tales* nail down hundreds of small, palpable details of life in San Francisco at the end of the twentieth century and the beginning of the twenty-first. Beach Blanket Babylon, Sam Woh's, the Mabuhay Gardens: these are names to conjure with, but so specific to their time and place that San Franciscans are often startled to learn how dearly the *Tales* are cherished by those who have never set foot in the place. Tour guides still lead visiting fans down Macondray Lane and to other sites that figure in the novels, but many of them have vanished. Along the way, Maupin's San Francisco really did become a fantasy. Silicon Valley wealth has priced out most of the bohemians, dreamers, and artists; today, someone like Mary Ann could never land an affordable room in Russian Hill at the spur of the moment, or at all. Then, in 2012, the cruelest blow of all fell: Maupin and his husband left the city for Santa Fe. San Francisco had lost its bard. But two years later, in a *Tales*-worthy twist, he moved back again, and announced the production of an updated sequel to the beloved television miniseries based on the books. The happiest ending is that the *Tales* never ended at all.

EARL LOVELACE

THE DRAGON CAN'T DANCE (1979)

Set among the shanty-town dwellers of Laventille in Port of Spain, Trinidad and Tobago's capital, the novel explores their dreams and resilient creativity, along with social, political, and ethnic tensions, through Carnival.

Exploring the profound meaning of Carnival for a range of characters at a time of political change, *The Dragon Can't Dance* is set in the shanty town in Laventille in Port of Spain. The eponymous dragon "mas player" is Aldrick Prospect, whose love for the 17-year-old mas princess Sylvia is a factor in his indecision as to whether to continue to masquerade as a warrior-rebel in dragon costume, as he does every year at Carnival. Sylvia, meanwhile, wavers romantically between the impoverished Aldrick and the landlord Guy, who buys her Carnival costume. The action begins during a lull in fighting between steelband gangs, when Aldrick and others mount a challenge to the government.

Laventille was the birthplace of steel pan music and steelbands. Drums were banned by the British colonial authorities in the nineteenth century, and steel pan evolved from first beating bamboo, pots, and dustbins, then converting oil drums into tuneable musical instruments. In the early 1960s, the author lived in a rented house in Laventille Road—the novel's "asphalt lane slashed across this mountain's face"—which meanders steeply up the eastern slopes of Port of Spain. Lovelace would hear steel pan beating up the hill, and was struck by how "muscular and energetic" the neighborhood was, "not just a placid place"*—a rhythm and energy that infuse *The Dragon Can't Dance.*

A Prologue in three parts, "The Hill", "Carnival" and "Calypso," sets the scene in the melodious, Creolized English of islands successively colonized by the Spanish, French, and British:

> This is the hill, Calvary Hill, where the sun set on starvation and rise on potholed roads … Laughter is not laughter; it is a groan coming from the bosom of these houses—no—not houses, shacks that leap out of the red dust and stone, thin like smoke, fragile like kite paper, balancing on their rickety pillars as broomsticks on the edge of a juggler's nose.

Born in 1935 in Trinidad, Earl Lovelace is one of few leading West Indian writers to have spent his life in the Caribbean. His work has been translated into German, Dutch, French, Hungarian, and Japanese.

This Caribbean classic was first published in 1979 by André Deutsch (London).

The Dragon Can't Dance was the author's third novel, following *While Gods Are Falling* (1965) and *The Schoolmaster* (1968).

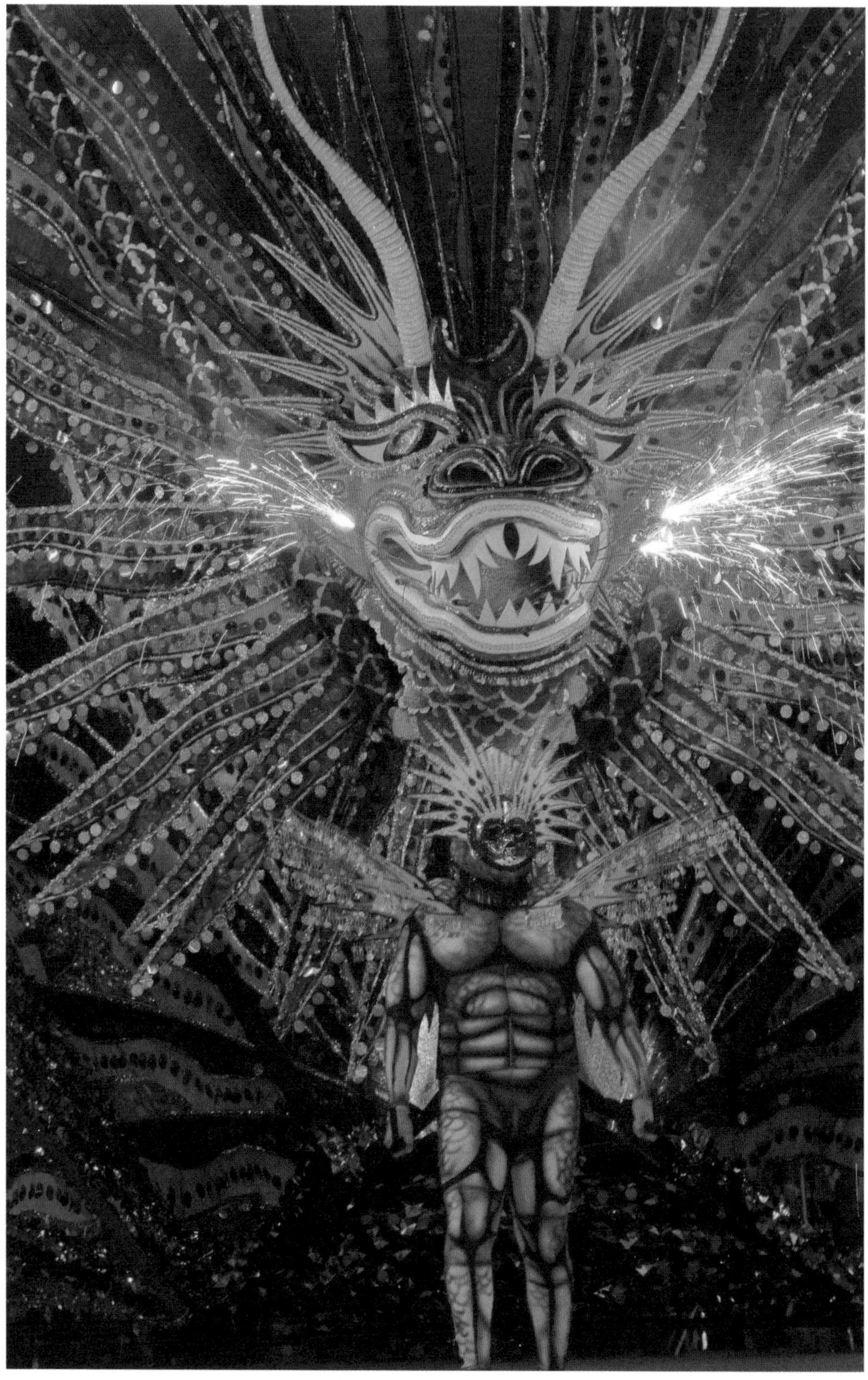

Set, with pointed irony, "one hundred and twenty-five years after Emancipation," and straddling Trinidad's independence in 1962, the novel is as firmly located in history as it is in place. Laventille was founded by formerly enslaved Africans who, lacking the land or compensation granted to slaveowners at Emancipation in 1834, abandoned the plantations to squat on the edge of the city. As the novel has it, "refusing to be grist for the mill of the colonial machinery that kept on grinding in its belly people to spit out sugar and cocoa and copra, they turned up this hill to pitch camp here on the eyebrow of the enemy." They were joined by other West Indian islanders seeking work, and by some descendants of indentured East Indians and Chinese—a cultural pluralism the novel scrutinizes. Emancipation, it suggests, was incomplete. Laventille's children, "their wise yellowed eyes filled with malnutrition and too early knowing," are heirs to "a resistance lived by their ancestors all through slavery, carried on in their unceasing escape—as Maroons, as Runways, as Bush Negroes, as Rebels."

Rebellion and cultural resistance are integral to Carnival, the annual pre-Lenten parade through Port of Spain that lends the novel its aesthetic form. It originated in parody of the eighteenth-century French plantocracy's masked balls—and was banned during the Second World War.

Carnival folk arts were largely banned under British colonial law when Lovelace was growing up. Yet, working in rural Trinidad as a forest ranger in the mid-1950s, and later for the agricultural department, he formed a "relationship with the countryside and the community's traditions—bongo, stick-fighting, dancing, songs, tales, which I'd have missed if I just went in a scholastic line. I gambled with the fellars on the corner, danced, played in the football team." He "learned who the people in the town were from knowing them intimately in the countryside. I could see them up close and that they were no different to me. That made me see who they were—people who'd been hard done by and were aggrieved; the rebelliousness of the youth who had every right to be rebellious."

Characters are introduced episodically as though in a masquerade procession—several at a point of crisis or dilemma. Aldrick, who walks with a "slow, cruising crawl which he quickened only at Carnival," is contemplating whether to abandon the role of artist-warrior and settle down. Yet he feels a sacred duty to the people of the hill, "to let them see their beauty, to uphold the unending rebellion they waged, huddled here on this stone and dirt hill hanging over the city like the open claws on a dragon's hand, threatening a destruction if they were not recognized as human beings." Philo the Calypsonian (modelled on The Mighty Sparrow) struggles to preserve the integrity of his art form's spontaneous political commentary amid debasing pressures to entertain. Fisheye, the dockworker and "bad John" (thug) stick-fighter, also wrestles as a steelband-man with commercial sponsorship that would separate warrior from musician. Drawn to the new political party but disillusioned by the PNM in power, he leads the thwarted revolt that lands Aldrick and himself in jail. This episode alludes to the failure of the black

Opposite: Elaborate costumes define the exuberant display at the carnival in Port of Spain, which takes place each year on the Monday and Tuesday before Ash Wednesday.

nationalist movement that swept the Caribbean in the late 1960s and early '70s, in which the author was an activist and commentator.

Besides Sylvia, residents of the novel's Alice Street, "named for Princess Alice, the Queen's aunt," include Miss Cleothilda, a "mulatto woman" with a parlor grocery store and snobbish pretensions as the Carnival Queen; and Pariag, an East Indian newcomer from rural New Lands. Pariag dreams of a world in which "flute, sitar and steel drum blend harmoniously," but "we didn't have to melt into one." Yet his ill-fated efforts to fit into the Creole community expose cracks in the fiction that "all o' we is one."

Though lightly fictionalized, the locales are real. Calvary Hill—recalled by the author as a "road with winding steps" which he used "as a hill for atonement"—is today a steep path with stations of the cross marked by bronze reliefs in brick niches. Much of the action centers on Miss Cleothilda's yard—a Caribbean open-air living space typically adjacent to tenements or shacks. Unlike Port of Spain's concrete barrack yards, Laventille's are dirt. This one was modelled on an "ordinary two-storey house with a courtyard to the side" where the author lived in another populous district, Belmont.

> Up on the hill with Carnival coming, radios go on full blast, trembling these shacks, booming out calypsos, the songs that announce in this season the new rhythms for people to walk in, rhythms that climb over the red dirt and stone, break-away rhythms that laugh through the groans of these sights, these smells, that swim through the bones of these enduring people so that they shout: Life!

The "Savannah" alludes to the Queen's Park Savannah, the city's green expanse where Carnival culminates. Its grand Edwardian mansions are now joined by the steel-and-glass curves of the National Academy for the Performing Arts, clearly visible from Laventille's slopes.

With improved infrastructure and amenities, big houses as well as teetering shacks, today's Laventille is a cradle of talent, from soca (soul-calypso) singers to soccer stars. Yet it has high unemployment and the stigma of danger—not a place for tourists to "lime." At the summit stands an arena and panyard purpose built for the Desperadoes—a champion steelband that features in the novel. Their rehearsals used to stop traffic. Yet they abandoned the hill because of rising violence. The novel has gangs fighting over territory in the "war days, when every street corner was a garrison," and the "scream of police jeeps" bringing "ritual harassment."

This fictional masterpiece uncovers the profound meaning of Carnival for those who possess nothing but themselves. In so doing, it humanizes and historicizes an urban landscape more often dismissed as a perilous slum.

FERNANDO PESSOA

THE BOOK OF DISQUIET
(LIVRO DO DESASSOSSEGO) (1982)

A collection of musings, maxims and dark meanderings that maps Lisbon's own wandering thoroughfares, Pessoa's masterpiece is crowded with the thoughts and things of the Portuguese city.

The Book of Disquiet was first published in Lisbon in 1982, forty-two years after Pessoa's death. In 1991 the first English translation appeared. The book is a collection of about 500 fragmentary fictional ruminations by Bernardo Soares: he is one of Pessoa's "heteronyms," a term he used to refer to imaginary writers who signed his works, dismantling the notion of a unified writerly identity. Bernardo is an assistant bookkeeper, misogynous, and at times racist, who yearns for the Portuguese imperial past present in the buildings of Lisbon. He is also a writer. Pessoa describes Soares as a mutilated version of himself "without reason and emotion." Not coincidentally, Pessoa locates Soares's office in the Rua dos Douradores, where Pessoa once lived.

Fernando António Nogueira Pessoa (1888–1935) was a native of Lisbon and the best-known modern Portuguese author. A prolific writer, he only published one book in his lifetime: *Messagem*, in 1934, the year before his death.

Pessoa's enormous body of work (in English and French as well as in Portuguese) is still being published. *The Book of Disquiet*, considered Pessoa's most important work in prose, was never a book in his lifetime. It was arranged posthumously from 25,000 loose manuscripts found in three trunks. Each edition reorders and reinvents it.

Pessoa and Lisbon are inseparable, personally and symbolically. The city proclaims its devotion to the author in a museum, street plaques, and a famous statue of the writer sitting in the terrace of the renowned café A Brasileira. He lived in this hilly coastal city situated on the geographic and political periphery of Europe during most of his life, except for a few years of his youth spent in South Africa. He knew it intimately, loved it, walked it, observed it, and wrote in its cafés. He celebrated it in poems and wrote a guidebook in English. Indeed, the *Book*'s first sentence reads like a travel guide's description: "Há em Lisboa um pequeno número de restaurants ou casas de pasto que..." ("There are in Lisbon a small number of restaurants or eating houses that...").

In spite of the descriptive opening sentence, in *The Book of Disquiet* the real Lisbon vanishes into literature as both the target of a "pathetic fallacy" and the stage on which the condition of the artist in the emergent modern city is displayed. The reader is denied realistic access to Lisbon because the city is exclusively presented through the melancholic gaze of the protagonist for whom, in its liveliness, Lisbon appears as an "other." City gardens, balconies perched on the city, the mighty Tejo River, are excuses for his meditations, screens where he projects his mood.

Inevitably, the Lisbon that emerges is rainy, gloomy, full of *saudade*—that Portuguese version of nostalgia. Like *The Book of Disquiet* itself,

CAMPO GRANDE
ALVALADE
SETE RIOS
BAIRRO DO ALTO DA SARAFINA
BAIRRO DA CALÇADA DOS MESTRES
CAMPOLIDE
AMOREIRAS
ESTEFÂNIA
ANJOS
Parque
Eduardo VII
Rua Joaquim António de Aguiar
RATO
ESTRELA
MADRAGOA
LAPA
ALCÂNTARA
BAIXA
ALFAMA
Avenida Professor Egas Moniz

No, others don't exist...It's for me that this heavy-winged sunset lingers, its colours hard and hazy. It's for me that the great river shimmers below the sunset, even if I can't see it flow. It's for me that this square was built overlooking the river, whose waters are now rising.

this Lisbon, in the words of the famous critic George Steiner, "lovingly cultivates sadness."

The social and personal transformations in consciousness elicited by cities is a central theme in the works of writers that Pessoa admired, such as Charles Baudelaire, T. S. Eliot, and Edgar Allan Poe. Lisbon in the *Book* is both a metropolis that produces anonymous crowds, transience, and loneliness, and an "uncertain and silent" muse for the artist who wanders through it alone and observant. City dwellers also provide Soares with a sea of faces among which to hide as a flâneur in Lisbon. The flâneurs ("saunterers," "strollers") were a new type of urban artists who knew cities very well and wrote about them. French poet Baudelaire and German critic Walter Benjamin famously studied them in, respectively, the nineteenth and twentieth centuries.

The activity of exploring Lisbon as a flâneur provides a precise example of how to read *The Book of Disquiet*. Because of the "virtual" character of this book (Pessoa did not leave any indications as to how it should be edited), readers are invited to navigate it in whatever order they choose, to skip, to return, to never visit sections of it. In sum, they are invited to wander through this book as one should visit Lisbon, a city with an extremely distinct personality, full of narrow streets and unsuspected hidden corners: slowly, at ease, without direction, without expectations, open to discoveries. Some readers might, and do, consider *The Book of Disquiet* the work of a genius, a shaman of modernity; others might see it as a collection of decadent hallucinations by a depressed fictional writer. The *Book* can be either loved or hated at first sight. But those who wander through it with calm and open eyes encounter unforgettably luminous corners.

Opposite: Produced by BoWo Studio, this 'human cartography' map creates a portrait of Fernando Pessoa using the streets of Lisbon.

WEST AND EAST BERLIN, GERMANY

PETER SCHNEIDER

THE WALL JUMPER

(DER MAUERSPRINGER) (1983)

In Cold War Berlin, an unnamed narrator travels back and forth between East and West, meeting friends and collecting stories about the Wall that divides the city.

Born in the north German port of Lübeck in 1940, Peter Schneider started out as a political moderate, writing speeches in the mid-1960s for the future chancellor of West Germany Willy Brandt; but he took a sharp turn to the left. He trained as a teacher, but was banned for three years from working in West German schools because of his radical politics.

The Wall Jumper was the first of several books Schneider has written that revolve around the split between East and West Germany, including *The German Comedy* (1991) and *Berlin Now* (2014).

Though it is advertized as a novel, *The Wall Jumper* barely meets the criteria—not that that makes it any less enthralling. Over the course of 135 pages, the unnamed narrator travels back and forth between his home in West Berlin and friends in the East, looking for stories about people who have crossed the Berlin Wall. He hears the story of Willy, Willy, and Lutz, three boys in East Berlin who, shortly after the Wall was built, found a route over and took to making a weekly crossing to watch westerns at the cinema; he hears about the East German who came West to embark on a campaign of sabotage against Communism, and got so ensnared in the world of intelligence and double agents that he forgot which side he was on; and he hears about Mr Kabe, the wall jumper, an unemployed West Berliner who won't admit the Wall is any kind of obstacle and just can't stop hopping over it. The book has no proper beginning or ending; and while there are incidents comic and dramatic and hints of romance, they seem mostly to be happening to someone else, or at some other time.

But then, a plot would not be in keeping with the spirit of the book, which is about how Berlin became a city in a bubble, suspended from the world and time. After Germany was split in two at the end of the Second World War, Berlin remained an island of capitalism in the Communist East. In 1961, the East German government closed the border and threw up the Wall, cutting the city in two and leaving the capitalist Western half isolated. For nearly 30 years, until November 1989, Berlin remained what Peter Schneider's narrator calls a "Siamese city," each half with its distinct character, but locked together.

The book starts as a conventional travelogue, describing how Berlin appears to the traveler arriving from the west by air, as the plane circles over the city to approach the airport from the east:

> Seen from the air, the city appears perfectly homogeneous. Nothing suggests to the stranger that he is nearing a region where two political continents collide. The overriding impression is of a linear order, which derives from the rectangle and rules out any bending. In the centre of

> the city, the apartment buildings are massed like fortresses. ... Berliners commonly call these apartments houses apartment barracks, an expression which accurately conveys the architects' inspiration.

Even on the ground, the Wall that divides the city can seem elusive: on maps in West Berlin, it is shown as a dotted, delicate pink band, while East Berlin maps simply stop short at the Wall, refusing to acknowledge that anything lies beyond.

In spy films of the 1960s and 1970s, the East is dingy and straitlaced compared with the prosperous, fun-loving West. In keeping with that, on his first trips over the Wall, the narrator notices the characteristic odor: "a smell of fuel mix, disinfectants, hot railroad tracks, mixed vegetables, and railroad terminal." But as he passes over the border more often, he starts to notice symmetries, to feel that perhaps the citizens of both halves are interchangeable.

At times, he describes the city in the most concrete, precise terms possible. The Wall, for instance:

> The ring around West Berlin is 102.5 miles in length. Of this, 65.8 miles consist of concrete slabs topped with pipe; another 34 miles is constructed of stamped metal fencing. Two hundred sixty watchtowers stand along the border ring, manned day and night by twice that many border guards. The towers are linked by a tarred military road, which runs within the border strip. To the right and left of the road, a carefully raked stretch of sand conceals trip wires; flares go off if anything touches them. Should this happen, jeeps stand ready for the borders troops, and dogs are stationed at 267 dog runs along the way.

But this only emphasizes the shadowy, abstract atmosphere that hangs over the book. This is a place of rumors, stories that may or may not be true—does it matter, as along as they make a point? The narrator lives surrounded by shadow people, neighbors whose footsteps he hears, but who he never sees. A friend in the East points out the graffiti—blotted out by the authorities before the artist could write more than four letters; but sometimes they even make it to five: the narrator tries in vain to guess the hidden word.

Easterners who have come West bring with them a scepticism—when the narrator and his friend Robert are caught up in a violent demonstration, Robert, brought up in a world of informers and secret police, is convinced it must be fake, the police smashing things to justify their own authority. Passing back and forth in this looking-glass world, puzzling over what is real, the reader begins to share the narrator's sense of being stuck in a half-life, where nothing can ever change. But of course, in the end, it did.

Overleaf: A section of the Berlin Wall painted by Gabriel Heimler depicting a wall jumper, or "Mauerspringer." This mural forms part of the memorial known as the East Side Gallery, the longest stretch of the wall to have been preserved.

Heimler
Stuttgart

NEW YORK CITY, USA

JAY MCINERNEY

BRIGHT LIGHTS, BIG CITY (1984)

Set in early 1980s New York, this is a week in the life of a young would-be writer nursing a long list of private hurts that send him on a spree of club hopping and drug taking that costs him his job at a prestigious magazine and ultimately his self-respect.

Jay McInerney was born in 1955 in Connecticut. He moved to New York in 1979. He completed his first draft of *Bright Lights, Big City* in six weeks in 1983. The manuscript was accepted for publication by Random House, who offered a huge advance of $7500. It made him an instant literary celebrity at the age of twenty-four.

The novel has since been translated into French, Italian, Hebrew, Czech, and Chinese. It sits atop a very short list of second-person narratives. To this day, any writer who writes in the second person risks being accused of copying McInerney.

Among the many pleasures of Jay McInerney's *Bright Lights, Big City* is its capacity to transport readers back to the days when New York City was still its mad, bad, pre-gentrification self. In the pages of McInerney's breakout novel, the subways are still a riot of graffiti tags and Rastafarians reeking of reefer, Lower Manhattan is still edgy and dangerous, and you can buy anything—drugs, a fake Cartier watch, even a live ferret—on the streets of Midtown.

Now, more than four decades later, the graffiti has been scrubbed from the subways and the peep shows of Times Square have been replaced by cheesy tourist traps. This abrupt turn in the city's fortunes would shock McInerney's hard-partying characters, who are too busy admiring their reflections in the coke mirror to notice they are witnessing the end of an era. Set in the early 1980s, *Bright Lights, Big City* follows a nameless recent arrival to the city who works as a fact checker at a prestigious magazine while he writes stories he hopes will gain him entry to the magazine's fiction pages. In the course of one reckless week, the novel's hero drowns his grief over the abrupt collapse of his brief marriage to a fashion model in a spree of club hopping and drug taking that costs him his job and ultimately his self-respect.

The New York of McInerney's novel is balanced on the knife's edge of change. After enjoying decades as a world capital of business, arts, and media, New York's star had faded to the point that, in 1975, the municipal government came within a day of going bankrupt, only to be bailed out at the last minute by the teacher's union. Two years later, the city went dark for a full day when the power grid failed during an electrical storm, leading to widespread looting that ravaged neighborhoods and set entire city blocks on fire.

This is the city where McInerney's hero comes to make his mark, a post-industrial landscape riven by drugs and crime, where on his morning walk to work through Times Square his ears are assaulted by "the same spiel from the same old man: 'Girls, girls, girls—check 'em out, check 'em out….'"

At the same time, it's a city of bottomless possibility, where a nobody from nowhere can roll into town with his fashion model wife and land a job at a famous magazine.

This iconic illustration for the first edition of *Bright Lights, Big City* by Mark Tauss shows the neon promise of the Odeon restaurant, a Tribeca landmark where visitors can still dine today.

This is also, not incidentally, the city where McInerney himself hoped to make his mark when he arrived in the late 1970s. Like his narrator, McInerney was briefly married to a fashion model who threw him over shortly before he was fired as a fact checker at the *New Yorker*. And like his narrator, McInerney was in those days ingesting more than his fair share of illicit chemicals. In the 1980s memoirs remained the province of movie stars and aging statesmen, so McInerney tossed the facts of his dissolute life into a blender, seasoned it with healthy dollops of invention and social commentary, and poured out a delectable literary confection narrated by a mysterious and nameless "you."

"You are not the kind of guy who would be at a place like this at this time of the morning," the novel begins. From this bravura start, McInerney's "you" serves as a callow young Virgil leading readers on a tour of the sweaty downtown clubs and glittering loft parties that made up boho New York City. "You" stumble out of a club at six a.m., drug-sick and ashamed, to face the morning light whose "glare is like a mother's reproach." "You" pull up a stool at the Lion's Head Tavern, the old-school West Village writer's haunt where the waitress knows your name. "You" party till dawn in the back of a limo with a Jewish gangster named Bernie.

But here you are, and you cannot say the terrain is unfamiliar, although the details are fuzzy. You are at a nightclub talking to a girl with a shaved head. The club is either Heartbreak or the Lizard Lounge. All might come clear if you could just slip into the bathroom and do a little more Bolivian Marching Powder. Then again, it might not.

Good luck finding that city today. Any *Bright Lights*-themed tour of contemporary Manhattan is bound to run headlong into the spit-polishing effects of four decades of gentrification that have turned early 1980s Manhattan into an urban Brigadoon, a city that lives on only in stories. The after-hours club scene has moved uptown to Chelsea and out to Brooklyn neighborhoods like Bushwick that McInerney's characters couldn't have located on a map. The Lion's Head closed in the 1990s, and the once-murderous Lower East Side streets where gangster Bernie moved his product are now lined with trendy eateries and sun-splashed yoga studios.

But if much of Manhattan has become a theme-park version of itself, the old streets and neighborhoods remain. A visitor can still dine at the Odeon, the era-defining nightspot in Tribeca where McInerney's characters snort lines of cocaine off a toilet seat in the bathroom. Visitors can also wander the West Village, pausing on Cornelia Street, a single picturesque block between Bleecker Street and Sixth Avenue where the novel's narrator lived with his fashion model wife when they first moved to New York. In those days, McInerney writes, the West Village retained a scruffy charm, with local butcher shops hanging their wares—"unskinned rabbits, hairless fetal pigs, plucked fowl with yellow feet"—in their windows.

Today, the only yellow feet you're likely to see in that part of town will belong to stylish women striding out of the Louboutin boutique on Horatio Street in yellow stilettos. But New York is still a world capital, and if you step out of the subway at Sheridan Square or walk the streets of Midtown, you can still see armies of young, dreamy-eyed kids from the provinces come to the big city hoping to conquer it and claim it as their own.

HONGOEKA BAY, NORTH ISLAND, NEW ZEALAND

PATRICIA GRACE

POTIKI (1986)

A small coastal New Zealand Māori community is threatened by developers who would desecrate their lands, but they find strength in their relationships with the land, sea, their culture, and each other.

Potiki is iconic in the New Zealand literary landscape for its vivid evocations of contemporary coastal Māori life and its searing depiction of the way land and sea are seen and held so differently by indigenous and non-indigenous New Zealanders. It tells how a Māori community is threatened by a land developer who wants to purchase ancestral land and begin construction. Its narrators include Roimata, a woman who describes the community's concerns and their quiet, concerted efforts to rebel; her husband, Hemi, a man who has been laid off from his job but then has the opportunity to reconnect with the land, his culture, and his family; and Toko, Roimata and Hemi's adopted son, who is physically handicapped but also has the gift of supernatural sight or matakite.

The setting of the novel is ostensibly the seaside community where Grace and her family have lived for generations—Hongoeka, Plimmerton, which is just north of Wellington, the capital city of New Zealand. Says Roimata:

> We live by the sea, which hems and stiches the scalloped edges of the land... our houses stand close together on this, the papakainga, and they window the neatened curve of the sea. Towards this curve we pitch our eyes constantly, tides of eyes rolling in reverse action to the sea.

This sea constantly threads through the story like a tide, a rhythm particularly noticeable in the narration of characters Roimata and Toko, who is born on the beach and almost left to the sea. The book's multiple narrators suggest that no story can be told from only one point of view. As much as the novel is about land and sea, it is also about stories—how a people know themselves through stories, which are inextricably written in the land and transferred to ancestral houses or wharenui.

The wharenui is a particularly potent motif throughout *Potiki*. The carving of a house begins the book, and ends it, and the story of resistance against the incursion of developers is mirrored by the burning and rebuilding of a a wharenui. The physical and cultural setting of the book are enmeshed

Patricia Grace (born in 1937) is a novelist, short story writer, and children's writer of Ngati Toa, Ngati Raukawa, and Te Ati Awa tribal descent. She was the first Māori woman to publish a collection of short stories and has published more than twenty books. One of New Zealand's most celebrated writers, Grace is a Distinguished Companion of the New Zealand Order of Merit for her services to literature.

On publication, non-Māori readers were concerned that Māori words appeared in the book untranslated. Grace responded: "I didn't want Māori to be treated as a foreign language in its own country."

When Grace wrote *Potiki*, her community did not have a wharenui, or Māori ancestral home. Her novel put an end to harassment from developers and enabled the community to build their own wharenui, as shown here in a photograph by Tina Makereti, 2018.

throughout, reflecting a world view in which people are intimately connected to their environment. Toko describes this relationship at the same time as he describes the ancestral house:

> This house of his, of ours, carried forward the stories of the people of long ago, but told about our lives today as well. There were crayfish, eels, moki and codfish all made into patterns in our house. There were karaka trees, pohutukawa, ngaio, nikau and kakaho, and patterns made from sea waves, rocks and hills, sun, rain and stars.

For many Pākehā readers, *Potiki*'s inside view of Māori life was revelatory; for others it was politically confronting. Grace herself was somewhat surprised by this reaction, stating:

> When *Potiki* first came out there was quite a bit of criticism of it ... some people thought I was trying to stir up racial unrest. The book was described as political... The land issues and language issues were what Māori people lived with every day and still do. It was just everyday life to us, and the ordinary lives of ordinary people.

Perhaps this is the most extraordinary and confronting aspect of *Potiki*: that, as Grace states, it was just about ordinary, everyday people, who had, until then, been invisible to the majority of New Zealanders.

TORONTO, ONTARIO, CANADA

MICHAEL ONDAATJE

IN THE SKIN OF A LION (1987)

Following the life and love story of a second-generation Canadian from 1900 to the period before the Second World War, Ondaatje's chronicle of Toronto expresses the ambivalence the immigrant feels about being metamorphosed into a new nationality.

Examining the untold stories of those who toiled to bring the modern city of Toronto into being, *In the Skin of a Lion* puts pressure on the idea of the "melting pot" thesis, invented by Israel Zangwill. While politicians have always loved the idea that you can cook nationality into a homogeneous stew in the interests of the host nation, novelists, who look at things in a closer way than politicians, are typically skeptical. Does a new "skin" come with a new passport, the old one sloughed off like a snake's? Are you a lion if you put on a lion skin? These are the questions posed here by Ondaatje, as he narrates the life of Peter Lewis, a second-generation Canadian of British origins, whose story maps the disquieting truth that contribution by an immigrant community is rarely commemorated by history. Even though great nations are as dependent on immigrant labor as ancient Athens was on slaves, the Zangwillian "melting" does not often happen. The pot retains its different ingredients, and though the "New Canadian" labor "made" Toronto, it never was Toronto.

Peter's early life is spent in Ontario open country in the second decade of the twentieth century; the first chapter's title is "Little Seeds," with the proverbial echo, "from little seeds do great oaks grow." The great thing is, of course, Canada, and these preliminary chapters provide important context for Peter's subsequent actions. The novel's pulsatingly angry, subdued element of historical protest blooms when the action moves to Toronto, but it is here that we notice its beginnings. Sitting at the kitchen table, Patrick makes his first attempts to grasp, mentally and manually, what Canada is:

> He sits down at the long table and looks into his school geography book with the maps of the world, the white sweeps of currents, testing the names to himself, mouthing out the exotic. Caspian, Nepal, Durango. He closes the book and brushes it with his palms, feeling the texture of the pebbled cover and its coloured dyes which create a map of Canada.

Canada will most vividly be "mapped," however, by the experience of the 1929 Depression. Patrick moves to Toronto in 1923; after a brief stint as

Michael Ondaatje was born in 1943 in Sri Lanka, of mixed Dutch, Sinhalese, and Tamil ancestry. Moving to Canada in 1962, he became a New Canadian, a designation whose meaning his books ponder and question.

In the Skin of a Lion is the precursor (and in some ways continuation) of his Man Booker–winning novel, *The English Patient*.

The novel's title is taken from *The Epic of Gilgamesh*, located in the epigraph as "I will let my hair grow long for your sake, I will wander through the wilderness in the skin of a lion," echoing the theme of converging voices retelling history.

a "searcher" (a four-dollar-a-week finder of missing persons), he takes up work as a laborer on Toronto's iconic viaduct and tunnel systems that were to carry water, power, and traffic across the city, working specifically on the Bloor Street Bridge, at once mighty and murderous, a monument to human endeavor:

> The bridge goes up in a dream. It will link the east end with the centre of the city. It will carry traffic, water, and electricity across the Don Valley. It will carry trains that have not even been invented yet.
>
> Night and day. Fall light. Snow light. They are always working—horses and wagons and men arriving for work on the Danforth side at the far end of the valley.
>
> Men in a maze of wooden planks climb deep into the shattered light of blond wood. A man is an extension of a hammer, drill, flame. Drill smoke in his hair. A cap falls into the valley, gloves are buried in stone dust.
>
> Then the new men arrive, the "electricals," laying grids of wire across the five arches, carrying the exotic three-bowl lights, and on 18 October 1918 it is completed. Lounging in midair.
>
> The bridge. The bridge. Christened "Prince Edward." The Blood Street Viaduct.

Vast, sudden and costly in human life, the urban renewal of Toronto is the dream of Rowland Harris, a man who is gigantically selfish and driven. (Harris was a heroic real-life figure in Toronto history. If anyone "built" the town, it was he—using, of course, immigrant labor.) Grandiloquent in his schemes, ruthless in his determination to make his dream real, Harris is fanatical about even the smallest detail.

His perfectionism serves to radicalize Patrick, though it is the accidental death of the love of his life, Alice, in an explosion, which provokes him to action. Vowing revenge, he embarks on reprisal by attempting to dynamite the Muskoka Hotel, a haunt of Toronto's rich and famous. Though he is caught and sentenced to five years in prison, on his release he sets out again, totally unrehabilitated, this time with the intention of dynamiting the hated tunnel connecting the City's waterworks with the City. His desire is clear: he will unmake Toronto. Commissioner Harris, as he now is, lives and sleeps in his palatial industrial building he has brought into being. Thus, it will be two birds with one stick of dynamite for Patrick.

Ondaatje's novel does not allow Patrick an uncomplicated victory, however. He confronts Harris, blasting box in hand, at the waterwork complex, upbraiding his enemy for all the immigrant deaths his visionary rebuilding of Toronto has cost. He tells him, it is blood, not water, which

Photograph from the Toronto City Archives of the Bloor Street Viaduct under construction in July 1917. Ondaatje worked extensively with the archives when researching for the novel.

flows from Harris's works. And yet Harris succeeds in persuading Patrick that he (Patrick) is, at heart, no destroyer. He really belongs to the newly made Canada of bridges, tunnels, and conurbation: "You must realise you are like these places, Patrick. You're as much of the fabric as the aldermen and the millionaires." Patrick is, in one of the book's dominant images, despite himself, part of the mosaic of emergent Canada.

Ending with such haunting subtlety, the final message of Ondaatje's novel is, ambivalently, to ponder the constructive and destructive forces that mingle to create a great city like modern Toronto, without didactically proclaiming what that means for the Canadian "melting pot" today.

TURTLE MOUNTAIN RESERVATION, NORTH DAKOTA, USA

LOUISE ERDRICH

TRACKS (1988)

Hailed as "epic and timeless," Tracks *is the third in a planned tetralogy of the vanishing settlements of the Chippewa tribe during the course of the twentieth century. The group of novels includes* Love Medicine *(1984),* The Beet Queen *(1986), and* The Bingo Palace *(1994).*

Louise Erdrich was born in Minnesota in 1954, and raised in North Dakota, of Turtle Mountain Anishinaabe (also known as Ojibwe and Chippewa) American Indian heritage.

She is the author of fifteen novels as well as volumes of poetry, children's books, short stories, and a memoir of early motherhood.

Tracks is Erdrich's third novel. Some of the chapters had appeared previously as standalone short stories. The novel met with a mixed reception on first publication; its esoteric narrative structure polarized critics.

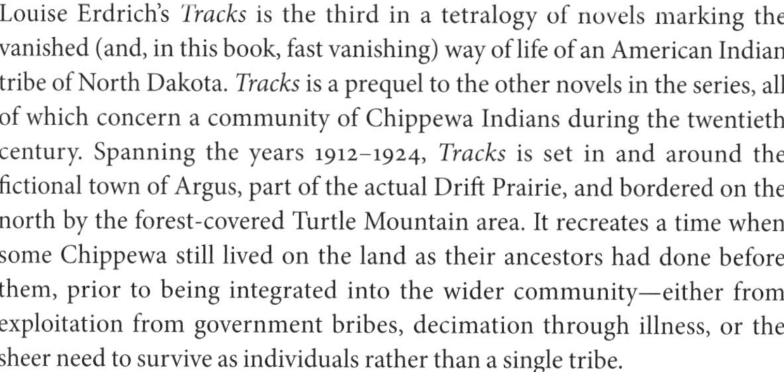
Louise Erdrich's *Tracks* is the third in a tetralogy of novels marking the vanished (and, in this book, fast vanishing) way of life of an American Indian tribe of North Dakota. *Tracks* is a prequel to the other novels in the series, all of which concern a community of Chippewa Indians during the twentieth century. Spanning the years 1912–1924, *Tracks* is set in and around the fictional town of Argus, part of the actual Drift Prairie, and bordered on the north by the forest-covered Turtle Mountain area. It recreates a time when some Chippewa still lived on the land as their ancestors had done before them, prior to being integrated into the wider community—either from exploitation from government bribes, decimation through illness, or the sheer need to survive as individuals rather than a single tribe.

The characters in the book are intrinsic to the land, as it is to them; they move in rhythm with the seasons, having journeyed across the great plains and wide, flat prairies of the upper Midwest, to reach this place of lakes and rich timber, teeming with deer, beaver, and moose—a fertile hunting ground steeped in myth and legend. While Erdrich brings this area richly to life, she also captures the essential isolation of an American Indian tribe whose smoky cabins dot the remote landscape, enduring the rawness of North Dakota's extremes of climate, from unbearably hot summers to brutal winters.

Tracks has two narrators: Nanapush, an elderly tribal leader, full of self-appointed wisdom, and Pauline, a young mixed-race convert to Roman Catholicism, although she carries the superstition of the Indian legends of her forebears into this new-found religion. At the heart of the book is a third major character, Fleur, magnetically attractive, rebellious, the last of the Pillager clan, rumored to be a witch. Fleur single-mindedly believes that through her own willpower (she can raise a whirlwind and cause thunderstorms) the old ways will remain: "It was as if the Manitous all through the woods spoke through Fleur, loose, arguing... Turtle's quavering scratch, the Eagle's high shriek, Loon's crazy bitterness, Otter, the howl of Wolf, Bear's low rasp." However, the land in this reimagined frontier region, containing the

A map from 1891 of North Dakota, showing the Indian reservations, mountains, lakes, and rivers of the region. The Turtle Mountain area, in which Erdrich's novel is set, is located at the top center.

natural resources and means of livelihood of the Chippewa, is under a threat they cannot resist:

> It began as a far-off murmur, a disturbance in the wind. We noticed an unusual number of birds and other animals that nested or burrowed in trees...Then one day we could hear them clearly. Ringing over the water and to our shore came the shouts of men, faint thump of steel axes. Their saws were rasping whispers, the turn of wooden wheels on ungreased axles was shrill as a far-off flock of gulls.

It is the tormented Pauline, subject to visions and hallucinations, who is the embodiment of the natural world around her, in particular the ancient forest and lake of myth and terror. "I was nothing human, nothing victorious, nothing like myself. I was no more than a piece of the woods."

Tracks is an intense work, threaded with aspects of magical realism and underpinned by a moral argument, which is highly critical of the way that the Chippewa, like other American Indian tribes, are becoming an anachronism. Written in cyclical form as the story moves from one season to the next, it describes a world where nature coexists with humans and the Chippewa's survival depends on the land, which, like their very existence, is being steadily eroded, yet memorialized by Erdrich in a gorgeous litany of words.

PERTH, AUSTRALIA

TIM WINTON

CLOUDSTREET (1991)

Taking its name from the crumbling house that sits at its heart, this is, above all, a novel about belonging—to a country, to a landscape, to a specific suburban environment, and to a family and the strength that this bestows.

Tim Winton (born 1960 in Perth, Western Australia) is his country's most popular contemporary novelist; four-times winner of its prestigious literary award (the Miles Franklin) and twice shortlisted for the Man Booker Prize.

Cloudstreet, Winton's acknowledged masterpiece, was awarded the Miles Franklin Prize in 1991, was adapted for the Australian stage in 1998 in a production that also toured overseas, became a TV mini-series in 2011 and an opera in 2016.

Winton expected *Cloudstreet* to sell only 10,000 copies; it sold almost that many in its first week, and has gone on to sell more than half a million copies worldwide.

Perhaps no other Australian writer apart from Tim Winton has so consistently and prolifically set his work within the landscape of his birth, the southwest corner of the continent. Winton's frequent acknowledgments of his geographical focus culminated in an autobiographical homage, subtitled "a landscape memoir," published in 2015: "I persisted with place as a starting point ... to draw a reader ... just as I was swept into ... Hardy's Wessex." A more localized literary mentor was Patrick White whose *Voss* (1957) marked "a turning point for me, a sign of what might be possible in writing poetically about figures in landscape."

Winton took these aims into his most popular novel to date, *Cloudstreet* (1991), which relocated his characters from a rural to a suburban setting. *Cloudstreet* is a nostalgic homage to his grandparents and their generation as Winton creates a suburban setting on the fringe of a city (Perth) that was still attempting to cast off its rural mantle.

From World War II and into the postwar years, Western Australia's capital is seen as the "most isolated country town in the world trying to be the most cut-off city in the world, trying desperately to hit the big time." After mid-century, as this transformation speeded up, upheaval was radical: "All the old houses were coming down and salmon-brick duplexes were going up in their place." However, when *Cloudstreet* opens and the saga of the Lamb and the Pickles families begins, the country and the city still coexist in an uneasy truce on each other's very doorstep.

Although close to the city center, the novel's setting is not merely suburban: it is triumphantly so. Its characters enjoy enough freedom to have a fowlhouse in their backyard built "from broken teachests and an old forty-four gallon drum." The novel still acknowledges the city's strong rural links.

This is a landscape where forgotten or nostalgic joys can rekindle memories of a lifestyle for many older Australians today: firecracker nights, building a cubbyhouse, playing marbles. Paperboys still sell newspapers in these streets, afternoon picture shows release their "squint-eyed patrons back to reality" and two-up games are conducted where "tired old tarts

Cover artwork by Andy Bridge for the 2008 Picador edition of *Cloudstreet*..

are calling sailors." All these attest to a lifestyle lived as much outdoors as indoors. Winton distils the essence of an era's suburban life in an Australia on the cusp of change, creating a landscape of rare value in his nation's literature.

This is because Australian writing, when it does inhabit a suburban landscape, has usually preferred to disparage its values and history. In *Cloudstreet*, however, if all is not idyllic at least a new life of great significance and value is capable of being forged. Winton is clear sighted enough not to make this a transplanted Garden of Eden. Its cast of characters is a marginalized mixture of gamblers, alcoholics, the mentally unsound, and the dispossessed. Furthermore, Winton centers this return to the past with a stern realization of its undercurrent: this is a serenity compromised by the Nedlands Monster. As a Perth journalist predicts, this serial killer embodies the urban conjunction that also fosters and allows "something nesting here, something horrible."

The novel is also a lament for the values that supported working-class people at the time. Inspired by Winton's grandparents, the book is dedicated to these forebears: "In the eighties I noticed that all the places my parents and so on talked about in their stories were disappearing … inside a generation Perth had been demolished and 'developed' into … a sort of try-hard, sterile city." Because Winton bemoaned that "he could find few of the places sacred to family memory" he unashamedly "tried to reimagine a lost town."

CLOUD ST

Initially the novel's two families, each sharing half an enormous house but only really intersecting after twenty years, are not attuned to their new landscape. Both families have been dispossessed. One by the husband's gambling losses, the other by "losing" a son. "We don't belong here" is their frequently held belief until gradually they form their own community, create "a new tribe." Eventually they become at one with their inner and outer countries.

Presiding over all is the sentient presence of Cloudstreet. Its very name is a mixture of the ethereal and the mundane and, ultimately, also the place where opposites can be reconciled. The house's previous history as one of great cruelty to its Aboriginal waifs makes it a symbol for the nation itself: hybrid and haunted by the past. The novel restores the house's lost innocence; its author has admitted that perhaps this is his "sentimental hopefulness about the nation."

The river sucked up the sky and went flat and glittery right down the middle of the place and people went to it in boats and britches and barebacked. Where the river met the sea, the beaches ran north and south, white and broad as highways in a dream…

Cloudstreet the house lives up to its duality and is as much a character in the novel as its residents. On its first sighting by the Lamb family it is "an enormous flaking mansion with eyes and ears." It is articulate with a "rumble and quake … going on all night like the bellyaches of a sleeping whale." The bush sounds that the Lamb family have been accustomed to are here replaced by "the house cracking its knuckles."

The Lambs open a typically makeshift Australian corner store in the house's front room, which eventually becomes a fixture in the landscape. As "a map point" to the neighborhood its integration parallels the acceptance both families achieve, of each another and by the house and, in return, by the country: "After a time the shop *was* Cloud Street, and people said it, Cloudstreet, in one word."

When a marriage is forged between the two families, the haunted souls still residing in Cloudstreet's walls are finally "forced on their way to oblivion … leaving a warm, clean sweet space among the living." The house and, as Winton hopes, the nation, "breathes its first painless breath." When the presiding Aboriginal spirit in the novel says, "Places are strong, important," this is echoed by the family's experience in creating their own tribe. Ultimate wisdom is vouchsafed at the close of the novel: "We all join up somewhere in the end." A landscape of belonging thus clearly manifests in this novel of wonders and miracles.

Opposite: Still from the Showcase adaptation of *Cloudstreet*, directed by Tim Winton. Photograph taken by David Dare Parker.

NEWFOUNDLAND, CANADA

E. ANNIE PROULX

THE SHIPPING NEWS (1993)

Quoyle, a "third-rate newspaperman," moves to the fog-wrapped island of Newfoundland, his ancestral family home, after his wife dies in a car crash.

E. Annie Proulx won the Pulitzer for this, her first novel, published when she was 57. It was filmed, starring Kevin Spacey and Judi Dench, in 2001.

Proulx is American, but has said in an interview that she was "physically shaken" on her first visit to the "hard, bare rock, the whistling wind'"of Newfoundland. "It wasn't so much a rush of energy as a rush of empathy."

A large island located off the east of Canada, Newfoundland (pronounced nyoo-fn-land) was found to be "swarming" with fish by a European in the fifteenth century. By the early 1990s, the cod fishing industry had collapsed after years of overfishing.

The reader's first glimpse of Annie Proulx's Newfoundland comes from the perspective of Quoyle's aunt, Agnis Hamm: she has propelled her nephew, who is heartbroken at the death of his unfaithful wife, to the home she left decades earlier. "This place, she thought, this rock, six thousand miles of coast blind-wrapped in fog. Sunkers under wrinkled water, boats threading tickles between ice-scabbed cliffs. Tundra and barrens, a land of stunted spruce men cut and drew away," she thinks, as they approach on the ferry. "The only cities were of ice, bergs with cores of beryl, blue gems within white gems, that some said gave off an odour of almonds." Quoyle, arriving for the first time in the land of his grubby, nasty ancestors, feels "as though he had dreamed this place once, forgot it later."

Described, with a wonderful off-handedness, as "an account of a few years in the life of Quoyle," *The Shipping News* follows our obese hero's devastatingly portrayed loneliness in America, his move with his children to take up a job working on the local newspaper, the Gammy Bird, in the tiny Newfoundland town of Killick-Claw, and his and his aunt's efforts to patch up her childhood home, a place which holds dark secrets. Assigned car crashes and the shipping news as his beat on the Gammy Bird, Quoyle is at first horrified—his wife was killed in a traffic accident—but slowly begins to settle into his new life in Newfoundland, and to seek out a love "without pain or misery."

Proulx published *The Shipping News* in 1993, around the time that the Canadian government was declaring an indefinite moratorium on cod fishing after severe depletion of stock. The novel charts the clash between the old and the new ways of life, but the island setting and its weather is the heart of *The Shipping News*—as important as a character, and in some ways almost turned into one. "The idea of the North was taking him. He needed something to brace against."

Proulx, not a native, but a lover of Newfoundland, evokes the cold, the fog, the starkness, the strangeness of this island balanced on the edge of Canada endlessly, and magically: "Fog against the window like milk." And:

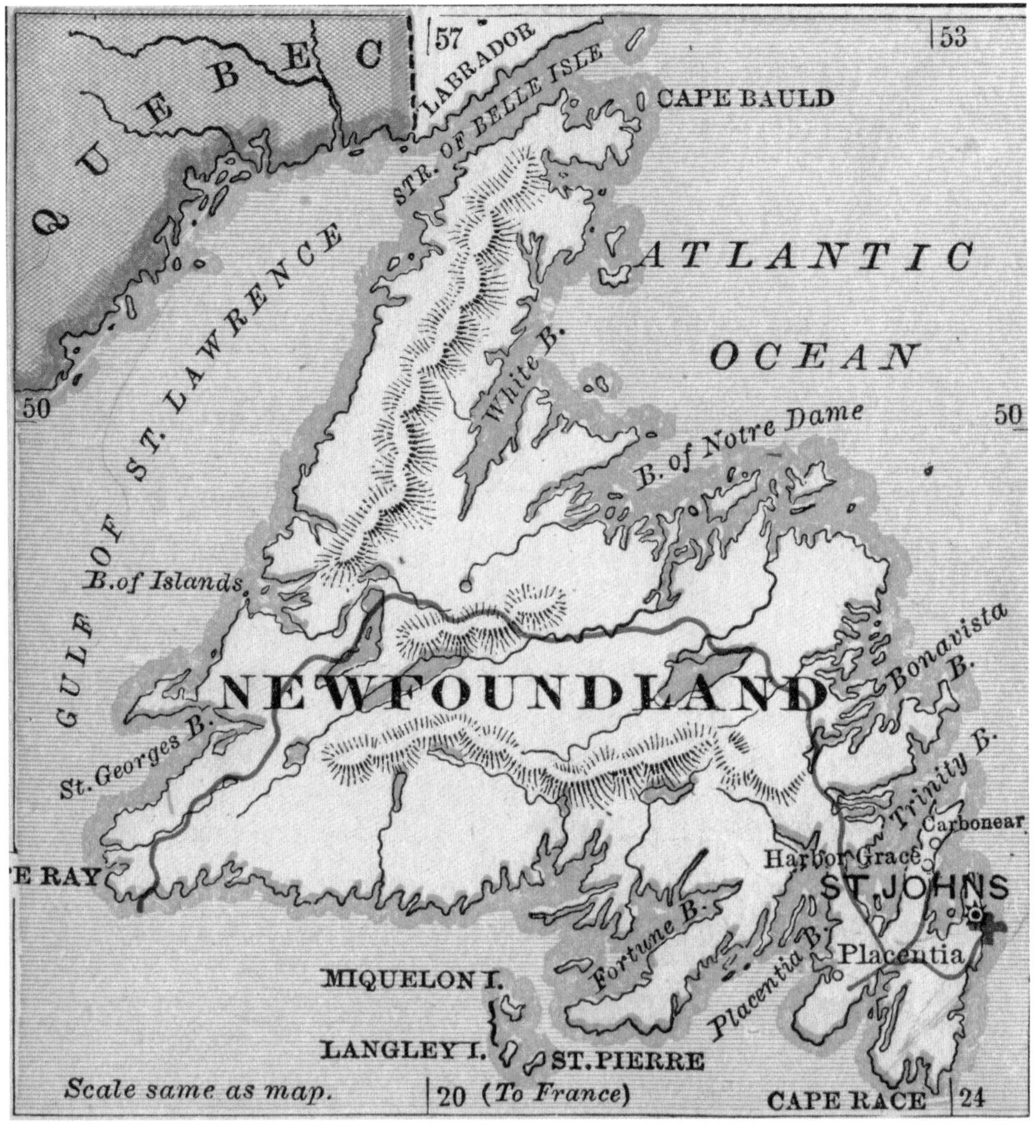

A map of Newfoundland (1903), a large island which sits off the east coast of Canada. Newfoundland and Labrador remained under British rule until 1949, when the province became part of Canada.

"Remember we had a yellow day on Monday—the sky cast was an ugly yellow like a jar of piss. Then yesterday, blue mist and blasting fog … there was a fall of frozen ducks on Water Street, eight or ten of them, feathers all on, eyes closed like they was dreaming, froze hard as polar cap ice. When that happens, look out boys."

The sea, the wind, the fog, the snow, the stunted trees, the sea again: Proulx's Newfoundland is stunningly harsh and heart-stoppingly stunning; the author herself once said that on her first visit to the island, "I liked this harsh, bony, bare, empty, cruel and beautiful place so much I could not bear it."

Hauling Job Sturges' House by David Blackwood, 1979. Blackwood is a Canadian artist famed for his portraits of Newfoundland life. This etching was featured on the cover of an American edition in 1993.

TOKYO, JAPAN

NATSUHIKO KYŌGOKU

THE SUMMER OF THE UBUME (1994)

The first of Kyōgoku's novels to be published follows Tatsumi Sekiguchi, a frustrated freelance writer, as he traverses postwar Tokyo desperate to unravel the mystery surrounding a cursed maternity clinic and the strange disappearance of a young doctor from a sealed room.

Natsuhiko Kyōgoku (born 1963) owned and ran a design company before writing novels. He takes an active role in the elaborate design of each book. He won the prestigious Japanese Naoki Prize in 2004 and is an expert in Japanese folklore.

The Summer of the Ubume was first published by Kodansha in 1994. It was translated into English by Alexander O. Smith and Elye J. Alexander, and published by Vertical in 2009.

A film adaption of the novel directed by Akio Jissōji was released in Japan in 2005.

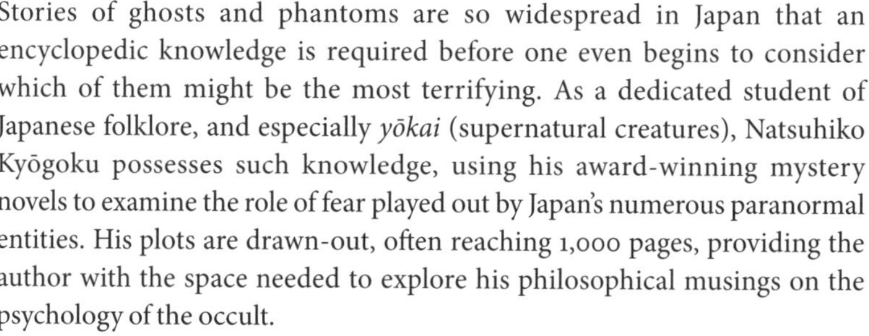

Stories of ghosts and phantoms are so widespread in Japan that an encyclopedic knowledge is required before one even begins to consider which of them might be the most terrifying. As a dedicated student of Japanese folklore, and especially *yōkai* (supernatural creatures), Natsuhiko Kyōgoku possesses such knowledge, using his award-winning mystery novels to examine the role of fear played out by Japan's numerous paranormal entities. His plots are drawn-out, often reaching 1,000 pages, providing the author with the space needed to explore his philosophical musings on the psychology of the occult.

Kyōgoku does not simply write ghost stories, though; instead his works are framed around hardboiled detective narratives, forming fantastically dark and complex plots that draw the reader into a criminal world that is at once both recognizable and uncanny in its rendering.

The Summer of the Ubume takes place in 1950s Tokyo; a city scarred by the air raids and firestorms of World War II and, like postwar Japan itself, still wrestling with its own fractured identity. Set against this somber backdrop, the story follows tabloid writer turned reluctant detective, Tatsumi Sekiguchi, as he is pulled further into the perplexing events surrounding the Kuonji family and their woodland maternity hospital, which has been the focus of growing rumor in the city. The clinic is shrouded in tales of disappearing babies, hideous frog-faced children, an ancient curse, and a bizarre twenty-month pregnancy.

The plot of the novel is disturbing enough to unsettle even the most hardened of readers, yet it is Kyōgoku's adroit use of the Tokyo landscape that truly brings this horrific tale to life. Kyōgoku describes the emotional impact of the environment upon the protagonist, Sekiguchi, transporting the reader into his world. The story opens and closes at the same pivotal location, *haka-no-machi memaizaka* (literally, "Vertigo-slope of grave-town"); a long, high-walled gradient that affects Sekiguchi, causing him to lose his balance, both physically and emotionally, at numerous points in the novel. The walls obstruct Sekiguchi's view of the cemetery that lies beyond them and

Graves in the Zoshigaya cemetery in Tokyo. Sekiguchi, the book's protagonist, walks through here in order to reach the "cursed" hospital.

so he forgets both its existence and his own proximity to death, mirroring Kyōgoku's theorizing of supernatural entities as barriers between perception and reality. Countless such hill paths can be found across Tokyo; many of them once referred to as *yūrei-zaka* (ghost slopes) due to the unsettling feelings they roused in passersby.

Kyōgoku draws upon site-specific knowledge to tie his characters further to the landscape they inhabit. He describes the fictionalized "*en-no-tsuki*" hill as a place long reputed for bringing "bad luck" and introduces the misfortune of its Itabashi location, a once thriving trade route that descended into ruin. Kyōgoku uses Tokyo's physical geography, particularly its undulating urban landscape, to manifest his character's physical and emotional discomfort. Sekiguchi describes the climbing of *en-no-tsuki* as "torturous" and comments on the disorientation he experiences in moving through the labyrinthine streets of a Tokyo that is familiar to him but in which he frequently loses himself as he becomes absorbed in his own repressed memories.

Together with his rich accounts of the novel's key locations, largely based on real places—Jinbōchō "book town," the Kuonji clinic, Kyōgōkudō's antiquarian bookstore and the Zōshigaya cemetery—Kyōgoku guides the reader through a semi-fictionalized Tokyo, which, like the phantoms he conjures throughout the book, is both real and imagined, and altogether haunting. *The Summer of the Ubume* provides an unsettling introduction to Japan's historically layered capital, evoking a city whose mystery can be explored both within and outside the pages of the novel.

JASPER, ALBERTA, CANADA

THOMAS WHARTON

ICEFIELDS (1995)

An impressive melding of history, geology, and myth, Thomas Wharton's first novel takes readers to the beautiful frozen world of the Athabasca Icefields where the landscape, although real, is also symbolic.

Thomas Wharton is a writer of fiction for adults, young adults, and children, born in Alberta in 1963. His work has been published in the US, UK, France, Germany, Italy, and Japan.

Icefields is Wharton's first novel. It began as his MA creative writing thesis, written under the supervision of Icelandic-Canadian novelist Kristjana Gunnars at the University of Alberta. It won the Commonwealth Writer's Prize for Best First Book, and the inaugural Banff Mountain Book grand prize.

His research projects include an interactive literary map of Edmonton, where he lives with his wife and children.

By mixing documented facts with his prodigious imagination, Thomas Wharton has created a literary landscape that is uniquely his own. The central character, Dr. Edward Byrne, is a British scientist. During an expedition in 1898 with the Royal Geological Society to the Columbia Icefields in the Canadian Rockies, he slips on a glacier and falls 60 feet into a crevasse. He is trapped hanging upside down, saved by his backpack that has prevented his further fall. While in this position, he sees a winged figure embedded in the ice wall and spends the duration of the novel wondering whether what he saw was an angel or merely a random pattern in the ice.

Byrne is rescued, but the experience continues to haunt him, and binds him profoundly and permanently to the glacier. He becomes obsessed by it, this fascinating natural formation, which "is not a liquid, nor [...] a solid. It flows like lava, like melting wax, like honey." He comes to see his nearly fatal accident as an act of fate. The glacier "has become the centre of his field of vision. And more than central: inevitable."

He settles into a shack at the edge of the glacier from where he makes studying the icefield his life's work. He also witnesses how over the 25-year span of the novel, Jasper, Alberta (the frontier town closest to the icefield) becomes, with the arrival of the railroad, a growing tourist attraction. The man who rescued Byrne, Frank Trask, is an entrepreneur determined to reap the financial rewards that tourism could bring. He builds a chalet and leads walking tours on the glacier, completely indifferent to the damage he might be causing.

The icefield is so much more, however, than a tourist destination. It represents the slow passage of time over the centuries, the unfolding of the Earth's history, predating humans. As Byrne writes in his journal: "The layers of ice deep within the fields may be hundreds of years old, formed from snow that fell here before the discovery of America, before the birth of Shakespeare, before the industrial revolution." In a later entry he writes that some scientists believe "that it is to the effects of the most recent ice age we owe the emergence of early civilization."

The alpine town of Jasper sits surrounded by the snow-topped Canadian Rockies, and acts as a center for Jasper National Park. Photograph from Jasper Yellowhead Museum & Archives, dating to 1945.

Byrne also has a deeply personal connection to his glacial environment: "I've learned a lot from the glacier itself. A way of looking at the rest of the world. Patience. Control of emotions." The glacier becomes the main character in the narrative, which is as slow moving as the ice itself. Thus *Icefields* can be seen as a compelling meditation on how human beings do not just affect their surroundings but how they are equally affected by them.

As a symbol, the icefields are powerful and poetic. Wharton emphasizes this by using scientific glacier terms and their definitions as his chapter headings. One in particular—Ablation Zone—rings especially poignant when one considers that since the novel was published in 1995, the icefields have shrunk by a third, and it is predicted that there is a danger that they might disappear entirely within a generation: "The line between the frozen and melting part of a glacier. Once past this point, the ice begins to die. Melting can be hastened even by a faint increase in heat at the lower extremity of a glacier, such as produced by the flash bulbs of hundreds of cameras."

Perhaps Wharton's greatest achievement in this book is that by placing one human being—one consciousness, as it were—into the vast, ancient glacial landscape, he creates awe and inspires us, as readers, to consider the immensity of our own smallness.

PARIS, FRANCE

PATRICK MODIANO

THE SEARCH WARRANT (DORA BRUDER) (1997)

An old newspaper announcement from the winter of 1941 sets the narrator on a trail to find a missing person, the teenage Dora Bruder from wartime Paris almost sixty years earlier, searching among the hidden byways of Paris's shabby arrondissements for clues, certainty, and closure.

Patrick Modiano was born in Paris in July 1945, almost a year after the city's liberation from German occupation. His Jewish father was of Italian origin, his mother, Flemish Belgian. During the war his father worked on the black market, refusing to wear the yellow star required of all Jews under Nazi rule. He narrowly escaped deportation.

Modiano won the Nobel Prize in Literature in 2014.

In 2015, the City of Paris named a promenade in the 18th arrondissement after Dora Bruder, the missing Jewish girl of Modiano's novel.

> PARIS: Missing, a young girl, Dora Bruder, age 15, height 1.55m, oval-shaped face, grey-brown eyes, grey sports jacket, maroon pullover, navy-blue skirt and hat, brown gym shoes. Address all information to M. and Mme. Bruder, 41 Boulevard Ornano, Paris.

A missing person notice from the darkest days of World War II, the identifying features hauntingly itemized, is chanced upon in a yellowing newspaper decades later by Parisian writer Patrick Modiano, becoming the catalyst for his novel *The Search Warrant*. A brooding, hybrid work, which like so many of the Nobel-winning author's books mixes autobiography, reportage, and fiction, it is set in an off-the-beaten-track Paris, away from the tourist sites: the shabby streets around Porte de Clignancourt in the 18th arrondissement, the "bas" de Montmartre, away from Le Sacré-Coeur basilica and the lights of the legendary Moulin Rouge. Modiano's narrator recognizes the Bruder's address immediately:

> I am trying to search for clues, going far, far back in time. When I was about twelve, on those visits to the Clignancourt flea markets with my mother, at the top of the right on one of those aisles boarded by stalls, the Marche Malik or the Marche Vernaison, there was a young Polish Jew who sold suitcases...

This would be 1957. Yet memory, though seemingly precise, is also elusive, unreliable: "With the passage of time, perspectives become blurred for me, one winter merging into another. That of 1965 and that of 1942."

The Paris of early 1942, the winter immediately after Dora Bruder disappeared, was a very different city to 1965, or to today, although so unchanged are its streets and architecture that one can seem to wander back in time very easily at the turn of a corner. Time, and the "mania" for looking back, are, quintessentially, what Modiano's novels are all about. In 1942 Paris was under German occupation, and a nightly curfew was imposed.

ON RECHERCHE une jeune fille, Dora Bruder, 15 ans, 1 m. 55, visage ovale, yeux gris marron, manteau sport gris, pull-over bordeaux, jupe et chapeau bleu marine, chaussures sport marron. Adresser toutes indications à M. et Mme Bruder, 41, boulevard Ornano, Paris.

The original missing persons advert for Dora Bruder, which appeared in *Paris-Soir* on 31 December 1941.

Dora Bruder's family was Jewish, and not well off. She had vanished from any official census—French Jews were being rounded up with the complicity of the Vichy government, and Dora's parents enrolled her in a Catholic boarding school in the heart of the city for her protection.

It was from here that she went missing in the bitter winter of 1941; her existence was revealed publicly in the newspaper plea from her desperate family. As Modiano's narrator discovers, 41 Boulevard Ornano is a hotel: "a five-storey block of flats, late nineteenth century." Nearby, at no. 43, is a cinema. The Metro station is Simplon. These are surface details, but, like an archaeologist, Modiano takes us further. "It takes time for what has been erased to resurface;" "I am a patient man. I can wait for hours in the rain." The months between Dora's disappearance, her unexpected return in April 1942 (how had she survived that ruthlessly cold winter?), her subsequent arrest in June, and the family's eventual departure to a place of no return—for Dora, internment at Tourelles in the 20th arrondissement, then the camp at Drancy, and from there to Auschwitz—form the bulk of the novel, interspersed with the narrator's overlaying of his own experiences.

It is a book of meanderings, of cigarettes smoked in half-empty cafes, watchfulness, blackout blinds, boulevards bordered with dusty plane trees, hidden passageways, interrogations behind faceless windows, secrets, codes, and registers. And fear, and the unquiet, lost voices of the Holocaust:

> I walk through empty streets. For me, they are always empty, even at dusk, during the rush-hour, when the crowds are hurrying towards the mouths of the metro. I think of her in spite of myself, sensing an echo of her presence in this neighbourhood or that. The other evening, it was near the Gare du Nord.

BARCELONA, CATALONIA, SPAIN

CARLOS RUIZ ZAFÓN

THE SHADOW OF THE WIND (LA SOMBRA DEL VIENTO) (2001)

A Cervantine combination of gothic adventure, detective novel, romance and melodrama, Zafón's bestseller offers a baroque portrait of 1940s Barcelona.

Carlos Ruiz Zafón, born in Barcelona in 1964, lives in Los Angeles and Barcelona. He was a successful publicist and author of young adult books before becoming a widely read author of popular novels.

His phenomenal success came with *La sombra del viento* (2001). First translated into English by Lucia Graves (*The Shadow of the Wind*, 2004), it has been translated for and published in more than forty countries with more than twenty-five million readers.

It is the first novel of the concluded tetralogy "The Cemetery of Forgotten Books."

In contrast to the lively Mediterranean city we know today, Zafón's Barcelona is a dark city, of crepuscular corners and crumbling streetscapes, as well as a city of darkness in a more spiritless sense, buried beneath the debris of the Spanish Civil War. Set in Barcelona between 1945 and 1956, the most brutally repressive years in postwar Spain, the novel narrates the coming of age of Daniel Sempere. When he is 10 years old, his father takes him to an abandoned book deposit called the "Cemetery of Forgotten Books." Any visitor to this secret library is allowed to take one book away with him—providing he vows to protect the volume he has chosen. Daniel discovers a novel entitled *The Shadow of the Wind* by a certain Julian Carax. From its first reading, it preoccupies Daniel's thoughts.

The plot that follows is labyrinthine, as stories within stories unfold and merge. Perceiving the parallels between his own situation and that of *The Shadow of the Wind*'s protagonist, Daniel becomes curious to unravel the mystery of the writer Carax. He cannot find any of his other novels; all but his copy and several others in the Cemetery have disappeared, and all he can learn of Carax's biography is that he was killed at the beginning of the Civil War. As Daniel deepens his search, it becomes an obsessive quest to discover and avenge the novelist's past. Supported by a memorable anarchist sidekick, Fermín, Daniel perseveres despite the threat of police officer Javier Fumero. Finally managing to build a life for himself and those he loves, Daniel is shown at the end of the book introducing his own 10-year-old son Julian to the selfsame secret book deposit.

The Barcelona that provides a backdrop to this story is authentic to the atmosphere of the 1940s, if not to the physical details of the city. It is not a realistic novel in the traditional nineteenth-century sense, mentioning geographical locations briefly to achieve a particular resonance, rather than characterizing them at length. The districts of Raval and Barceloneta are contrasted with Pedralbes and Sarrià to call attention to class division; the police station of Via Laietana is introduced to highlight the state-sanctioned nature of torture. Together these places function as synecdoches; like pieces in a

The Bridge of Sighs, or Pont del Bisbe, in Barcelona's Gothic Quarter. The "Shadow of the Wind Literary Walking Tour" takes visitors through this atmospheric area of the city.

puzzle, or the chunks of pottery re-assembled to make a mosaic, using the Catalan method *trencadís* made famous by Gaudí, they create a fragmented Barcelona—a city of ruins.

Fans of Zafón's book often opt to take a "Shadow of the Wind Tour." They wander down the iconic *ramblas* amidst stands of flowers, birds, and books, and visit the medieval Old City, as well as the port, the mountains of Montjuic and Tibidabo, and the medieval cathedral of Santa Maria del Mar. They cannot fully experience his version of Barcelona, however, which exists vividly in his imagination. Zafón composed his own piano melodies to inspire the writing of this book: to listen to this music is to enter the novel's atmosphere of melancholia. While its gothic elements promote a sense of threat, desolation, and horror, the novel's mist swathes the novel in further uncertainty. The past, Zafón suggests, is highly elusive—like the shadow of the wind, or the hurricane of history.

Zafón imagines a Barcelona that serves as emblematic of his central themes: death, disappearance, and memory. When, at the book's end, the city is reborn from the sea as a luminous, silent, and spectral Venus, we are reminded that books, even if dangerous and scary, are essential for survival—like Barcelona, which contains both a violent past insufficiently confronted, and a magnificent literary culture that has helped this wonderful city survive.

KARS, TURKEY

ORHAN PAMUK

SNOW (KARS) (2002)

Set in Anatolia in the remote border city of Kars, this work explores the tension between Turkey's secularism and its radical Islamist factions, following protagonist Ka's return to Turkey after a twelve-year period of political exile.

Orhan Pamuk, born in Istanbul in 1952, is the first Turkish Nobel laureate, having been awarded the Nobel Prize in Literature in 2006, four years after the publication of his fifth novel, *Snow*.

Faber and Faber published the first English translation in 2004; it was translated by Maureen Freely.

Of this work, Pamuk has commented: "I strongly feel that the art of the novel is based on the human capacity, though it's a limited capacity, to be able to identify with 'the other'."

A deceptively quixotic novel from the Nobel Prize-winning Turkish writer Orhan Pamuk, *Snow* is a heady, driven combination of political thriller, allegory, and intellectual meditation which, on its first English-language publication in 2004, was hailed for laying bare the complexity of Turkey's divided soul, specifically the tenuous balance between its secular outlook and radical Islamist elements. From the first pages the reader is drawn into a strangely submerged, alternate universe—that of Kars, (*Kar* is Turkish for "snow"), an isolated Anatolian city that has been arbitrarily cut off from the rest of the world by a three-day blizzard.

Into this snowstorm a bus is traveling precariously:

> The road signs caked with snow were impossible to read. Once the snowstorm began to rage in earnest, the driver turned off his full beam, and dimmed the lights inside the bus, hoping to conjure the road out of the semi-darkness. The passengers fell into a fearful silence, with their eyes on the scene outside: the snow-covered streets of derelict villages, the dimly lit, ramshackle one-storey houses, the roads to farther villages that were already closed; and the ravines barely visible among the streetlamps. If they spoke, it was in whispers.

One of these passengers is a stranger, Ka, whom the unseen narrator of the novel (claiming to be an old friend of Ka's named Orhan) refers to conspiratorially as "our traveller." Ka, a forty-two-year-old poet, has returned to Istanbul for his mother's funeral after twelve years of political exile in Germany. Somewhat discombobulated by this sudden homecoming amid personal loss, he decides on impulse to journey to Kars.

Yet Kars is not wholly a dreamlike, poetic destination but one in the grip of a terrible phenomenon: an unusual, and increasing, rate of suicide among its young female population, in protest at a mandatory instruction to remove their headscarves at school. These young women form a kind of Greek chorus to the narrative. Politically, too, Kars is at a crucial moment: Islamists

Years later, he could still recall the extraordinary beauty of the snow that night: the pleasure it brought him was far greater than any he'd known, in Istanbul. He was a poet, and, as he himself had written ... it snows only once in our dreams.

are set to sweep the imminent local elections. And Ka's pilgrimage is not one of idle curiosity: he is posing as a journalist, which makes him the ideal recipient for information the narrator wants to impart to the reader; and he is in search of Ipcek, a former girlfriend from student days, and for the answers to the divisions within himself, which echo Turkey's divisions: the emptiness of Westernization, which Ka has experienced throughout his German exile; the repellence of Islamic fundamentalism. There is a strong thread of individualism versus nationalism running through the book. We learn, as he contemplates this polarized city, which has evolved from many assimilations and influences, that Ka has visited twenty years earlier, as a young man. Nostalgically he surveys the diverse hinterland that history has wrought: the decaying ruins from the days of the Ottoman empire, the thousand-year-old Armenian churches, the castle occupied by the Russian army in the late nineteenth century, giving way to "modernization" under Ataturk:

> The streets and the large cobblestone pavements, the plane trees and the oleanders that had been planted after the founding of the Turkish republic. They gave the city a melancholy air unknown in the Ottoman cities whose wooden houses were burned down during the years of national struggle and tribal warfare.

Almost immediately on arrival in Kars, Ka witnesses an assassination, an act of extreme violence, and it is this seemingly random brutality set against a bittersweet love story that propels the novel. Set in 1992, it is as near to realism as Pamuk, a renowned weaver of tales, had achieved at this point in his writing career: an extraordinary foreshadowing of Turkey today with its controversial, authoritarian leadership and jailing of journalists, academics, poets, and writers. Pamuk as writer, observer, and shadowy narrator mixes satire and subterfuge in this ravishing "ghost city" strikingly emblematic of Turkey's past, present, and future.

Overleaf: Pamuk illustrated a first edition of his novel with his own drawing of Kars for a charity auction in December 2014. The auction, organized by Christie's to benefit the PEN American Center in New York, raised $13,000 from the drawing.

Ne zaman Kars'ı
hatırlasam böyle
bir resim geliyor gözü
ve yalnız köpek...

n önüne 2014

HAWKESBURY RIVER, NEW SOUTH WALES, AUSTRALIA

KATE GRENVILLE

THE SECRET RIVER (2005)

A highly acclaimed realist historical novel set in the colony of New South Wales that explores the convicts' reactions to the alien landscape and to its indigenous inhabitants.

Kate Grenville was born in 1950 in Sydney. She is one of Australia's most celebrated authors and has published fifteen books. She has won the Commonwealth Writers' Prize and the Orange Prize. In 2018 she was awarded an Officer (AO) for distinguished service to literature and the publishing ind ustry.

The Secret River forms a loose trilogy with *The Lieutenant* (2009) and *Sarah Thornhill* (2012) about the first three generations of colonial Australia.

The novel was shortlisted for the Man Booker Prize, and short- and long-listed for fifteen other national and international awards.

The significance and even sacred stature that landscape can assume; the human need to own or to simply belong to a landscape and the dual nature of both promise and threat that landscape can hold: all these reactions figure large in Kate Grenville's *The Secret River*, which is set on the Hawkesbury River, 47 miles northwest of Sydney. This is an area that was settled by one of Grenville's ancestors, Solomon Wiseman, later known as the "King of the Hawkesbury."

This internationally acclaimed realist historical novel chronicles the life of William Thornhill, from his poverty-stricken days in London in the late eighteenth century to his convict transportation to New South Wales in 1806 and his final transformation into a prosperous colonial landholder.

As an experienced riverman on the Thames, Thornhill is able to read his landscape, to "guess the state of the river, the tides, the wind." However, when faced with his country of exile Thornhill is utterly confounded: "This place was like nothing he had ever seen … different everywhere and yet everywhere the same." Eventually, however, the secret river overlays the Thames in his imagination. But what still confounds Thornhill comes from his determination to own part of this landscape that, to European eyes, lacks any visible marks of previous ownership: "There were no signs that the blacks felt the place belonged to them … no fences that said this is mine."

Because questions of the white settlers' relationships with the Aboriginal inhabitants and with the land loom over this saga, Grenville addresses the themes of racial atrocity and reconciliation. While this has made her book contentious to some academics, the reading public have embraced it, finding its history emotionally engaging rather than dry and distant.

While *The Secret River* can be read as part of a colonial trilogy that Grenville published between 2005 and 2011, it can also be read in conjunction with her journey through its creative writing process, *Searching for the Secret River* (2006). Here she acknowledges the pivotal role of landscape, confessing that she had found herself describing landscape in human terms: "the golden flesh of the rocks beneath their dark skin, the trees gesturing, the

bush watchful and alive." Grenville's rationale for this vision was insightful: "Humanising the landscape could be a way of showing the link between indigenous people and their land because … the country *was* the people." In Thornhill's voice this becomes: "The eye could peer but not know if it was a couple of branches … or a man with a spear, watching."

This 1822 painting by J. Lycett, *North View of Sydney New South Wales*, shows the broad mouth of the Hawkesbury River. It is held by the State Library of New South Wales.

The book's deeper purpose is to question white Australia's relationship with the land and to its Aboriginal inhabitants. Thornhill is haunted by the book's climactic massacre of Aborigines, which creates another secret river, a river of blood and a tragic undercurrent within white Australia's history. Thornhill's "ownership" of land thus becomes a hollow achievement and he even dies unreconciled with his son Dick whose sympathy toward the local Aboriginal people alienates him from his family.

Early in this novel the crucial dilemma facing its characters in coming to terms with an utterly new vision of landscape is made unequivocally clear: "This place was like nothing he had ever seen." And for this reader, as someone Australian-born and bred, what *The Secret River* achieves is implicit in this dichotomy. This is a novel that allows even a native Australian to re-engage with his own country and to see it with new eyes. It is Grenville's crowning achievement.

NAPLES, ITALY

ELENA FERRANTE

MY BRILLIANT FRIEND
(L'AMICA GENIALE) (2011)

A bestselling Bildungsroman by the pseudonymous author Elena Ferrante, My Brilliant Friend *follows the thread of a friendship between two girls from Naples over many years.*

Elena Ferrante is a pseudonym. Many attempts have been made to unmask Ferrante, including a widely shared exposé by Claudio Gatti in 2016, but none have been confirmed by Ferrante or her publishing house.

Ferrante's quartet of Neapolitan books has sold more than 5.5 million copies worldwide, and *My Brilliant Friend* is currently being turned into a television mini-series by HBO.

The unnamed Neapolitan neighborhood where *My Brilliant Friend* is set is based on a real district in Naples called the Rione Luzzatti.

My Brilliant Friend, the first in Elena Ferrante's series of Neapolitan novels, is a book of binaries. Lenù Greco, our narrator, is perennially "anxious;" Lila Cerullo, her best friend, is "terrible, dazzling." From modest beginnings in a down-at-heel neighborhood in Naples, they remake themselves by different means. Lenù furthers her education, while Lila marries a wealthy young grocer. They are jealous of each other, drawn to each other, opposites in everything they do. Aptly, the city they live in is a place of contrasts, reflecting the extremes of the two girls' personalities.

In Ferrante's hands, Naples in the 1950s is both alluring and sordid, impoverished and wealthy. The neighborhood Lenù and Lila inhabit embodies one extreme; it is established from the start as a site of violence, gang-riddled and lawless. "We lived in a world," Lenù observes, "in which children and adults were often wounded, blood flowed from the wounds, they festered, and sometimes people died." Families are crammed into tall apartment buildings; the air is thick with "*disperazione*—a word that in dialect meant having lost all hope but also being broke."

For Lenù and Lila, wealth becomes an "obsession." They plan for a future of carefree luxuriance; "to listen to us," Lenù remarks sardonically, "you might think that the wealth was hidden somewhere in the neighborhood." In their adolescence, they witness this ideal of wealth in other Neapolitan districts: "It was like crossing a border… [The women] seemed to have breathed another air, to have eaten other food, to have dressed on some other planet, to have learned to walk on wisps of wind."

Boundaries are essential to the novel, and the transgression of boundaries, both physical and social, becomes a recurring theme. As children, Lenù and Lila venture through the tunnel that leads them out of their neighborhood, but on the other side they grow fearful and soon turn back. Later, Lenù transcends the expectations of her parents by attending high school; "I had crossed the boundaries of the neighborhood," she writes.

One of *My Brilliant Friend*'s most significant episodes occurs when Lenù travels to Ischia one summer. "For the first time I was leaving home,"

Above: Four young women do their *passeggiata* on the streets of Naples, showing off their best clothes. In the novel, Lenù and Lila long for the wealth of Naples's more prosperous districts. Photograph, 1955.

Previous page: The profusion of laundry in these Naples alleyways is an indicator of the close physical proximity in which Ferrante's characters grow up. With limited apartment space, residents share communal washing lines to dry their clothes. Photograph by Laura Di Base, 2013.

she says. "I was going on a journey, a journey by sea. The large body of my mother—along with the neighborhood, and Lila's troubles—grew distant, and vanished." Ischia works its magic on Lenù's unruly, adolescent body—she becomes sun-kissed and confident in this place removed from the claustrophobia of her home, and finds herself falling in love with a boy named Nino.

Subsequent books in the series see Lenù journeying still farther beyond the parameters of the neighborhood. Her education opens doors in distinguished homes in Naples and other cities; with this "sudden widening of [her] world," the rift between Lenù and her childhood environment grows even more gaping. Looking back at Naples, she is preoccupied by its malignance: "The city seemed to harbour in its guts a fury that couldn't get out," she writes in *The Story of a New Name*, "and therefore eroded it from the inside, or erupted in pustules on the surface, swollen with venom against everyone." Yet she comes to realize that she is "bound" to Naples, just as she is bound to Lila, who, we are told in the opening pages of *My Brilliant Friend*, "never left Naples in her life."

Like Lila, like Lenù, Naples wears many faces. It is a place of wealth, of extravagance, as well as darkness, violence, and despair. In some areas, it seems rich with opportunity; elsewhere, deep in the heart of the neighborhood, it feels inescapably small. A fascinating creation, it is as layered and volatile as Ferrante's engaging cast of characters.

HENAN PROVINCE, PEOPLE'S REPUBLIC OF CHINA

YAN LIANKE

THE EXPLOSION CHRONICLES (ZHÀLIÈ ZHÌ) (2013)

A high-stakes satirical novel set in the author's native Henan province, The Explosion Chronicles *tells the story of the fictional village of Explosion, from its accidental creation as the result of volcanic eruption to its extraordinary rise to a megacity which is home to millions.*

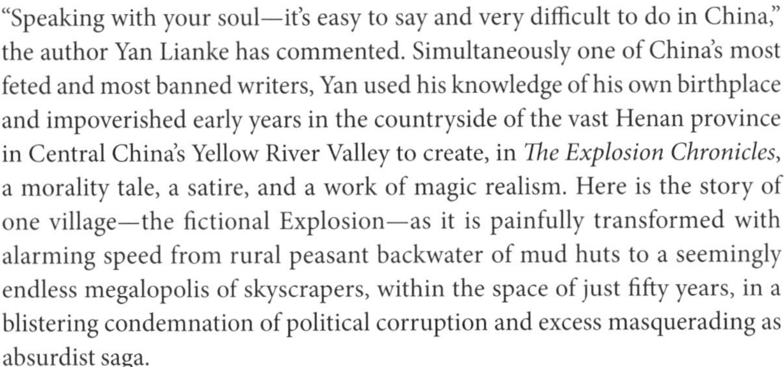

"Speaking with your soul—it's easy to say and very difficult to do in China," the author Yan Lianke has commented. Simultaneously one of China's most feted and most banned writers, Yan used his knowledge of his own birthplace and impoverished early years in the countryside of the vast Henan province in Central China's Yellow River Valley to create, in *The Explosion Chronicles*, a morality tale, a satire, and a work of magic realism. Here is the story of one village—the fictional Explosion—as it is painfully transformed with alarming speed from rural peasant backwater of mud huts to a seemingly endless megalopolis of skyscrapers, within the space of just fifty years, in a blistering condemnation of political corruption and excess masquerading as absurdist saga.

Explosion is so called for its original settlement by a group of refugees fleeing a volcano eruption during the Song Dynasty (960–1279), yet the name is also a metaphor for its rapid evolution. The main focus of the novel is on the years following the founding of the new China in 1949, when the history of Explosion Village "replicated in miniature the pain and prosperity undergone by the nation itself," according to Yan, who fictionalizes himself as a designated literary personage commissioned to write the history of the village's extraordinary metamorphosis. That change is at first geographical—and then social. Yan places the village in the real landscape of Henan province specifically, almost affectionately, as someone with deep ties to the area: "When Explosion village was founded ... the fields were wide and flat [and] farmers would often gather there to buy and sell goods."

Henan province, with its capital Zhengzhou, has huge significance as the place where Chinese civilization originated. Its temples are among the first Buddhist temples in China. In one gruesome, poignant moment in the novel, like several based on real incidents, elderly people commit suicide so that they will be buried in tombs according to their Buddhist faith, before new cremation laws forbidding such practices take effect. This reportedly occurred in the city of Anxing. In another, thousands of dead pigs float down the contaminated river of a megacity that supplies drinking water to millions

Renowned as one of China's greatest living writers, Yan Lianke was born in Song County, Henan Province, in 1958. Based in Beijing where he is a professor of literature, Yan has said that his heart remains in Henan, the setting for many of his novels and short stories.

Originally published in China in 2013, the first English translation was published by Chatto & Windus (UK) in 2016 and Grove Atlantic (US) in 2016.

Lianke has admitted to self-censoring some of his own highly controversial works in order that they themselves not be censored.

Detail from "Along the River During the Qingming Festival," painted by Shen Yuan, which shows the very rural beginnings of Henan province. The painting depicts the landscape of Bianjing, the ancient capital of the Song Dynasty, now present-day Kaifeng.

of its inhabitants. This environmental disaster happened in the Huangpu River, just before Yan concluded his writing of the *Chronicles*. The reasoning behind what he coins as his "mythorealism" becomes clear—an exaggerated reality of deliberate, collective stupidity and counterfactuality. What is fact, and what is myth?

As the novel progresses and the village transforms, nature reflects the tumultuous events taking place. Yan reminds the reader in his author's note: "contemporary China is currently hurtling past a series of economic and developmental milestones that took Europe over two centuries to achieve." That bewildering speed of economic and social reform is represented by the natural world's confusion over Explosion's unprecedented changes: "the chickens started laying goose eggs and the geese started laying duck eggs."

The other aspect of myth versus reality is harder to separate or beautify, and that is of the inevitable driving force of power and its all too familiar companion, corruption. Yan shows this early in the novel, a sign of grimness to follow, in the gruesome drowning in spittle of Zhi Quinlang, Explosion's old village chief. Zhu Qinglang's horrible public demise is the catalyst for the human drama of the novel, and also for the almost cataclysmic "progression" of change in this backwater landscape. One unforgettable exchange between the mayor and an associate sums up the bewildering transformation from agriculture to industry and its depersonalizing effect.

> When they were halfway up the mountain, they turned and the mayor noted with surprise that buildings had suddenly sprouted up everywhere, and the streets were bustling with activity that was quite different from the kind of rustic excitement the town had enjoyed when it was a mere village. Streetlamps now lined the streets like chopsticks, and each house's chimney spat out thick smoke like clouds on an overcast day. Everywhere, the ground had been opened up and revealed, like a patient randomly cut up by a surgeon, and things were vibrant but also covered in scars.

The capital of Henan province, Zhengzhou, has developed into an epicenter for industry, manufacturing, and technology. With a population of nearly 100 million people, the province is one of the most populous areas in the world.

Yan's preoccupation in the novel is with the recurrent nature of "progress," and the lamenting of the loss of the bedrock of ancient Chinese culture as the rush to advancement becomes ever more frenzied. When Explosion's elevation to megacity is complete; it is rendered almost unrecognizable.

HOKITIKA, SOUTH ISLAND, NEW ZEALAND

ELEANOR CATTON

THE LUMINARIES (2013)

Catton's richly evocative Victorianesque novel tells the lesser-known story of the West Coast New Zealand gold rush, capturing an intricate world of shifting fortunes, both monetary and astrological.

Eleanor Catton was born in Canada in 1985, but grew up in Christchurch, New Zealand. *The Luminaries* is her second novel.

It won the Man Booker Prize in 2013, breaking several records: Catton was the youngest ever recipient of the award at 28 years old. At 832 pages long, the novel was the longest work ever to secure the prize, and it was also a first for the publishing house, Granta Books.

We all know the American gold rushes of the mid-nineteenth century. Images from those years leap to mind: somewhere in the Californian desert, a prospector hammers in wooden pegs to stake his claim. Deep in the Yukon at dusk, a wolf howls in the blue distance, then one by one the rest of the pack join in. Miners huddle round the low-burnt fire, touch their rifles for reassurance. Sergio Leone and Jack London are the laureates of these landscapes.

But the New Zealand gold rush? Not many people will know of its existence until they read Eleanor Catton's vast and intricate novel *The Luminaries*, set in the township of Hokitika in 1866. Out of Catton's patient prose emerges a world so completely realized that you feel part of its population. Gold has been found in the sands and rivers of the South Island, and Hokitika teems with speculators, aggregators, bankers, and outfitters. Up and down the west coast the diggers toil, delving for the sly glint of ore. Eastward of Hokitika the land rises into totara forests, rolling hills, and clear-watered rivers whose beds are cobbled with "smooth, milky-grey stones that, when split, showed a glassy-green interior, harder than steel"—the sacred Maori stone known as *pounamu*. And over all of this loom the Southern Alps, ice-capped and incorruptible.

The novel unfolds a mystery. A haul of gold has been discovered in a hermit's cottage: its provenance is unclear, its ownership disputed. Death stalks the land in the guise of lucre. The reader's first task is—as Lester Freamon puts it in *The Wire*—to follow the money. That pursuit takes us forward and backward in time, and through the varied landscapes of the South Island. As we move from place to place, expanding our imagined geography, so the plot whirs on—gorgeous and complex as an orrery.

For a novel set in such wild country, it often takes us indoors: in barrooms, billiard-rooms, and courtrooms, in shanty-shacks and opium dens where smokers lie supine. These interiors are evoked in exceptional detail. Catton's narrator seems to notice everything, down to the seam that runs through the center of the billiard-table baize, from when it "had been sawn in two on the Sydney docks to better survive the crossing."

Readers might be put off by the book's cubical bulk and astrological armature. What a loss that would be! Each reading of its 2,496 pages has yielded new dividends. And its consequences enact its concerns, for Catton takes such pains not only for the joy of evocation, but also to carry out a huge thought-experiment into the nature of value.

Early archival photo of a Westland digger in Hokitika during the West Coast Gold Rush. Coastal Hokitika was one of New Zealand's most populous centers in the late nineteenth century as an important river port. Today it is a small township with a population of around 2,000.

Almost everyone in Hokitika is dedicated to the acquisition of wealth and the maximization of profit. It is a community driven by capital, in which relationships are ruled by cost-benefit analysis. One of the few transactions to defeat this fierce logic is the unconditional love that develops between two characters: a young prospector and a "whore." Their love eventually emerges as a gold standard: a touchstone with which to test the value of all things.

And so this phenomenal book, apparently about digging into the Earth's innards in search of wealth, ends up delving into the heart's interior to find true worth. All the while the landscape goes about its business: rain clatters fatly onto the roofs of Hokitika's 100 pubs, storms pummel the sand-bars, the snowmelt of the high peaks swells the rivers, and the rivers crash down toward the sea, carrying gold that shines in their eddy-pools, as one early prospector put it, "like the stars of Orion on a dark, frosty night."

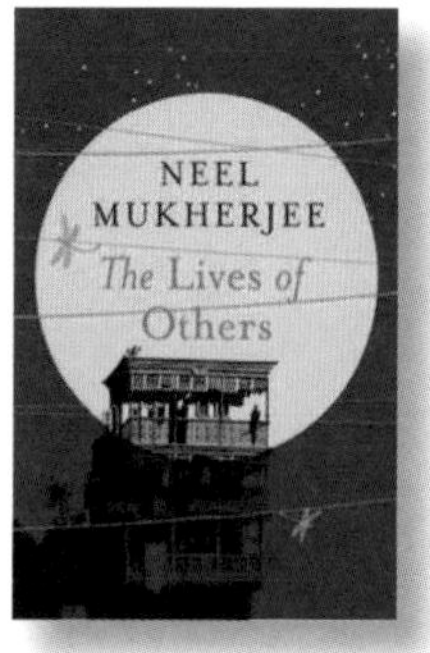

KOLKATA, WEST BENGAL, INDIA

NEEL MUKHERJEE

THE LIVES OF OTHERS (2014)

Set in Calcutta in 1967 in the midst of political tumult, this hymn to a home city is epic in ambition, rich in compassion, and comprehensive in its anatomization of a place and a people.

Neel Mukherjee was born in Calcutta in 1970. Educated at Jadavpur, Oxford and Cambridge he trained to become a Renaissance scholar before becoming a writer at the age of 40.

This is Mukherjee's second novel and it was shortlisted for the Man Booker Prize 2014 and the Costa Novel Award, winning the Encore Award for best second novel in 2015.

Set in Calcutta (now Kolkata), the capital of the state of West Bengal, the novel focuses on the events of Naxalite insurgency. The name derives from the name of the village of Naxalbari in West Bengal, the first center of the uprisings.

In an interview in 2018, Neel Mukherjee confessed his desire, conceiving *The Lives of Others*, to write a book that grappled with his own origins: "Most writers need to have at least one reckoning with the place they grew up in. … This is my 'Bengali novel.'" The book that results is sprawling but never messy, tender in its attention to the nuances of familiar relationships and yet violent in the extremes of deprivation and cruelty that it so compellingly displays.

At the heart of this complex history sits a house and a family: the Ghoshes of Calcutta, whose members (and squabbles) are many, the internal hierarchy of the family spatialized in their confinement to different floors of the house. The patriarch, now a grandfather, commands the top with his wife while the servants and the widow of the youngest son, who is herself of lower caste, make do with the bottom level, in proximity to the stink and noise of the street.Where it might have felt sufficient to concentrate only on that household as a microcosm of Bengali society, the novel is more ambitious, set at a critical juncture in Indian political history and underpinned by a fundamental binary: "Inside-outside: the world forever and always divided into those two categories." This is highlighted by two separate strands of narrative, removed both socially and geographically from one another: city versus country; haves versus have-nots; and a third-person narrative versus an unreliable first-person.

With a hypersensitive attention to "the torrent of ordinary life," he roams to scenes beyond the household at Number 22/6 Basanta Bose Road: the punishing poverty of the rural countryside, the realities of the slums in Calcutta, the sadism of police brutality. His portrait of a family becomes a chronicle of the Naxalite insurgency in West Bengal in 1968, which becomes in turn a meditation on essential questions of social justice, equality, and the limits of empathy.

The bourgeois "interior" living of the Goshe family, kettled in their home, seems far removed from the external world. Supratik, the radicalized eldest grandson, labels their existence a "cushioned vacuum" and leaves the family to engage with the activities of the CPI(M) (Communist Party of India—Marxist). "My concern is not with the inside … the world is my concern." His narrative, which intercuts the comfort of the account of the family and its history, duly

Contemporary photograph of the streets of Calcutta in 1962, whose 'ampitheatre' of noise prompts the Ghosh family into wakefulness each day: "The clatter of metal buckets; uninterrupted cawing of crows; wrangling stray dogs..."

deals with this big beyond. But back in Calcutta, the experience of the city is not comfortable, a sensuous assault of sounds and smells around which the humidity "congeals into [a] suffocating blanket." Family secrets take us to the squalid slums that exist in proximity to the splendour of Chowringhee. A raw urgency accompanies the description of these scenes. In one horrific episode, we see a young boy stand transfixed by the body of a dead woman. Her body is "all vertices and angles like a collapsible contraption" as she is attacked by crows; the boy himself "helpless in the face of the intrepid crow's desecration of his mother." This is a place that is not only physically repugnant, "all open drains and squalid houses," but also a site where darkness becomes animate: "the dark retreated only insufficiently into corners, waiting impatiently to flow out and take over entirely again."

At the end of the novel, Supratik discovers that the rigid demarcation of "inside-outside" is less about geography than perspective. Selfishness has many faces; it is foolish to think that family and politics don't intersect in their rival demands for our attention; and the agency of the individual in the fabric of a collective structure is, at best, only tenuous. "If you are so full of kindness and sympathy for the powerless, why don't you look closer to home," his mother Sandhya admonishes him on his return.

Empathy is finally not only a bridge across the distance separating "us" and "them," but an invitation to consider each inner life. Mukherjee's depiction of "the opera of Bengali life" is unfailingly dedicated across his spectrum of characters—whether he is describing beauty, "the rice fields as parcels of bright emerald during the monsoon," or painting darker realities. "We are so much creatures of our context, I feel," he continues in the interview, and this book is the vivid, unflinching demonstration of that belief.

NEW YORK CITY, USA

FRANCIS SPUFFORD
GOLDEN HILL (2016)

A mysterious young Englishman arrives in pre-revolutionary New York bearing fabulous wealth and refusing to say what his purpose is.

Francis Spufford (born 1964) had turned 50 and was the author of five non-fiction books—on subjects as diverse as polar exploration, the economics of the Soviet Union, and what it feels like to be a Christian in the modern world—before he wrote this, his first novel.

Rapturously reviewed on publication in 2016, *Golden Hill* was shortlisted for the Walter Scott Prize for Historical Fiction and the Folio Prize, and won the Costa Award and the Desmond Elliot Prize for first novels, and the Royal Society of Literature Ondaatje Prize for a book that evokes the "spirit of a place."

For Richard Smith, the young Englishman who arrives in New York on the first page of Francis Spufford's novel, the city is a bewildering place, every doorway holding the promise of danger, pleasure, or bliss (he encounters plenty of the first, a little of the second—and the third...?). New York is almost as bewildered by Smith, who comes with a note of credit for £1,000 sterling ($1,300), a fabulous sum of money; and Smith's refusal to say how he came by it or what he intends stirs suspicion and rumor: he could be a swindler or a spy. He will turn out to be something more unexpected, and more scandalous.

This New York is disconcerting for the reader, too. The year is 1746: Americans are still subjects of King George. New York, population 7,000, is an anthill next to the London Smith has left, the largest metropolis in Europe with 700,000 souls. The skyline Smith sees out of his window on his first morning isn't the towering amalgam of concrete and steel familiar from countless films and television programs: instead, "rooftops and bell towers greeted him; a jumble, not much elevated, of stepped Dutchwork eaves and ordinary English tile ... and behind a slow-swaying fretwork of masts."

Spufford is known as a supremely versatile and original writer of non-fiction, one who uses all the weapons of the novelist—unexpected similes, metaphors, speculations, parables, rich description—to conquer the reader's imagination. In *Golden Hill*, he uses a similarly wide range of techniques to help the reader see New York afresh, forgetting everything we know about what would come afterward. It is more like science-fiction novel than a historical novel, building this new world piece by piece, letting the reader learn with the traveler how everything works—money, manners, the rigid hierarchies of wealth and status, and the factions (governor versus magistrate, English versus Dutch) that cut across them. Not that Smith learns quickly enough: treading on toes, blundering through politics and high finance, he finds himself at odds with the establishment; he makes an unexpected friend, falls in love, becomes a star of the stage, is thrown into prison, fights a duel—and shows in the end that he can spring a bigger surprise on New York than the town can spring on him.

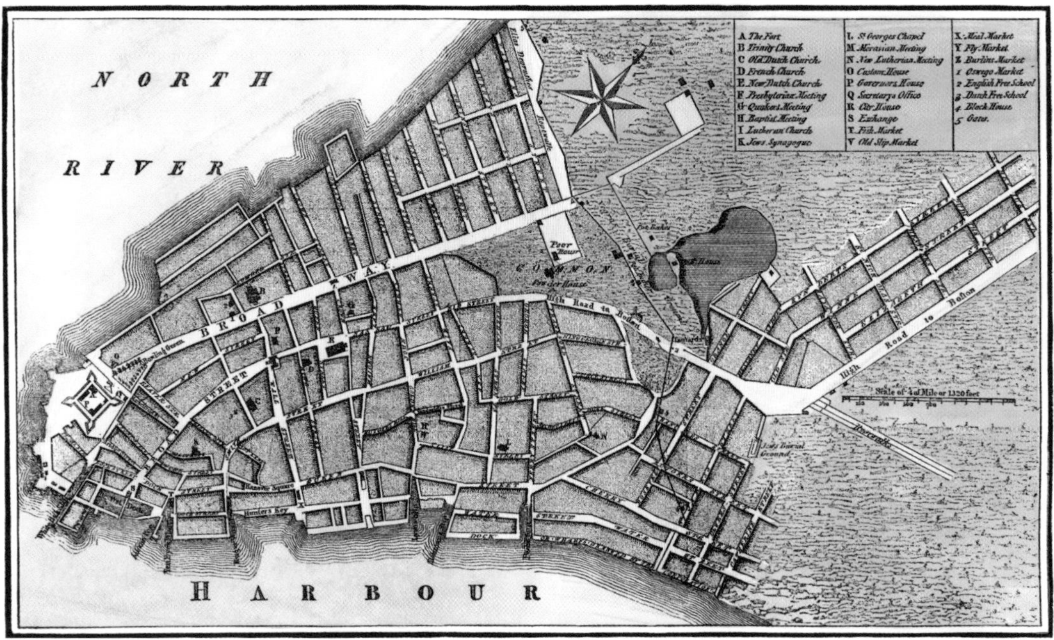

Archival map of Manhattan in 1767, when New York was just "a small town on the tip of Manhattan Island."

Part of the trick is to match the Smith's surprise and puzzlement with the reader's: Smith, like the modern reader, is struck by how small and countryfied New York seems—the street called "the Broad Way" is not that broad, and lined with trees. At times, though, the reader may be taken aback where Smith isn't: Smith contrasts the mazy streets and sometimes shabby buildings of New York unfavorably with the wide open squares in the fashionable West End of London, turning upside down the difference we have become used to.

Spufford's talent for metaphor is let off the leash—so that a fog contains and muffles sounds "as a jewel-box with a cushioned lid presses all within into the smothering clasp of velvet." But as well as the look of the place, *Golden Hill* gives you its sounds, its stinks (so much cleaner than filthy London), the bone-deep chill of its winters and the draftiness of its wooden building, and the fear that never quite goes away. This New York isn't the gateway to a great nation, but to an unmapped, hostile continent. On Guy Fawkes Night—when the New Yorkers proudly show off their loyalty to the British crown, and toast the confounding of dastardly Roman Catholic plots—Smith sees the celebratory bonfire as a tiny spark against the vast dark continent of America. The town has its own darkness, a barely suppressed violence that almost does Smith in, and though it is a pious place, with thirty churches, it has its share of sins, carnal and otherwise, including America's original sin: slavery. The book's achievement, in the end, is not simply that it brings alive the New York of the eighteenth century, but that it brings a richer life, deepened by the past, to the America of today.

AMAZON RAINFOREST, VENEZUELA

MIGUEL BONNEFOY

BLACK SUGAR

(AZÚCAR NEGRA) (2017)

A vivacious portrait of his mother's homeland, Bonnefoy's generational saga does more than just speak up for the country we now call Venezuela. This novel talks of the spirit of the South American rainforest, and a people emerging "not as a tribe, but not yet a country."

Miguel Bonnefoy was born in France in 1986; his mother is Venezuelan and his father, Chilean. He holds an MA from the Sorbonne, and spent time teaching French in Venezuela.

Black Sugar is his second novel; his first, *Octavio's Journey (Le voyage d'Octavio,* 2015) was shortlisted for the Goncourt first novel award.

Black Sugar was originally published in France by Rivages. The first English edition was translated by Emily Boyce, published by Gallic Books in 2018.

We start with a shipwreck. Already history is snagged on the Amazon rainforest itself, "its stern wedged in the crown of a mango tree many metres tall … fruits hung amid the rigging." Immediately we are in a rich canopy of rainforest:

> A breeze heavy with the scent of dried almonds blew in and the whole carcass of the ship ... creaked like an old treasure chest being lowered into the ground.

This literary lanscape has no name, only a symbol. The book's epicenter is literally the cross on the map of the treasure buried by the privateer Captain Henry Morgan. This cross also represents the mark of man's greed. Three hundred years after the shipwreck the promise of its riches still lures adventurers. The forest has reclaimed and hidden its treasures, and yielded up other wealths—like sugar and rum and oil.

Here now lives Serena Otero, an only child to elderly, distant parents, who is overjoyed at the arrival of the modern radio and its small adverts that link up the communities around. She is an instinctive botanist, entranced by and in tune with the natural world and all things organic.

> Every morning she set out across the fields armed with a shovel and a pruning knife, cutting bulbs and pressing leaves between her fingers as she went.
>
> In the forest she picked lobster-claw and bird-of-paradise plants, west Indian jasmine and porcelain roses and collected herbariums. She carried under her arm a sketchbook she had bound from textured paper and sticks of charcoal that blackened her pockets.

At night, she dreams of a lover who might answer her small ad: "Has drowned her heart in a barrel of rum. Reward offered to whoever comes to drink it."

A banyan ficus tree in the Henri Pittier National Park. Venezuela is one of the ten most bio-diverse countries in the world, with over 21,000 species of plants. Forests and plantations cover two-thirds of its land mass.

When finally someone does arrive at the small sugar plantation, he is not what she had in mind; a gold digger who comes looking for the treasure from which a panoply of postcolonial allusions and nightmares are unleashed. Yet soon Serena bewitches him.

The rainforest provides the novel with its senusous surroundings.

> They [stomped] through piles of sticky mud-covered leaves, delving into the undergrowth. They climbed a mound and leapt across a stream, their clothes spattered with earth.

At heart, this is a biography of a woman and by inference a nation confronting the greed and lust of the modern world, her story a fast-growing vine that twists around the jungle trunks with as many turns. To give away too much too early would spoil the entertainment.

Bonnefoy does not let his characters stray too far though; they are only allowed so much dialogue for themselves because he is the main storyteller, this is his jungle, not so much history as iridescent, raw, sometimes cruel fable.

Like a matrix his images move around and reappear before locking back into place, tightly. The prose is, rather like the forest itself, superficially all green, but it is a camouflage hiding many things, not least the heartbeat and travails of Venezuela. What the writing does yield up is the spirit and colors of what another South American nation, the Costa Rica, calls pura vida. In that sense, it is a novel that speaks up for a continent.

CONTRIBUTOR BIOGRAPHIES

JOHN SUTHERLAND—GENERAL EDITOR

John Andrew Sutherland is an English academic, columnist, and author. Emeritus Lord Northcliffe Professor of Modern English Literature at University College London, John began his academic career as a lecturer in Edinburgh in 1964 after graduating from the University of Leicester. He taught for many years at the California Institute of Technology with a specialist interest in Victorian fiction, twentieth-century literature, popular fiction, and the history of publishing. His books include *How to Read a Novel: A User's Guide* (2006) and *Curiosities of Literature: A Feast for Book Lovers* (2008), and he was a major contributor to *Literary Wonderlands* (2016). He is a regular contributor to *The Times, Guardian, New Statesman, New York Times* and *London Review of Books.*
Wuthering Heights (page 24), *The Return of the Native* (page 38), *In the Skin of a Lion* (page 205)

LAWRENCE BATTERSBY

A graduate of University of Glasgow with a Masters in Literature (Creative Writing), Lawrence Battersby also has an MBA and BA in Psychology. He lives in Paris, where he writes in diverse genres and has recently completed a historical novel set in nineteenth-century Spain and a Second World War novella set in 1940s Europe.
Kidnapped (page 46), *Sunset Song* (page 104)

MICHAEL BOURNE

Michael Bourne is a contributing editor for *Poets & Writers* magazine, whose work has appeared in the *New York Times, The Economist*, and *Salon*. A long-time New Yorker, he now lives in Vancouver, where he teaches at Simon Fraser University and the British Columbia Institute of Technology.
Bright Lights, Big City (page 200)

MARIAROSA BRICCHI

Mariarosa Bricchi is a linguist and a freelance editor. She teaches at the Universities of Milan and Pavia, and was a visiting scholar at Columbia University in New York.
The Betrothed (page 18)

JULIE CURTIS

Julie Curtis is a Professor of Russian Literature at Wolfson College, Oxford, and has written four books (biographies and interpretative studies) about Bulgakov, as well as others about his friend and contemporary Evgeny Zamiatin. She currently works on twenty-first-century drama written in Russian.
The Master & Margarita (page 170)

GARY DALKIN

Gary Dalkin a freelance editor and writer. Recent projects include a new anthology of stories, *Improbable Botany* (2017), and edits of books by Andrew David Barker, Ben Graff, Lynne Chitty, Sarah Tyley, and David Lawrence-Young. He contributes every month to *Writing Magazine* and is a founder of Gateway Writers.
Persuasion (page 16)

TONY EARNSHAW

Writer, editor, and film historian based in Yorkshire, UK, Tony Earnshaw has written a number of books including *An Actor and a Rare One: Peter Cushing as Sherlock Holmes* (2001), *The Christmas Ghost Stories of Lawrence Gordon Clark* (2014), *Under Milk Wood Revisited: The Wales of Dylan Thomas*, (2014), and *FANTASTIQUE: Interviews with Horror, Sci-Fi & Fantasy Filmmakers* (2016). He holds a Masters in English by Research from Sheffield Hallam University.
Under Milk Wood (page 140)

ALISON FLOOD

Alison Flood is a books critic for the *Guardian*. She loved *The Shipping News* so much that she went to Newfoundland on her honeymoon.
The Shipping News (page 214)

WAYNE GOODERHAM

W. B. Gooderham is a freelance writer for the *Guardian*, *Observer*, and *Wasafiri*. He was shortlisted for the Dinesh Allirajah Prize for Short Fiction and his first book, *Dedicated To...* (a collection of found inscriptions inside second-hand books) was published by Transworld in 2013. He is currently working on his second.
The Magic Mountain (page 78)

RUTH GRAHAM

Ruth Graham is a contributing writer at *Slate*. She has written for the *New York Times Magazine*, *Wall Street Journal*, *Boston Globe*, *Politico Magazine*, TheAtlantic.com, and many other publications. She lives in a small town in northern New England.
Kristin Lavransdatter (page 67)

DANIEL HAHN

Daniel Hahn is a writer, editor, and translator with fifty-something books to his name. His work has won the International Dublin Literary Award and the Blue Peter Book Award, and been shortlisted for the Man Booker International Prize, among others. Recent books include the new *Oxford Companion to Children's Literature*.
Les Misérables (page 32), *Winnie-the-Pooh* (page 89)

ROBERT HANKS

Robert Hanks is a freelance journalist and broadcaster based in Cambridge. He contributes to, among other things, the *London Review of Books* and the film magazine *Sight & Sound*; for BBC radio he has written and presented programs about the relationship between writing and pubs and the place of dogs in human lives.
The Wall Jumper (page 196), *Golden Hill* (page 242)

ROBERT HOLDEN

Australia-based lecturer, curator, and historian, and the author of over thirty books, Robert Holden has received awards from the Literature Board of the Australia Council, held a Mitchell Library Fellowship, and has spoken at numerous conferences in Australia and at the Universities of Oxford and Cambridge. He also contributed to *Literary Wonderlands* (2016).
Voss (page 154), *Cloudstreet* (page 210), *The Secret River* (230)

JON HUGHES

Jon Hughes is Senior Lecturer in German and Cultural Studies at Royal Holloway, University of London. He has published on many aspects of German literature, history, and culture, and has a particular interest in Berlin and the Weimar Republic. His latest book is *Max Schmeling and the Making of a National Hero in Twentieth-Century Germany* (2017).
Berlin Alexanderplatz (page 96)

MAYA JAGGI

Maya Jaggi is an award-winning global cultural journalist, writer, and editor. A contributing art critic to the *Financial Times*, she was an arts profile writer and book critic for the *Guardian Review* for more than a decade. Educated at Oxford University and the London School of Economics, she has reported on culture from five continents, and was awarded an honorary doctorate by the UK's Open University for "extending the map of international writing." All author quotations are from Maya Jaggi's interviews with Earl Lovelace in 1990, 1998 and 2018.
The Dragon Can't Dance (page 189)

DECLAN KIBERD

Declan Kiberd is author of *Ulysses and Us: The Art of Everyday Living* (2009). He has written many books about the Irish revival, including the trilogy *Inventing Ireland* (1995), *Irish Classics* (2000), and *After Ireland* (2017). He has introduced the Penguin Modern Classics *Ulysses* and published an Annotated Student's Edition also in that series. He is a former Director of the Abbey Theatre in Dublin and has appeared in many film and radio documentaries about Ireland. He is currently Keough Professor of Irish Studies at the University of Notre Dame.
Ulysses (page 74)

REYES LAZARO

Associate Professor of Spanish and Portuguese at Smith College in Massachusetts, Reyes Lazaro holds a PhD in Spanish and a Masters in Philosophy from the University of Massachusetts, Amherst, and a BA in Philosophy from the University of Deusto, Bilbao, Spain. She was also a student of Journalism at the Universitat Autònoma of Barcelona.

The Hive (page 133), *The Book of Disquiet* (page 193), *The Shadow of the Wind* (page 224),

NICHOLAS LEZARD

Nicholas Lezard is an English journalist and literary critic. He writes regularly for *The Guardian*, *The Independent*, and the *New Statesman* and has published two books, *The Nolympics: One Man's Struggle Against Sporting Hysteria* (2012) and a memoir, *Bitter Experience Has Taught Me* (2013).

Bleak House (page 28)

ROBERT MACFARLANE

Robert Macfarlane is the author of a number of books about landscape, language, and nature, including *The Wild Places* (2007), *The Old Ways* (2012), *Landmarks* (2015), and *The Lost Words* (2017). His work has been widely adapted for film, radio, television, and performance. He is a Fellow of Emmanuel College, Cambridge.

For Whom the Bell Tolls (page 116), *The Luminaries* (page 238),

TINA MAKERETI

Tina Makereti is a fiction writer, essayist, and creative writing lecturer in New Zealand. Her books include *Where the Rēkohu Bone Sings* (2014), *Black Marks on the White Page* (2017), and *The Imaginary Lives of James Pōneke* (2018), and she is lucky to live close enough to Hongoeka to visit sometimes.

Potiki (page 203)

IAIN MALONEY

Iain Maloney is the author of three novels and a collection of poetry. He is also an editor, journalist, and teacher. He lives in Japan where he writes as "The Only Gaijin in the Village."

The Sound of Waves (page 142)

KATE MCNAUGHTON

Kate McNaughton is an author, translator, filmmaker and self-professed fan of *The Lonely Londoners*. Born and raised in Paris by British parents, and currently living in Berlin, Kate is fascinated with the role of place in literature. Her debut novel *How I Lose You* (2018) was published in the UK and in France.

The Lonely Londoners (page 148)

SARAH MESLE

Sarah Mesle (Ph.D., Northwestern University) is a professor of writing at the University of Southern California and Senior Editor at the *Los Angeles Review of Books*, where she also writes regularly about television, literature, and popular culture. With Sarah Blackwood, she is the co-editor of *Avidly* and the forthcoming *Avidly Reads* series from NYU Press.

Anne of Green Gables (page 56)

LAURA MILLER

Laura Miller was the general editor of *Literary Wonderlands* and co-founded Salon.com, where she worked as an editor and writer for twenty years. She is currently a books and culture columnist at *Slate*. A journalist and a critic, her work has appeared in the *New Yorker*, *Harper's*, the *Guardian*, and the *New York Times Book Review*, where she wrote the "Last Word" column for two years.

Tales of the City (page 186)

MAHVESH MURAD

Mahvesh Murad is an editor, critic, and voice artist from Karachi, Pakistan. She is the editor of the *Apex Book of World Science Fiction: Volume 4* (2015), and co-editor of the *Djinn Falls in Love* (2017) with Jared Shurin.

Things Fall Apart (page 161)

MARGARET OAKES

Margaret Oakes is a Professor of English at Furman University in Greenville, South Carolina, specializing in early modern British poetry and drama. She holds a BA in English, a JD from the University of Illinois at Urbana-Champaign, and a Ph.D. in English from Stanford University.

O Pioneers! (page 60), *To Kill a Mockingbird* (page 164)

TIM PARKS

Tim Parks grew up in London and studied at Cambridge and Harvard. In 1981 he moved to Italy where he has lived ever since. Tim has translated works by Moravia, Calvino, Calasso, Machiavelli, and Leopardi. He is a regular contributor to the *New York Review of Books* and the *London Review of Books* and has written fourteen novels including *Europa* (1997), shortlisted for the Booker prize, *Destiny* (1999), *Cleaver* (2006), *Sex Is Forbidden* (2013), and, most recently, *In Extremis* (2017).
The Evenings (page 126), *Arturo's Island* (page 158)

DANIEL POLANSKY

Daniel Polansky was born in Baltimore in 1984. His first novel, *Low Town* (2011), was a rather transparent attempt to reproduce Chandler's prose in a low-fantasy setting, but since then he likes to think he's rather improved. By habit and inclination an aimless wanderer, he currently lives above a tattoo parlor in Venice Beach, and believes himself to be the only inhabitant of Los Angeles who walks anywhere.
The Long Goodbye (page 136)

XENOBE PURVIS

Xenobe Purvis, who studied English Literature at Oxford and has an MA in Creative Writing from Royal Holloway, is a writer, researcher and critic. Her writing has been published in the *Independent* and the *Glasgow Review of Books*. In 2017, she was accepted onto the London Library's Emerging Writers Programme.
The Ice Palace (page 168), *My Brilliant Friend* (page 232)

ERIC RABKIN

Eric S. Rabkin, University of Michigan Professor Emeritus of English Language and Literature and of Art & Design, includes among his books works on fantasy, science fiction, literary theory, and pedagogy. His current book project explores the visual aspects of language.
The Great Gatsby (page 86)

RACHAEL REVESZ

Rachael Revesz is a journalist and writer who spent a year in New York covering the 2016 presidential election for the *Independent*. She is writing her first novel.
The Age of Innocence (page 70)

ADAM ROBERTS

Adam Roberts is a writer and critic, author of *The Palgrave History of Science Fiction* (2006) and seventeen science fiction novels among many other things. He is currently writing a literary biography of H. G. Wells. He lives not far from Wells's Woking, just over the Surrey border in Berkshire.
War of the Worlds (page 52)

MAURICIO SELLMANN OLIVEIRA

Mauricio Sellmann Oliveira received a PhD from the University of Manchester (UK) for his research on the city in Jorge Amado's urban novels. He is currently a visiting scholar in the Department of Spanish and Portuguese at Dartmouth College.
The Violent Land (page 118)

SUSAN SHILLINGLAW

Susan Shillinglaw is the Director of the National Steinbeck Center in Salinas, California, and a Professor of American Literature at San José State University. She has published widely on Steinbeck, most recently *Carol and John Steinbeck: Portrait of a Marriage* (2013) and *On Reading The Grapes of Wrath* (2014).
Cannery Row (page 120)

JARED SHURIN

Jared Shurin is the editor of the award-winning pop culture website *Pornokitsch* and over a dozen anthologies, including *The Djinn Falls in Love* (co-edited with Mahvesh Murad).
The Adventures of Huckleberry Finn (page 42), The *French Lieutenant's Woman* (page 174)

DREW SMITH

Drew Smith is an author and editor who curates the blog www.101greatreads.com, which focuses on twentieth-century writing. He began his journalistic career on *Argosy* short story magazine editing William Trevor and Sean O'Faolain. He is the author of *Oyster: A Gastronomic History* (2015).
Peyton Place (page 152), *Black Sugar* (page 244)

ALYSON TAPP
Alyson Tapp teaches Russian literature at the University of Cambridge and is the author of essays on Tolstoy, Dostoevsky, the tram in Russia's literary imagination, and elegiac poetry.
Anna Karenina (page 35), *The Gulag Archipelago* (page 181)

ANDREW TAYLOR
Andrew Taylor is a journalist and author based in the UK, who lived and worked in the Middle East for several years. He studied English at Oxford University, and now lives near Stratford-upon-Avon.
Midaq Alley (page 130)

CATHERINE TAYLOR
Catherine Taylor is a writer, editor, and critic based in London. She has been publisher at the Folio Society and is the former deputy director of English PEN, the founding center (1921) of the global organization for literature and freedom of expression.
The People of Hemsö (page 49), *The Rainbow* (page 64), *Mrs Dalloway* (page 82), *Odessa Stories* (page 99), *Bonjour Tristesse* (page 145), *The Bluest Eye* (page 177), *Tracks* (page 208), *The Search Warrant* (page 222), *Snow* (page 226), *The Explosion Chronicles* (page 235)

IAN THOMSON
Ian Thomson is a writer and critic, author of Primo Levi's biography, works of travel, and other non-fiction, including a study of Dante. He is currently writing a book set in the Baltic city of Tallinn during World War II.
The Time of Indifference (page 94)

JAMES THURGILL
James Thurgill works as a Project Associate Professor at the University of Tokyo. His current research examines literary geographies of absence in the ghost stories of M.R. James and Lafcadio Hearn. James lives in Tokyo with his wife, Kät, and their adopted cat, TanTan.
The Summer of the Ubume (page 218)

EVA TIHANYI
Eva Tihanyi lives in St. Catharines, Ontario, Canada, and teaches at Niagara College. She has published eight volumes of poetry, including, most recently, *The Largeness of Rescue* (2016), and a collection of short stories, *Truth and Other Fictions* (2009).
Icefields (page 220)

LISA TUTTLE
Lisa Tuttle is an award-winning author of science fiction, fantasy, and horror. She has also written for children, and her non-fiction includes *Encyclopedia of Feminism*. Born and raised in Texas, she has lived in Scotland for more than twenty-five years.
Little House on the Prairie (page 106), *The Summer Book* (page 179)

ANDREW WATTS
Andrew Watts is Senior Lecturer in French Studies at the University of Birmingham. He is the author of *Preserving the Provinces: Small Town and Countryside in the Work of Honoré de Balzac* (2007) and the co-editor (with Owen Heathcote) of *The Cambridge Companion to Balzac* (2017).
La Comédie humaine (page 21)

ELLA WESTLAND
Ella Westland lived for many years on the south coast of Cornwall, where she was co-founder of the annual Daphne du Maurier Festival (now Fowey Festival). She has published *Reading Daphne* (2007) and written extensively on Victorian literature, romantic fiction, and Cornish culture.
Rebecca (page 112)

BENJAMIN WIDISS
Benjamin Widiss teaches literature at Hamilton College. He is the author of *Obscure Invitations: The Persistence of the Author in Twentieth-Century American Literature* (2011). His writing on Faulkner has appeared in *The New Cambridge Companion to William Faulkner* (2015) and *Novel: A Forum on Fiction*.
Absalom, Absalom! (page 108)

Opposite: "Portrait of Fernando Pessoa" by José de Almada Negreiros, 1954.

ORPHEU
2

INDEX

Page numbers in *italics* refer to illustrations.

CREDITS

Every effort has been made to trace copyright holders and to obtain their permission for the use of copyright material. The publisher apologises for any errors or omissions in the following list and would be grateful if notified of any corrections that should be incorporated in future reprints or editions of this book.

Edited and with additional text by Jessica Payn.

A version of Robert Macfarlane's essays on *For Whom the Bell Tolls* and *The Luminaries* appeared first in *Intelligent Life* magazine.

Page 4-5: The seventeenth-century painter Claude Lorrain was one of the first artists to pay attention to landscape as a subject in its own right (see Introduction, page 11). This oil painting illustrates a scene from Greek mythology, 'Landscape with Ascanius Shooting the Stag of Sylvia',

Page 14-15: Don Rodrigo speaking to Lucia, in a scene from Alessandro Manzoni's *The Betrothed*. Print of nineteenth century wall painting by Nicola Cianfanelli.

Page 62-63: George Grosz's German Expressionist work Metropolis, 1916–1917, captures the energy and chaos of a modernist urban environment. Oil on canvas.

Page 124-125: John Standing's photograph of the London roofscape in 1959, showing the postwar development of the city.

Page 184-185: Photograph of colorful San Francisco in 1960, at the height of the hippie movement.

Other images as follows:
Alamy Stock Photo: © AF archive, 32, 118; © age fotostock, 245; © Aled Llywelyn, 141; © Andrew Fare, 87; © Antiqua Print Gallery, 65, 75, 84, 103, 131; © Art Collection 2, 52; © Artepics, 251; © AugustSnow, 215; © Barry Iverson, 130; © Ben Wyeth, 235; © Chronicle, 39, 54, 55, 67, 239; © Classic Image, 49; © dpa picture alliance, 160, 224, 238; © Entertainment Pictures, 71; © Everett Collection Historical, 94; © Everett Collection Inc, 52, 162, 174, 177, 200; © GL Archive, 86; © Granger Historical Picture Archive, 29, 133, 140, 164, 168; © Geraint Lewis, 205, 240, 242; © Heritage Image Partnership Ltd, 104, 144; © Historic Collection, 143; © Historic Images, 223; © Hi-Story, 28; © IanDagnall Computing, 82, 121; © INTERFOTO, 14, 18,19, 96, 116, 142, 155, 226; © ITAR-TASS News Agency, 170; © Jeff Gilbert, 180; © jeremy sutton-hibbert, 219; © John Standing, 124; © Kathy deWitt, 210; © Keystone Pictures USA, 89; © Lebrecht Music and Arts Photo Library, 24, 33, 46, 78, 156; © Michael Dwyer, 153; © Moviestore collection Ltd, 176; © Newscom, 218; © Niday Picture Library, 35; © North Wind Picture Archives, 243; © NPC Collection, 44; © Old Images, 72; © Oldtime, 169; © Paul Fearn, 106, 158; © Peter Horree, 62; © Photo 12, 64, 99; © Pictorial Press Ltd, 16, 21, 37, 70, 74, 93, 108, 112, 120, 136, 145, 181; © Realy Easy Star 18; © The Picture Art Collection, 22, 154, 236; © Science History Images, 38, 60; © Splash News, 26; © SPUTNIK, 183; © The Protected Art Archive, 42, 165; © UtCon Collection, 179; © Vintage Book Collection, 57; © Westend61 GmbH, 245; © Xinhua, 222; ZUMA Press Inc, 208, 214. © Albert Bonniers Forlag, 1972, 179. © Alfaguara, 1950, 133. © Courtesy of Allen and Unwin Book Publishers, 230. © Andy Bridge for Picador, 2008, 211.© Aschehoug & Co, 2011, 67. © Australian Penguin Books, 1963. 156. © Courtesy of Belgravia Books, 244. © Illustration by Bill Bragg, art direction Clare Skeats for the cover of *The Evenings* published by Pushkin Press (2016), 128. © Photo by Bob Sandberg, *LOOK* magazine, 18 March 1958. *LOOK* magazine Photograph Collection, Library of Congress, Prints & Photographs Division, LC-DIG-ds-04279], 152. Bridgeman Art Library: © Ashmolean Museum, University of Oxford, UK, 4; © British Library Board, 40; © Gamborg Collection, 171; © Granger, 43, 47; © Hereford City Museum and Art Gallery, Herefordshire, UK, 114; © Kunstmuseum, Basel, Switzerland, 80; © Look and Learn, 30; © Mario De Biasi per

Mondadori Portfolio, 241; © Private Collection / The Stapleton Collection, 17; © SZ Photo, 182. © Charles Scribner's Sons, 1925, 86, 116. © Charles Scribner's Sons, 1993, 214. © Chatto & Windus: 1979, 177; 2014, 240. © Circulo de Lectores cover design, 1989, 134. © City of Toronto Archives, 207. © D. Appleton & Company, 1920, 70. © David Blackwood, *Hauling Job Sturges House*, 1979. Etching and aquatint on wove paper, Overall: 43.9 x 88 cm. Art Gallery of Ontario, Gift of David and Anita Blackwood, Port Hope, Ontario, 1999. Digital file courtesy of Art Gallery of Ontario, Port Hope, Ontario, 216. © De Bexige Bij, 1947, 126. © Editions Cremille, 1991, 32. © Editions Mornay, 1933, 21. © Editora Ulisseia, 1958, 110. © Editorial Planeta, 2011, 224. © Edizioni e/o, 2011, 230. © 1926 E. H. Shepard, reproduced with permission of Curtis Brown Group Limited, London on behalf of The Shepard Trust, 90, 92. © Einaudi, 1957, 158. © By permission of the Estate of Sam Selvon, 150. © Eyre and Spottiswoode, 1957, 156, 156. © Faber and Faber, 2016, 242. © Copyright 2018, Faulkner Literary Rights, LLC. All rights reserved. Used with permission, William Faulkner Literary Estate, Lee Caplin, Executor. © Gabler Edition, 1984, Penguin Books, 1986, 76. © Garth Williams Estate, 107. Getty Images: © Buyenlarge / Contributor, 123; © Chris Ware / Stringer, 149; © Howell Walker / Contributor. National Geographic Collection, 146; © Hulton Deutsch / Contributor, 117; © Keystone-France / Contributor, 119; © Laura Di Biase / Contributor, 231; © Mondadori Portfolio / Contributor, 232; © Photo by The Print Collector/Print Collector, 157; © Sino Images, 237; © Stephen Spraggon, 175. © Granta Books, 2013, 238. © Hamish Hamilton, 1953, 136. © Harper & Brothers, 1935, 106. © HarperCollins, 2006, 230. © Henry Holt & Co., 1988, 208. © Hogarth Press, 1925, 82. © Jamie Whyte, 172. © Jasper Yellowhead Museum and Archives (PA 7/26), 221. © J.B. Lippincott Company, 1960, 164. © J.M Dent, 1954, 140. © Julliard, 1954, 145. © Julian Messner, Inc. 1956, 152.© Jonatahn Cape, 1976, 156. © Jonathan Cape and Harrison, 1929, 110. © Joost Evers, National Archives of the Netherlands/Anefo, 126. © Kodansha, 1991, 218. © Lanterne, 1971, 168. © İletişim, 2002, 226. © Little Brown 1969, 174. © Longman, 1989, 148. © Looking Glass Library, 1960, 42. © Courtesy of Lorain Historical Society, 178. © 2014 Loren Latker http://shamustown.com/store.html. Originally published by Metropolitan Surveys of Los Angeles. Base map drawn by Karl Moritz Leuschner 1932, 138. © MacMillan & Co Ltd, 1958, 38. Photo Illustration by Marc Tauss Copyright © 1984, 201. Mary Evans Images: © Glasshouse Images, 97; © IDA KAR, 148; © Illustrated London News Ltd, 113. © Painting by Matthew Joseph Peak, 68. © McClelland & Stewart, 1987, 205. © McPhee Gribble, 1991, 210. © Methuen & Co. Ltd., 1926, 89. © Nebraska State Historical Society image RG2639, 61. © NeWest Press, 1995, 220. Copyright © 2014, Orhan Pamuk, used by permission of The Wylie Agency (UK) Limited, 228. Image courtesy: Bridgeman Art Library. © Penguin, 1961, 156. © Penguin, 1975, 154. © Courtesy of Patricia Grace, 203. © Random House, 1936, 108. © Random House, 1938, 110. © Random House, 1948, 110. © Random House, 1951, 110. © Random House, 1957, 110. © Random House, 1959, 110. © Record, 1976, 118. © Rivages, 2017, 244. © Cover artwork by Ronald Glendenning (1959) for Collins edition, 159. © Courtesy of the private collection of Roy Winkelman, 209. © Screentime Australia, photograph by and courtesy of David Dare Parker, 212. © S. Fischer Verlag, 1929, 96. © Shakespeare and Company, 1922, 74. © Shanghai Literature and Art Publishing House, 2013, 235. Shutterstock Images: © Shutterstock, 230; © ValerioMei, 95; © V.I. Vernadskyi National Library of Ukraine (VNUL), 101. © Smith & Haas, 1932, 110. © State Library of New South Wales, Mitchell Library, DG V1/11, 231. © Courtesy of Thomas Wharton, 220. © Photograph by Tina Makereti, 2018, 204. © University of California Press, 1999, 222. © University of Hawaii Press, 1995, 203. © Victor Gollancz, 1938, 112. © Viking Press, 1945, 120. © Vintage, 2009, 110. © Vintage Books, 1962, 110. © Vintage Books, 1964, 110. © Vintage Classics, 2011, 110. © Vintage Contemporaries, 1984, 200. © Vintage International, 1954, 142. © Map by Virginia Norey reprinted from *Kristen Lavransdatter, I: The Wreath* by Penguin Books, 79. © William Heinemann, 1958, 160. © YMCA-Press, 1967, 170. © YMCA-Press, 1973, 181.